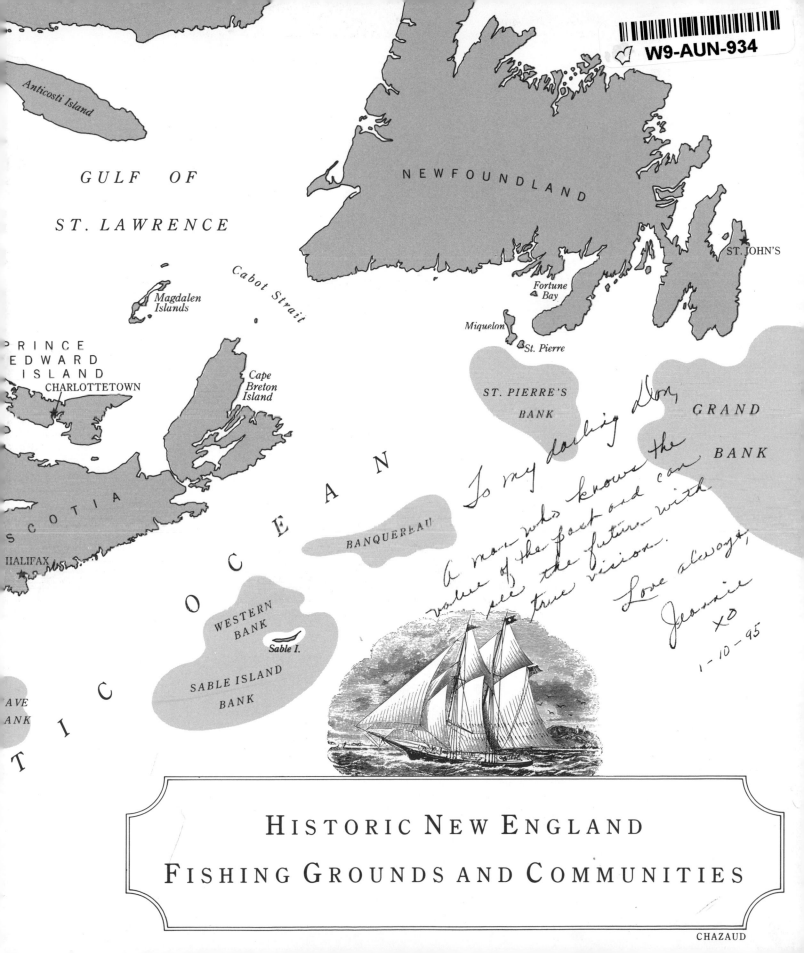

HISTORIC NEW ENGLAND
FISHING GROUNDS AND COMMUNITIES

THE VIEW FROM FRONT STREET

TRAVELS THROUGH NEW ENGLAND'S

HISTORIC FISHING COMMUNITIES

W·W·NORTON & COMPANY

New York   London

THE VIEW FROM FRONT STREET

TRAVELS THROUGH NEW ENGLAND'S HISTORIC FISHING COMMUNITIES

RUSSELL BOURNE

Published simultaneously in Canada by Penguin Books Canada Ltd.,
2801 John Street, Markham, Ontario L3R 1B4.
Printed in the United States of America.

The text of this book is composed in 11.5/15 Century Old Style, with
display type set in Century Old Style. Composition by PennSet, Inc.
Manufacturing by the Murray Printing Company.
Book design by Margaret McCutcheon Wagner.

First Edition

Library of Congress Cataloging-in-Publication Data

Bourne, Russell.

The view from Front Street.

Includes index.
1. Fishing villages—New England—History.   I. Title.
SH221.5.N4B68   1989   974   88–12524

ISBN 0-393-02577-2

W. W. Norton & Company, Inc., 500 Fifth Avenue, New York, N.Y. 10110
W. W. Norton & Company Ltd., 37 Great Russell Street, London WC1B 3NU
1 2 3 4 5 6 7 8 9 0

TITLE PAGE. *View of New Bedford: In 1852 Charles
Bosworth sketched the comfortable houses above the
waterfront of his cousin's city, then approaching its peak.
The Whaling Museum of New Bedford.*

FOR POP

Again, the kingdom of Heaven is like
a net let down into the sea,
where fish of every kind were caught in it.
When it was full, it was dragged ashore.
The men sat down
and collected the good fish into pails,
and threw the worthless away.

MATTHEW 13:47–49

*Cushing, Maine,
lobsterman: Looking out to
his boat in the harbor, a
fishermen stands amid the
technology of his industry.
Maine State Archives;
George French photo.*

CONTENTS

PREFACE

IT WOULD be "a narrative of heroic daring." That's what fisheries historian Raymond McFarland said of the first *social history* of the New England fishermen—if ever it would be written. No such analysis came into existence in McFarland's own time—the late nineteenth century, when tall-masted schooners were the subject of ballads and magazine chronicles. And none exists to this day—when New England fishermen fight against competing interests on the waterfront for the preservation of their space and their heritage.

What an ancient battle this is, for the New England waterfront. As early as 1657 Richard Mather complained that Massachusetts' seaport towns were "exceedingly exposed and deprav'd by the Powring in of Trade and Strangers." Greater understanding was needed, even then, of the essential role played by the fishermen in the health of the community and the state.

While this book is not McFarland's desired, definitive social history, it does visit many of the sea-fronting communities in which the fishermen and their families worked out their social destinies. It's the View from Front Street. And although it does not contribute much tourist data for the benefit of contemporary visitors, it does focus on what made those fishing ports important in their own day.

Probably McFarland's yearned-for social history of these people and their lifeways will never be written. The first reason is that the fisherman has traditionally been a slave in New England—both in earliest colonial times (when chronicler John Josselyn described how seventeenth-century merchants trapped the men in bondage of drink and indebtedness) and up through the nineteenth century. Today when the death rate on board fishing vessels is seven times the national average, fishermen are still in jeopardy. Their ways are *not* viewed as heroic. A culture has a difficult time writing the appreciation of its former slaves, as Tacitus observed.

The second reason is more complex: we have romanticized the New England fisherman and his family out of existence (perhaps because we don't much like their nonconforming reality). The fisherman is locked into the bronze statue upon the Gloucester shore, peering nobly seaward from beneath his faithful sou'wester (which was not the "Cape Ann hat" he actually wore). The fisherman's home, hung with nets and pots, is subjected to so many watercolor paintings that it becomes the clichéd shack. The fisherwife stands perpetually on the shore, in verse or engraving, scanning the seas for her home-sailing husband (having nothing better to do on her own hook). From those romantic enslavements, this book seeks to release the fisher families and their communities.

In that attempt, I've been assisted immeasurably by the respective towns' historical societies and museums. Indeed, this is their story, their liberation of real people, if not heroes. In almost no case did my guides at these societies and museums fail to appreciate that fishing was the business and the spirit that lay at the heart of all growth and activity—the essential bond to the sea. The societies and their interlocutors are named, community by community, in the Acknowledgments section of the book, along with pertinent reference works.

As this work progressed, continual help and guidance were given to me by

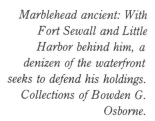

Marblehead ancient: With Fort Sewall and Little Harbor behind him, a denizen of the waterfront seeks to defend his holdings. Collections of Bowden G. Osborne.

certain institutions, focal points of New England waterfront research. These were, from south to north, the Maritime Center, Norwalk, Connecticut; Mystic Seaport, Mystic, Connecticut; the Whaling Museums of New Bedford and Nantucket, Massachusetts; the Peabody Museum, Salem, Massachusetts; the Maine Maritime Museum, Bath, Maine; the Penobscot Maritime Museum, Searsport, Maine; and the Maine Maritime Academy, Castine, Maine. To these centers and their staffs, particularly their library staffs, I would like to extend special thanks.

Near the head of any list of institutions making significant contributions to research among the fisheries must stand the Northeast Folklore Society at the University of Maine in Orono, whose archives (the conception of Edward D. "Sandy" Ives) contain increasing numbers of fishermen's recollections in interview form, compiled by students and graduate assistants. In company with the conversations I was privileged to have in the waterfront communities, these interviews represent my most valuable sources.

Professor John F. Battick of the University of Maine's History Department has been my friendly mentor through the course of writing the book—a push here, a lead there. Also of stalwart assistance have been Richard C. Kugler of New Bedford's Whaling Museum, Andrew German of Mystic Seaport, and Russell Handsman of the American Indian Archaeological Institute; I thank them all for their patience, and for their challenges.

My editor at W. W. Norton, Eric Swenson, deserves a flag dipped in salute for his encouragement and support, as does Norton's newest sailor, Jim Mairs. Because my wife merits a similar salute for her many contributions, and because she appears throughout the following pages anonymously and in somewhat shadowy form, I want to recognize her here, with love and appreciation—Miriam Anne Bourne.

To them all as well as to my readers, I extend the hope that these waterfront travels will deepen their regard for New England's fish-powered heritage.

—RUSSELL BOURNE

On Front Street: Rattling along cobblestones, freight wagons once passed here between New Bedford's humming ship chandleries and grog shops. Mystic Seaport Museum, W. H. Tripp Collection.

THE VIEW FROM FRONT STREET

TRAVELS THROUGH NEW ENGLAND'S

HISTORIC FISHING COMMUNITIES

WHERE ONCE THEY FISHED

THE most ancient, most historically vital fishing communities of New England cannot, fortunately, be visited by car or bicycle. You cannot drive down the hill and find stubbly fishermen at the "liars' bench," waiting for the fog to lift; you cannot pedal along elm-hung streets above the waterfront and scan dignified sea captains' mansions or hear the tones of the church bell softened by salt air. Nor can you hang out on the waterfront of these particular locations until the men sail in on their net-hung vessels, seagulls whirling in the wake; no chance to watch as boxes of silvery catch are hoisted wharfward and buyers muscle in to point out wanted whiting or hake or cod.

For in these communities of which I speak—so closely related to the villages up and down the coast—life is ordered differently. They are a hundred miles or so out to sea, just under water. An amphibian creature might not notice the difference: the land beneath the water is arranged just as it is on the continent proper; eroded hills and deeply glaciated valleys run southwest-to-northeast. But there beneath the seas the weather is totally controlled by the seasons of the Atlantic Ocean, with a year-round temperature variation of no more than 20 degrees Fahrenheit.

Out there—in these fish-populated communities I have on my mind—a major factor of life is the Gulf Stream as it rushes north but is bent eastward by the shoals. Ben Franklin drafted a map of this crucial junction of land and water, using his Nantucket grandfather's data and noting where the herring tended to be found. And out there on the shoals the Arctic Current surges in from the north with its companies of pelagic fish. Yes, these are the fish-rich New England Banks, extending from Georges (out to sea from Nantucket) to Browns and La Have (off the mouth of the Gulf of Maine). As part of the coastal shelf, they lead on to the Banks of Nova Scotia and Newfoundland, grounds that have also been associated with our fishermen since long before Plymouth.

OPPOSITE. *Stonington, Maine: Ladling out herring bait to a waiting fisherman, about 1940. Maine State Archives; George French photo.*

Out to these storm-wracked, current-swept shoals have sailed more pinkies and "dogboddies," more schooners and draggers than have ever returned. The grounds are as much a part of New England as if they were above water (as, indeed, once they were); this front step of the continent drowned only a few thousand years ago, when the glaciers melted. And some of it has been magically, geologically, restored to sunlight in the intervening millennia: certain rocky peninsulas of Maine look by twilight as if they had but recently emerged from the depths, rough rock still struggling up from the sea.

Although the sunken lands cannot be explored by those of us equipped only with land vehicles, they remain essential, causative parts of the New England scene. They are the fish-farmers' fields, the fishermen's reason for being. The fisherman knows these pieces of territory as intimately as he knows his own back pasture. He knows them if only because each species of bottom fish has its preferred type of bottom—catfish like a rocky bottom, halibut are found only in gravel. Also, the ground has always been a better aide to the navigator than compass or star; its bumps and bendings neither gyrate nor fade with the fog. The skipper feels his way across the bottom with the canniness of a crab and the sensitivity of a blindman's cane—though the device used here was for centuries lead-and-line and is now sonar of the most sophisticated breed.

From Nantucket (and many other communities) comes the story of the nineteenth-century skipper who had an unfortunate tendency to stay below with his bottle rather than on deck with his nose in the wind. His habits resulted in a wandering wake, the schooner more and more off course in the foggy sea. The hapless crew heaved the lead day after day to test the bottom but could not figure out from the samples of mud brought forth where in the world they were. Finally, determined to rouse their skipper and to force him to find the way, the crew's jokester took a bit of soil from the geranium in the captain's cabin and put it on the bottom of the heaved lead. Well, when that lead was pulled up from the bottom and the besotted captain was summoned to analyze it, he exclaimed: "Glory be, boys . . . Nantucket's sunk and we be right over Marm Hacket's garden! Ready about!!"

That the heirs of those old-time fishermen find their way safely out and back from the Banks continues to be vitally important. New England's coastline may comprise only 7.3 percent of the total United States coast, but more than one-third of America's supply of finfish and shellfish comes from this uniquely productive territory. Among all professional American fishermen, 35 percent are employed in the North Atlantic fisheries. This is the ancient and continuing home of American fishing—a $350 million business annually. My interest lies in the historic communities—on land and at sea—in which the fishermen and their families continue to dwell. I've been attracted by their secretive, withholding air. Something seems to lurk here . . . a kind of hidden history too valuable to be lost as the villages give way to modern improvements.

For example, I've driven through, and been intrigued by, two very different New England Stoningtons. These two regions have been sending boats out to the fishing grounds for centuries, one from the southeastern corner of Connecticut, the other from the eastern side of Maine's Penobscot Bay. But they're so different one from the other: Whereas the Connecticut Stonington blossoms with gift shops down along narrow streets and luxuriates in houses of mellow pride and substance, the Maine Stonington looks like a rough-and-tumble outpost on a hard-luck planet.

Stonington, Maine, is, primarily, a lobster town, with a rather impressive command of this fishery. Four of the awkward, long-legged wharves that aim out at the island-strewn Deer Island Thorofare have active buyers' stations at their heads, to which the individual lobstermen bring in their daily catch. Then there's the State Fish Pier, to which a variety of gill-netters and mussel-draggers bring in a variety of fin- and shellfish. Altogether, they do something like $2.5 million worth of business a year—not too bad for a town that looks too poor for a tourist to get a flat fixed.

Yet there seemed to be no place to stay here, and my wife and I could find no pottery candlesticks to buy. There was a certain shabby aloofness. One writer on the Maine mind concluded after a number of similar visits that Down Easterners "have necessarily been on guard against unexpected attacks from Indians, the weather, the wrath of God, and smooth-talking, out-of-state salesmen." I wanted to know more.

By contrast with the Maine shabbiness, the fishing fleet at Stonington, Connecticut, ties up to a very substantial, steamship-era Town Dock. Here the view from Front Street—you'll find a Front Street along the waterfront of just about every fishing community—sparkles with dollar signs. Hefty draggers fitted out for the Banks and slim seiners readied for local waters roll contentedly in the swell, each worth several hundred thousand dollars. These are corporation-financed vessels, some managed by descendants of Portuguese seamen who had served on the town's former whaling and sealing vessels. But the polished pride that's so evident in the town, Federalist houses with fanlights and a Doric-porticoed church, has not much to do with the activity on the waterfront. For in this town there's the awesome presence of what Yankees call old money; those places behind walls and hedges were built by shipowners and shoremen who profited from the seal oil trade before the Civil War. Yet this proud Stonington is reported to be the last of Connecticut's historic ports still engaged in off-shore fishing.

Probing to the north and east, I learned that in the same era of the 1840s, that formative time in our republic's development, Stonington, Maine, was hardly visible. But its close neighbor, South Deer Isle, had then embarked on an exciting voyage in the fisheries, sending its schooners off for mackerel in the Gulf of St. Lawrence, for cod upon the Grand Bank of Newfoundland, and for cod and halibut along the coast of Labrador. The little town boasted seven stores, a Customs House, and a Methodist church among other busy structures (many of which faded away when the cod fisheries died in the late 1860s). A modest place but one that gave a good life to its inhabitants.

It was only later, in the 1870s, that next-door Stonington, Maine, came to the fore, booming with wealth from its granite quarries. Victorian houses sprang up, bristling with turrets and mansard dormers—buildings whose spruced-up remains still line Main Street. The town swarmed with quarrymen demanding booze, whores, and a good time. But after all this passed with the decline of the market for granite, Stonington cautiously turned toward fishing; it became the seat of canneries, then lobstering and market fishing. Unlike its Connecticut namesake, this place still depends totally on the sea's harvest.

Despite all the differences that one can recount from history and can feel when exploring the two towns, what's remarkable is that both stand forth as representative New England fishing communities. They provide bi-focal glimpses of that elusive heritage. Both towns are creations of the sea and of the particular sea animals which lured the men in boats out after them. The way the buildings stand, the streets curve, the vessels ride at mooring in the harbor—these all reflect the mind of the fisherman.

It cuts even deeper than that. Who are these people, native Americans or Yankees or immigrants? What about the women, the churches, the relations between rich and poor? Don't human engineerings shape the towns, too? Yes, of course; but everything responds to the fate of a particular fishery. A fisherman from the one Stonington could not find a job in the other Stonington (nor would he seek that job). It's such a close business that a fisherman's berth as well as his proper port is determined by his clan. It's always been that way, in harbors small and large—a fisherman from Boston would be out of luck in New Bedford.

This, I began to realize, is the main point as one looks at fishing communities: their individuality and their strict dedication to the respective fishery. In the words of anthropologist Susan Peterson, the men seek to "catch [only] what they catch. They don't want to learn new species. Their identity is bound up in that kind of fish." The inshore fisherman (like one from Stonington, Maine) has invested a whole, proud life in figuring out the patterns of his prey in local waters, aided only slightly by science and industrial intelligence. Ditto with the offshore dragger—who reads the ridges and valleys of the Banks by means of his electronic gear.

Yet for all its parochialism and specialization, fishing in New England has not been, will not be displaced as an economic foundation stone of the American republic. Beyond that, it has helped shape the way we think and vote and pray or curse. Though fragile and needing support from time to time, it has given the nation basic food for its hunger and fundamental experience for its character.

THOMAS JEFFERSON thought that New England fishermen and their way of life mattered very much, not because that society was polite but because it was extraordinarily productive. As secretary of state soon after the Revolution, he wrote of "the superiority of our mariners in skill, activity, enterprise, sobriety, and order." (Forgive the Virginian, I implore you, if some of his words sound rather generalized.) He was deeply aware of the damages the war had inflicted on the fleets, and reported that both whalemen and codfishermen labored "under heavy embarrassments which, if not removed or lessened will render the fisheries every year less extensive and important." To augment their chances for survival (and to encourage their output), he instituted a bounty for their catch of cod, a small but key subsidy that lasted from 1791 to 1866.

And before Jefferson, the statesmen on the other side of the aisle, the Federalists (today's Republicans) also spoke up for the fishermen. Fisher Ames, redoubtable bulldog of a Massachusetts conservative, declaimed in 1783 against a tax on this essential but always marginal industry:

> Unless some extraordinary measures are taken to support our fisheries, I do not see what is to prevent their inevitable ruin. If instead of protection, we extend to them oppression, I shudder for the consequences. . . . [The fishermen] are very poor: they are in a sinking state; they carry on their business in despair. But gentlemen will ask us, "Why then, do they not quit their profession?" I answer, in the words that are often used in the eastern country respecting the inhabitants of Cape Cod, they are too poor to live there, and too poor to remove.

Thus not a tax but a subsidy was given, backed by all sectors of the new democracy. And for nearly a century this provided the extra boost that kept the codfishing vessels afloat. As augmented by Congress after Jefferson's time, the "bounties" awarded annually to codfishermen rose to $3.50 per ton for small vessels (30 tons or less) and $4.00 a ton for larger vessels. Thanks to this subsidy, codfishing—which had long supplied the primary item of foreign trade for New England merchants—became recognized as a special interest of the entire republic.

Recognition of the fisherman's value to the state had long roots in New England history. As early as 1639, the Puritan forefathers had relieved fishermen from military duty because their catches were essential both to the Massachusetts colony's early survival and to its future trading potential. One historian summed it up as follows: "There is not industry in America that antedates the fisheries. [They] at once became the chief industry of the people . . . the principal article of trade between [America] and the West Indies and Europe . . . the main source of wealth for the Revolution." Another historian added: "The Revolution itself was . . . a by-product of the New England fisheries. For it was to serve her fishermen that New England colonists had built their own ships and so had begun to justify British jealousy."

Their work and their independent spirit were vital to the War for Independence as well as to the building of the young republic. And so it remains today, as we shall see in a diversity of visited communities. Although Massachusetts' theocracy imposed a certain communal similarity upon its settlements (central church, close-gathered houses), this was soon contradicted by independent-minded communities in neighboring Rhode Island and provincial Maine. And even within Massachusetts, early fishing/farming settlements like Westport (near the Rhode Island border) and Dartmouth—where Quakers and Baptists asserted individualistic apartness from Plymouth—look nothing like the conventional church-on-the-commons model. On the contrary: in Westport and Dartmouth the old, gray-shingled houses have a tendency to scatter away from the center, down the rivers and into the woods. They are almost anticommunities.

Connecticut never developed a seabord metropolis of the size of Boston or New York, preferring to scale its communities to the discrete harbors on narrow waterways that lead down to Long Island Sound. If you want a city at sea, however, look to Nantucket, which, like New Bedford, has always thought of itself as quintessentially urbane. Along with urbanity, heterogeneity reigns in New Bedford and Gloucester—which is precisely what differentiates them from the communities farther east along the coast. There you'll find a homogeneity so intense that it can surround you in a way more enveloping than fog.

Various sociological reasons doubtless exist to explain these differences among New England fishing communities. But the chief reason for their diversity is that the fish were different. The whalemen of Nantucket or New Bedford lived differently from the oystermen of South Norwalk, Connecticut, and the codfishermen of Vinalhaven, Maine. The deep-water fishermen from Gloucester, who went off in March to keep their rendezvous with the denizens of the Banks, left behind them residential worlds organized quite differently from those of the mackerelers of sandy-shored Wellfleet, who went after their skittish prey in the summer (and carried baby oysters from Chesapeake Bay to Cape Cod in winter and spring). Different fish: different lives.

Yet there were constants in the business of fishing, and these themes shaped the internal structures of the communities. For example, there's the ages-old pattern of the successful Yankees abandoning the fo'c's'le berths and the Front Street shanties, giving them up to workers from Portugal, Nova Scotia, and other fisher homelands. This social displacement (minority advancement or exploitation, however you see it) occurred from the earliest, colonial times. Remarked one labor historian: "On the edge of the wilderness, where labor was in demand, liberty for some implied, in New England as in the Southern colonies, a restriction of freedom for others." Those others were usually of a different skin color, lingo, or religious belief from the original settlers, as we all learned in our cradles. They were swept into the ports of New England by a dearth of fish or by the winds of starvation at home. Here, initially, they became components in a postfeudal form of debt peonage; later they were statistics in a more complex industrial system of class repression.

When asked about native-born Americans in the New England fisheries of the nineteenth century, Captain Thomas Fulham, a Newfoundlander whose reminiscences are on file at the Northeast Folklore Archives in Orono, Maine, put it this way: "Well, uh, there really weren't any Americans, except the . . . Portuguese [descendants, who] had been in Provincetown many, many years." He went on to talk about fishing in general. "It seems to be kind of a hard-luck occupation or a . . . basically immigrant occupation."

Historian Samuel Eliot Morison, never one to whitewash our New England social scene, caused storms of controversy by his depictions of waterfront exploitation, particularly among the whalemen. He made a distinction between the worker systems within whaling and codfishing:

> Although the fisheries made a smaller contribution than whaling to the production statistics of Massachusetts, the worker got a much larger share of the profits. In cod and mackerel fishing the "share system" [about which more later] has continued to this day, and has never become the caricature of Communism that it did in [whaling's capital,] New Bedford.

Suspecting that he might not have made his points sharply enough, Morison went on to say that New Bedford's Oil Kings, the venerable Quakers who owned the ships and set the wages (or actually, the shares) "were as tight-fisted, cruel, and ruthless a set of exploiters as you can find in American history."

But whaling's a different game, let me protest mildly. It demands different capitalization and different agreements with the men engaged. (Whales, as mammals, are not, strictly speaking, fish—they propel themselves by up-down motions rather than by sidewise wiggles, as with fish—but whaling is a "fishery.") Perhaps

I feel excessively defensive about whaling's reputation, stemming as I do from grandparent-places in New Bedford decorated with whale oil lamps and pictures of delicious slaughters at sea. This will all have to be looked into and worked out in the subsequent chapters on Nantucket and New Bedford.

Whether north or south of the New Bedford–Cape Cod–Nantucket line, communities tend to be particularized (let me repeat) by the fish that swim in the nearby waters. The towns along the sounds to the south are quite different from the towns along the bays to the north. To test out that proposition in place and time, it might be well to range backward from a hundred years ago to earliest New England history, and to focus on three different communities from Rhode Island to New Hampshire, between the Stoningtons.

THE GREATEST ANALYST of the American fisheries, Dr. George B. Goode (whose multivolume report on the industry at midcentury was published by the Smithsonian in 1885), described in vivid detail the specific fish pursued at Rhode Island's Sakonnet Point. Although some pelagic (oceanic) fish swim through his lists—cod and hake and pollock—and although some bethnic (bottom-dwelling) fish are also featured—flounders and flat fish—most of those he spotted were strictly local characters. Some of these—the tautog and the scup—were here in such numbers because they sought these warm waters for their regular, summertime place of residence; others—the striped bass, shad, sturgeon, and alewives—were here because they were fond of running up and down the local rivers.

Dr. Goode's researcher found one Rhode Island pound trap at the mouth of the Sakonnet River that was so successful in bagging the abundant scup that 3,000 barrels of that fish alone were taken in the year 1879. "The traps were so full they could not be raised," he reported. Yet what makes this fishery particularly notable is that Dr. Goode, in commenting on the associated behavior of the Rhode Islanders, wrote that they were "more intelligent than fishermen generally; and many of them are landowners and quite well-to-do." Does he perhaps mean that these good folk were intelligent-seeming because they were of the landowning class?

Sakonnet Point today is a landscape blasted by hurricanes. My wife and I, eating our lunch on a couple of rocks that had not yet been blown seaward, watched a small group of mackerel seiners in their king-sized dories setting out nets in the river current. Whether intelligent or not, they worked with the everlasting hope that the fish might choose to cooperate. All the fishing shacks that stretched along these beaches in Dr. Goode's day have long since disappeared, as has any true memory of the life of the people.

Carleton Brownell, the acknowledged town historian of nearby Little Compton, showed me documents and pictures, however, that did much to bring the last-century scene back into the light. Sakonnet Point was by no means a town, it was a specialized fishing encampment. Landowners who had erected barracks down on the point would post notices up in the big town of Tiverton advertising that fishermen were needed: they were invited to apply for positions and to live in the barracks and to work at the nets. Most of those who responded were "Newfies" and Nova Scotians, men who drifted in and out, families rife with schoolchildren, of even lower social rank than the Portuguese. The Portuguese at least had the pertinacity to stay and succeed in establishing farms.

This social drama occurred in the heyday of the nonmechanized American fisheries, about 1862, when there were fourteen companies of fishermen working the nets at Sakonnet Point. "Business Nearly Incredible," proclaimed a local newspaper. The fish—led by scup—were sold to markets in New York and Philadelphia; what could not be sold at market price was let go to farmers for manure. For those who owned the business, it was tremendous—until the rivers became polluted, the fish diminished, and the competition with other transportation-blessed centers became unbearable. The owners then intelligently put their money elsewhere and the fishermen went back home . . . to be followed by other fishermen who kept hoping.

All of this contrasts sharply with the fish-inspired way of life in another, simultaneously active, New England fishing community: Rockport, Massachusetts. Although that craggy town then stood within the first dozen of the regions's ports

Mackerel seining: As tall schooners jockey for position, seine-boatmen charge forth to circle the school with their net (1860). Peabody Museum of Salem; William D. Stille oil painting.

in terms of volume of fish caught, it ranked even higher in terms of historic position. From here and a few other early Massachusetts towns, fisherman had made fortunes for fish shippers since earliest settlement times. New England's "Cod Aristocracy" counted Rockport among its favorite possessions.

And those gentlemen honored the cod for their fortune. In the Bulfinch-designed hall of the Massachusetts legislature, they hung up a great, gleaming image of the cod to symbolize its value to the state. And it *is* a splendid-looking fish, with a fascinating barbel hanging down from its lower jaw, which the cod uses (along with smell) to find sea worms and other provender along the bottom. Samuel Eliot Morison, more impressed by the Atlantic cod's durability than by its appearance, noted that "the firm-fleshed codfish of northern waters is unsurpassed for salting and drying." It was that quality that made it the hero of Massachusetts.

Rockport, as the farthest-out fishing harbor on Cape Ann (the nub of land that juts forth at the junction of Massachusetts Bay and the Gulf of Maine), became a center of the codfishery. Snapping back from the destructions of the Revolution, and benefiting from the cod bounty endorsed by Federalists and Republicans alike, the harbor hosted upward of 150 vessels by the early 1800s. Shipbuilding and ancillary industries arose around the central enterprise—a fair chance for all who participated. A local writer of the time observed, however, that for seamen from these rocky coves, there were other than honest ways of earning a living: "Our fishing interests, with some little interruptions, proved highly profitable and the mass of people obtained a comfortable living in peaceful pursuits; but some, for purposes of plunder and more rapid gains, embark[ed] on privateering."

As portrayed in the eloquent town history by Marshall W. Swann, Rockport's more law-abiding citizens not only set out after cod in inshore waters and among the shallows of nearby Jeffreys Ledges, they also sailed forth to Browns Bank and the Banks beyond. Sandy Bay, as Rockport was called in those early times, harbored four long-distance Bankers even before the Revolution. With the new century, that number rose geometrically. And the sixty-five fishermen's houses that had lined the shores, sheltering some two hundred people, doubled and tripled, as did the assemblage of sheds and fish houses. Soon, however, the small compass of the harbor began to militate against expansion; nearby Gloucester's harbor, though also limited, offered far greater potential.

Yet Rockport had another seemingly attractive way to turn: toward the mining of its own rock. In the second half of the nineteenth century, Rockport went off booming in that direction while Gloucester and other New England ports continued after the cod. Then the granite boom busted, leaving the quarry-pocked region looking like a Cubist painting of planes and angles.

At nearly the same time, Rockport was hit by the endemic New England disease, tourism. "Rusticators" flocked to enjoy the vacated charm of the village, many of them eager to paint the listing sheds, the net-hung shacks, and the rocky backgrounds. By the first decades of this century, a certain, wonderfully picturesque fisherman's hut had become an oft-repeated, almost obligatory painter's theme. Rockport boosters jacked up this hut, draped with its nets and buoys and markers, onto a float and took it to Chicago as their exhibit at the American Legion Fair of 1920. Called "Motif No. 1," it won the fair's first prize.

When my wife and I visited the town, a few fishing boats bobbed quietly in the granite-walled harbor. On the neck called Bearskin Point for reason of legend,

Rockport, Massachusetts: The fishing schooner Oddfellow, *bow-heavy, awaits unloading in the rock-hewn harbor. Mystic Seaport Museum, Hudson Collection.*

there was a veritable frenzy of activity. Here in a jumble of former shanties, purveyors of seasonal junk and jewelry had found shelters for themselves and their enterprises. Now, the season having ended, merchants were piling leftover trinkets and canvases into cartons and buzzing off; the Cadillacs bore out-of-state license plates.

At the chowder place, I asked our waitress whether she wasn't glad to have the season come to a close. "Not really," she answered. "What bucks you get here come with the season." To my wife on this blustery day she served a tuna melt that had not recovered from its sojourn in the refrigerator. All these seemed signs that Rockport had long since gone the careless way of tourist traps, having died unto real life for lack of fishing.

Before the Revolution, when American self-opinion was still formless, the largest and most productive fishing outpost was on New Hampshire's Isles of Shoals. Offering minimal harbor refuge, lashed with sea winds from the open Atlantic, these little islands might seem an unlikely place for any type of settlement. But they provided precisely what the seventeenth-century fishermen needed: easy access to the grounds where the cod and the haddock foraged as well as to the currents where the mackerel and the pollock swarmed. (Schooling fish tend to be smaller, incidentally, than bottom fish.) The fishermen also needed plenty of room on shore to dry their catch in the summer sun, for this had long been the preferred way of processing the product. On the Isles of Shoals there were ample acres for the fishing companies' "flakes" to be set up—light wooden frames on which the fish were dried and turned and turned and dried. Among certain connoisseurs, the Isles of Shoals had a reputation for producing slightly ripe, brown-tinged pollock, called dun fish.

As the fishing community settled in, others arrived: farmers, sheepherders, and their families. The fishermen, perennially the lowest of the low, lost their control of the land, squeezed on all sides. And the newcomers scorned them, calling them a "riotous collection" of humanity, and taking special note of their untidy sexual habits (adultery, incest, etc.). The local "fishwives," always shocking characters by others' perceptions, were said to scold and swear—even to smoke pipes!

But in the suit that was eventually brought to resolve this social clash, the judgment fell to the fishermen. The farmers' pigs had to leave the islands because they despoiled the drying fish. The farmers' wives, however, could stay. Nonetheless it was clear that as colonial society gained confidence and definition, power was surrendered by the fishermen. Though they had brought forth the wealth from the sea, they did not own it. And, possessing no wealth, they were subjects of disrepute.

Although the Isles of Shoals continued to be utilized as an outpost and storm shelter for New England fishermen into the nineteenth century, the original purpose of the location (to be a seasonal camp) no longer existed. And like many codfishing ports when the Congress terminated the subsidy after the Civil War (interior states of the nation having perceived that codfishermen were really not marlinspike sailors for the new, mechanized navy), the islands gradually reverted to their natural form—or were occupied by summer hotels. In 1873, Celia Thaxter, a eulogist of coastal New England, wrote nostalgically of her favorite island:

> Star Island Cove was charming with its tumble-down fish houses, and ancient cottages with low, shelving roofs, and porches covered with the golden lichen that so loves to embroider old weather-worn wood. Now there is not a vestige of those delapidated buildings to be seen; almost everything is white and square and new; and they have even cleaned out the Cove, and removed the great accumulation of fishbones which made the beach so curious.

The desire of the summer crowd to build something new and white in the place of what was old and gray is seldom to be denied.

BY SAILING not much farther northeast into the Gulf of Maine, one arrives at Monhegan Island, perhaps the earliest fishing outpost in what became New England. Here camped another group of "riotous," freedom-loving fishermen, removed from most mainland concerns—other than who owned the station and allowed them to fish there for their share of the catch. They were their own men, but under those nonownership circumstances. For more than two centuries they were able to maintain their loose and individualistic life style, disdained by the Commonwealth's Puritans, scorned by the post-Revolutionary merchants whom they supplied with fish.

In his researchings, Dr. Goode found a report on Monhegan's society that dated back to 1832 and that sheds additional light on formative fisher society. It stated (without much pleasure) that Monhegan had

> no officers of any kind, not even a justice of the peace. The people's affairs are governed and guided by themselves conformably to certain prudential rules and useages which have been mutually established. They have paid one U.S. direct tax, otherwise they are strangers to taxation, except that they pay toward the support of their schools.

The mothers of the children who went to those schools were obviously playing a civilizing, creative role in the community. But the pipe-smoking "fishwives" whom one meets in reports of the period continue to be held in contempt for their loudness and contentiousness. Perhaps they were merely speaking up for their rights? As my wife and I began to travel more widely in New England to study more fisher-built communities, this theme of women fighting along with their men for better lives became increasingly prominent.

Under nineteenth-century circumstances, the women tended to be short-changed and chivvied by the "company stores" run by the businessmen on the respective waterfronts. And whereas male workers in the Maine canneries of the 1880s earned regular blue collar wages, women were paid at half that rate. This injustice occurred when women had partially emerged from the "fishwife" stereotype, when (according to one contemporary writer) "a respectable class of women is engaged." Nonetheless they were put down, not because of their deportment or their productivity but because of their gender.

With what means they could command, the women fought back. And in many communities they won their law suits, forced the stores and landlords to treat them and their husbands squarely, and turned long-promised, season-end wages (which burned-out husbands often had difficulty collecting from the fishing companies) into cash-in-hand. In a trenchant paragraph about home life in the fishing towns, Dr. Goode remarked:

> The man being away so much, his wife had to act as his agent. And generally being the more capable of the two [perhaps because of greater education], she controls matters at home. He comes home often in the capacity of a border. Her world is considered better than his, and she is not infrequently the leader.

Did it always work that way? One wonders, and one yearns to hear not an outside analyst but a participant from within describe the quality of the life.

One such participant whose words live on is Martha's Vineyard's Tom Tilton, whose salty tales have fortunately been preserved by the Northeast Folklore Society. He was born on that little gravel pile just off the Vineyard called Nomansland, in 1887. And he remembered in full detail those years on Nomans when he and his family fished for cod spring and fall and concentrated on lobsters summertimes.

> The boats were hauled up on the beach on so-called ladders. The cross-members of the ladders were grooved and greased for the keels of the boats to run in. One man on each side of the boat steadied it as the oxen hauled it up on the beach. In the morning the boats were run down into the water without the use of oxen but with two or three men on each side. On Nomansland the fishermen always helped one another, even to giving away the spots where they had found the best fishing. Sometimes some of the fishermen brought their wives to Nomansland with them, and for the women that seems to have been like a beautiful vacation.

I must admit that Tom, in the way of men, was far more interested in chronicling his life at sea—his boats and the particular fish that called him in pursuit—than in portraying family life. But, since the historians, the women, and the fish themselves have all helped me introduce the fishing communities, let us now hear it from one of the men himself. Tom learned to box the compass "as soon as I could talk—no'th, no'th by east, and so on." On his first real boat, a catboat named *Ospray* (which followed after his first make-believe boat, which had been a washtub), he carried fish to New Bedford from his father's trap on the north shore of the Vineyard. To do that, he had to learn how to navigate through the current-crazed "holes," or straits, that connect Vineyard Sound with Buzzards Bay.

But Tom's preferred activity and favorite vessel was "coasting" on board the swift schooner *Alice S. Wentworth*. Sailing with his uncle, he served as mate on this "pretty" (his word), seventy-three-foot center-boarder. I think I recall seeing her on the ways in Fairhaven, across the river from New Bedford, and I'm delighted to learn that she may be reconstructed by the naval historical team at Mystic Seaport. And perhaps she will also be on display, thereafter, in South Norwalk, Connecticut, one of the many ports she regularly visited during her long life.

Gay Head, Martha's Vineyard: Upon the dory-hauling beach at "Lobsterville," a fisherman contemplates his seasonal community. Peabody Museum of Salem.

The most frequent cargo for the coaster *Alice S. Wentworth* was oysters—which South Norwalk produced lavishly, as did New Haven—oysters in varying stages of development, freighted to Long Island and Cape Cod. This highly perishable cargo required extra-rapid shipment, and was worth the seamen's tenderest care, for it was the seafood of choice up and down the coast as the century ended. (Perhaps it should be pointed out that though whaling and cod-fishing, as well as mackereling and other prominent fisheries, enjoyed their days of dominance, it is the finicky oyster business, and the shell fisheries all together, that have led for decades in U.S. economic importance.) Quite capable of living up to those demands, Tom Tilton's shallow-drafted schooner had the fine lines and tall rig of a racing yacht. It was one day's passage for the 100 miles between Greenport, Long Island ("breakfast"), and Vineyard Haven ("supper at home").

So high-flying with canvas was the *Alice S. Wentworth* that one day her topmast and upper tier of sails was carried away. As a shipmate of Tom's recalled,

That meant that there was no foretopsail and no flying jib, but actually that did not hurt her sailing ability to any great extent; and it meant that one did not have to go

Alice S. Wentworth: *This legendary New England schooner made up in brisk speed what she lacked in new sails; lowered from davits, her boat tows astern. Mystic Seaport Museum.*

aloft to shift tacks when she came about. [I.e., one did not have to go aloft to transfer the topsail to the other side of the triatic stay, standing at masthead as the vessel plunged up and down in the waves.] From my point of view, that was a blessing. Once off Newport she actually passed a cup defender . . . but the wind was on the quarter.

Wellfleet, Massachusetts: BELOW. *Topmasts seemingly slanted forward, oyster schooner* Three Sisters, *ties up below the town and railhead,* LEFT, *to which oysters brought prosperity in the 1880s. Both, Mystic Seaport Museum.*

Tom left the faithful *Alice S. Wentworth* only when it became clear that coasting days were over, trucks and highways having conquered the land.

This meant that Tom was out of a job. But, no matter, he could go back to fishing at home; there, other fish called him on to other careers. When there wasn't trap fishing, there was bull-raking for quahaugs; when there wasn't offshore dragging, there was rumrunning (a peculiar fishery that will not be examined here). Such sudden shifts in the fortunes of fisherfolk were another constant theme discovered in our coastal travels. Wipeout gales and hurricanes, overwhelming losses at sea, and sudden disappearances of the particular fish most depended on by a certain town—these were all characteristics of the communities' economic destinies. Reasons have been searched and debated for the last of these phenomena. And surely the most haunting, least talked-about reason for the death of this or that fishery has been depletion. Extirpation of the species.

You'll hear different explanations for a sudden stillness on the Maine coast after 1866 (the removal of the bounty being but one), or for the forced shift in New Bedford from whaling to cotton manufacturing, or for the conversion of Cape Cod towns from proud fishing towns to quaint tourist spots. But you won't hear much about overfishing—with the possible exception of the whale, our mammalian cousin, whose passing strikes a sympathetic chord. Tom Tilton, however, is bold to put the finger on depletion as the across-the-board cause. And I'm inclined to agree. He states: "No fisherman will admit that any kind of fishing ended because of over-fishing. But it's my firm belief that that's why trapfishing [for one] came to an end. . . . But don't try to tell any fisherman that."

For a while industrial specialists pinned the blame for the fishes' disappearance on super-efficient East European trawlers (and the modest recovery of certain species since the imposition of the 200-mile limit for foreign ships proves them partially right). Others complained that scientists had been lax in studying the effects of water temperature change on fish supply (I heard this charge in Maine). Many faulted destructive, modern fishing techniques like dragging or gill-netting. But, one way or another, it's still overfishing—which is what happens when man ceases to balance his needs with those of nature. Though not a feature of the historic fishing communities, that is certainly an aspect of our mechanized century.

The happy news is that something *may* have been learned from history. In those relationships between fishing communities and fish populations which have been intelligently managed, the fish seem not to have been extirpated or scared away. For New Bedford, now New England's fishing capital, yellowtail flounder and sea scallops have held up magnificently, like the fishermen's best companions (scallops' value rose from very little in 1945 to more than $8 million twenty years

OPPOSITE. *Evolution of oyster craft: Hand adzed dugouts from Connecticut,* BELOW, *had become sleek, competitive craft,* ABOVE, *by the time of the "Great Oyster Excitment" at the end of the nineteenth century. Both, Mystic Seaport Museum.*

later). For Gloucester, cod and haddock in the same period remained constant in value, about $3.5 million, though the number of pounds taken annually declined slightly.

KILLING OFF the fisheries and the fishing communities by excessive indulgence would have struck New England's founding fathers as unusually stupid. As early as 1652, the Puritan legislators decreed that codfish, haddock, hake, and pollock could not be taken during the winter months because that was their time for spawning. And in 1684 the General Court outlawed private citizens' right to take mackerel by seines. Later, Caleb Cushing of Newburyport sought to ban trawling, saying that that technique would exterminate haddock, just as salmon had been eliminated.

From earliest times Rhode Island's fishing communities regulated their oyster business; Connecticut also controlled shellfish and river fishing. Maine restricted the taking of herring with spawn in certain coastal areas during the fall. And of course for many years lobstermen have been required to measure their lobsters down to the ultimate centimeter to ensure that they're large enough, but not too large. (Amusingly, the Maine town of St. George passed a bizarre counter-law, whereby any citizens who had been caught taking short lobsters could deduct their fines from property taxes.) Conservation lurched along in the communities, without much science or popular support behind it.

Another factor in the death of many former fishing towns was the nature of capitalism—the forward push of capitalists on to other, richer territories when the old ground seemed no longer productive. The dollar, it seems, has no local loyalty; it works not for the locality but for the bank. For centuries, however, smart money had backed the towns' fishing efforts. Captain John Smith had said that New England's fisheries would be more valuable for Mother England than the gold and silver mines possessed by the King of Spain. John Hancock and Joseph Rotch entered into titanic struggles to corner the market for sperm whale oil during the peak of the colonial era. Capitalists were more than willing to fund the railroad to Gloucester and the canneries of Maine when those fisheries looked hot in the nineteenth and early twentieth centuries. Indeed, the increasingly massive investments succeeded in concentrating the total business at a few advantageous locations. In the melancholy words of William F. Robinson: "The little fishing hamlets like Marblehead or those on the Isles of Shoals were gradually overshadowed by [the big] fishing industries."

In earlier times, there had seemed to be a rather neat and natural relationship between the investment and the return. If all went well, the cost of a Banks schooner (approximately $8,000) could be paid off in the first voyage. Ditto for a whaler ($40,000). Thereafter the profits could flow freely to the owners. To be sure, there were risks—but the vessels could be insured against loss at sea; and the men, well, the men could be replaced. But even before the end of the nineteenth century that easy relationship had been warped and strained by greater costs—and by the lust for greater profits. Fortunes could be made more easily by investing in railroads and in the new and distant industries of oil and steel. The big money left town; supporting the local fishery became something of a fool's game.

Nonetheless, in those New England communities where fishermen inventively sought out new fisheries (offshore lobstering, seed-bedded mussels, even shrimp and tuna) and succeeded in staying on top of their own business by cooperatives and other creative agreements, waterfront life has continued to flourish in all the decades of this century. I'm thinking first and foremost of Gloucester and Provincetown and New Bedford, then of a score and more smaller places like the two Stoningtons. I also have in mind such revitalized cities as South Norwalk and Portland, where fishing makes the critical difference between phoniness and real life (and where federal allowances have helped make reconstruction work). I give a special salute to the host of communities down the Maine coast, like Beals Island, where financial interests and the fishermen and women themselves are in creative synchronization. There a very special way of life endures for yet another century and old charges of inflexibility go by the board.

These are the New Englanders, the venturers and the fishermen, who will not abandon the sea. They have a special means of communication with the communities beneath the sea on which we everlastingly depend. And because that communication system works, they continue to feed us almost eucharistically—with provender and with life examples.

I want to show you the men and the fish, the families and the businesses, the boats and the buildings. Most of all I want to show you the towns, the typical towns, in which the themes of this maritime history are best represented, beginning with tiny Noank, Connecticut, not far from Stonington, where nothing has yet drowned out the voices of the last century; then ancient Marblehead, where New England's first great fleet ran into heavy weather. All of the major places to which I've referred will also be visited—with an opportunity to consider the magnificence and cruelty of whaling versus the hazards and rewards of life on the Banks in the "Golden Years" of fishing (1870–1900).

Although I cannot take you to the communities where fish spawn human destinies, I will take you to fabled towns where you can feel the pull of those lines into the deep.

NOANK: EACH ON HIS OWN HOOK

WHEN I drove down the hill from the west into Mystic, Connecticut (not the "Seaport," but the real place), something exciting seemed to be happening. Freshly painted buildings, graphically sharp signs, Oriental kites tied to the posts of second-floor porches greeted me as if to an advertised festival.

Gleaming Mystic was a turned-on village that day, rich with profferings. It invited me and all passers-through to visit its beguiling shops and salty-fare restaurants—seen against a humdrum backdrop of railroad tracks and last-century warehouses. The river glistened; the cars jockeyed to get over the bridge to the Seaport.

But what caught my eye was a patch of tasteful lettering up on a brick wall: "Future Site of Luxury Waterfront Condominiums." A pair of bulldozers was disposing of the former building's insides while the exterior shell was set aside for later use, the way my wife saves Christmas wrappings.

The propped up façade also reminded me of faded photos of Gold Rush towns, hastily built in a panic of avidity. Luxury waterfront condominiums; the new El Dorado. I drove over the bridge.

Mystic, long epitomizing Yankee enterprise (maritime department), extends on both sides of its eponymous river. The area once harbored the most active shipbuilding center on the Atlantic Coast; now it hosts New England's leading tourist attraction. Condominiums certainly seemed in keeping with that spirit. But on the day described, I preferred sleepy Noank, Connecticut—the little community that I'd just discovered a few miles back, on its own arm of the Mystic River. I had found that it faced out upon Block Island Sound, and that it was thus of the Atlantic, not of Long Island Sound. Quiet and a little shabby, Noank glowed dully in the manner of a dusty silver prize that was put away long ago on a hard-to-reach shelf. There were here some intriguing structures, bespeaking a modest economic boom that must have lasted a generation or two in the 1800s; a lovely harbor.

OPPOSITE. *Noank perspective: A fisherman ascends to his house via a handline from his shoreside occupations. Mystic Seaport Museum, Leavitt Collection.*

But, besides a "Sundries" store (one side of which seemed to have had an accident with a truck), there was very little here to deter a stranger from continuing on. The eyes of the town were closed, the visage private; the doors of the big Baptist church were locked, no one seemed to be around. No filling station or antiques shop invited me to spend a buck. Mysterious.

Fortunately, I succeeded in arranging an appointment at the local historical society a few weeks later: a morning in October which resolved some of Noank's mysteries. The president of the society, Mary Anderson, and Captain Adrian Lane met me at the door of the deconsecrated Episcopal chapel which serves as the society's headquarters. In front of the chapel now stands a flagpole made from the topmast of Captain Lane's grandfather's fishing schooner. Inside, they introduced me to a special exhibition the society had prepared on the community's fisheries.

While I walked around the exhibits and listened to Captain Lane's yarns (in between his lightings of cigarettes, which he almost immediately put out, as if trying to get rid of the things), a very unusual community began to assert itself. Here was a place removed from the high-stepping themes of American history; here was something isolated and rough and . . . innocent. Pictures of the slatted ramps for hauling up the fishermen's boats, the unpainted shacks and barnacled slips and gaff-rigged smacks began to come into focus for me. But the scenic beauty and long-ago charm of this shorefront complex—no more than fifty yards in extent and built, it seemed, out of matchsticks—were not all that enraptured me. It was the way of life. When looked at closely, all those piled-up lobster pots, those nets draped over barrels, those spars and floats and cribs represented scores of enterprises, a humming dynamo of human endeavor. Yet all could be blown or washed away in a single storm (which was precisely why the sheds were built so lightly—let 'em go).

Here was an intense encampment, hammered together by hand, activated by muscle and guts, impelled by the lure of fish and the promise that you could be your own boss. You could bring back a big haul, with just your son or your nephew helping you, and you could look anyone in the eye. Here were men and boys doing what they could against the sea with wood and rope and iron and no real money. I was drawn into their world.

As expressed in one of the exhibit's captions, Noank in those days was "a close community of independent yet cooperative people." The twin industries of fishing and boat building leaned companionably against each other, it appeared, not unlike the walls of one of those gradually collapsing shanties. Rich and poor, everyone worked competetively with each other, joked or cursed at each other in this democratic, nineteenth-century village of some eight hundred souls, no matter what was going on elsewhere.

Later, while driving away from the exhibition, I spotted a sign on Noank's Pearl Street which indicated that the informal but prideful spirit still prevailed here. The sign said:

WE THINK OUR TOWN IS HEAVEN.
PLEASE DON'T DRIVE LIKE HELL THROUGH IT.

But of course you normally *don't* drive through Noank if you're a stranger, unless you've turned off I-95 too early, taken the wrong Seaport exit; or if you've deliberately chosen to approach Mystic by the wandering road that leads to its back door.

I began to see normally bypassed Noank as the surviving representative of many other vanished fishing villages—a chapter expunged from our national history. Voices from the past that I had ceased to listen to (if I had ever heard them) now got through to me, voices from the waterfront that informed me differently about being an American. But why has this historic way of life been erased and forgotten? From subsequent readings, key facts came together, making that question all the more urgent. Given the tremendous loss of life at sea from ports like Noank (from one famous New England port 382 vessels and 2,454 fishermen were lost in 24 years), given also the indomitable building and launching of new vessels to replace those lost, why is this scene not viewed as a frontier of American heroism?

It's possibly because these communities were poor, smelly, and the people removed from the general concept of Progress. Impiously, we've turned our backs on what's not "successful." Yet perhaps that could be turned back around, and we could gain a more realistic understanding of how Americans built their country, if we paid attention to these nostalgic communities. Better do it fast, before Noank, and its sisters are swept away by the rising tide of condominiums and artificial land values.

FLAWS of the complexion would probably disqualify Noank from any suburban beauty contest. Paint peels, gutters sag, fences lack pickets. Nonetheless, if you happen to have taken that back way into Mystic (Route #215), I'll wager the place will have caught your eye. There's a balance of nature and man's works, a harmony of scale that approaches perfection. Can this be accidental, or is it possibly an expression of the life here? Beyond that, you may have noticed the piquant architectural contrast between the humble but beautifully detailed and proportioned fishermen's cottages near the waterfront and the superb, somewhat miniaturized Greek Revival houses on the crest of the ridge. Even in that contrast, there's a sensitive harmony.

The houses are all of the lonesome, underlandscaped sort that encourages the viewer to think: "Boy, I could get that baby for a song." Watching out over other roofs is a tall, whimsical palazzo that is what the term *Carpenter Gothic* is all about. This house, with its mansard-roofed tower and its multiplicity of porches, had just been sold to out-of-towners for an "undisclosed figure," I was informed at the Sundries store.

On its ground-floor level, the lofty Victorian structure boasts a side porch decorated with a paint-peeled, twelve-paneled wood screen depicting either the Labors of Hercules or Aesop's fables (interpretations vary), one panel of which is missing. The house was built by the hands at Deacon Palmer's shipyard, in between vessels, along about 1894. "The Deacon knew everyone in town, and everyone worked for him," one native told me, in an apt but not quite accurate phrase.

Three-quarter Cape Cod cottage: Males loll about the fisherman's house on a Sunday; his wife, in apron, stands at the door. Mystic Seaport Museum, Scholfield Collection.

Most of those who did not work at Palmer's Yard went off to sea in fishing boats. They were the men who lived with their families down on Front Street in one-and-a-half story cottages like that owned by John Beach. When I called upon John, with an introduction from the historical society, I saw that his typical cottage of the 1840s was far from mean. Though originally small of measure (roughly 30′ × 40′) and now enlarged, it has always displayed an amazing amount of flexibility. It was a "three-quarter Cape"—one window on this side and two on the other of the front door instead of two windows on either side—thus symmetry never mattered. Irregularity and innovation could reign.

The large room at front, on the right, was the parlor by the original plan, with the kitchen (family room) at back left. Running back to the kitchen from the front door was a narrow passageway, illuminated but dimly by daylight through the little panes over the door; into that darkness plunged a perilously steep stairway from above the visitor's left shoulder. A confusion of doorways: one to the parlor; another to the kitchen; but the other? Ah, a bedroom at back right. But what about the front left? Oh, that's another bedroom, accessible through a door from the kitchen. Upstairs they squeezed in two or three more bedrooms (depending on how the walls were jiggered around the central chimney), beneath a ceiling no more than six feet high. "Not much room to swing a cat," as John said. But plenty of spaces for a three-generation family.

Who lived in such flexible nonshanties? A fisherman named George Brown was the first occupant of the house down the way at 65 Front Street. He might be considered the model: Anglo-Saxon, unrelated to anybody of importance, independent, and unmemorialized. He (or the assessors) evaluated his small holding at $700 at the time of the 1850 census, when his house was eleven years old. Brown lived in the house now owned by John Beach. The captain had at some point managed to acquire a degree of wealth as a result of salvage work, so he charted his course toward a more up-and-coming part of town. His wife objected, out of fondness for the old neighborhood (as the story is told on Front Street), but they moved anyway.

John feels no call to move—despite having gone through six sump pumps during his tenancy, in a vain effort to control the flooding in his basement. And his wife, who initially had seen Noank as a community to stay away from because of its lack of public water and sewage systems, now agrees that the house is a treasure. It became all the more so, in her eyes (and others') when Noank installed the missing systems in the 1960s, enabling her to tap into something more regular than a cistern filled by ground and heaven water.

The Beaches recently noted with amusement that, when their married daughter looked at a similar house in Noank with vacation-times in mind, the asking price for that "unimproved" Cape turned out to be $275,000. "And see that brown house, cater-corner across the street?" John asked me. "That just sold for $810,000. It has a pretty nice front yard, though."

As a result of the time spent with John, and the realization that big money was knocking at Noank's door, I pondered more intently what precisely was being threatened here by the changes that now loomed. Another new cross-street neighbor of the Beaches had built a Marin County-type ranch house, with ranch house-type plantings, out into the harbor—a breach of something or other. Taste? Or ethics? Surely a psychological wrench of geological proportions to a village where harmony has been the mode.

THE streets run through the blocks in Noank from one end to another more or less where they may. And the houses disincline to line up the way the streets go; they'd rather face this way or that, hunkered down out of the weather or enjoying a particular view of the harbor. As a result, there is no feeling here of the mythical New England town center with its common and its diatonically presented, white buildings (black shutters). Nor the broad avenue lined with Federalist elms, pilastered houses set back on capacious lawns. Noank's Main Street does slide down in a more or less direct way to where the Old Landing Place used to be. But the streets off to either side are irrationally positioned and have a tendency to change names in the telling; inhabitants hesitate to advise how to get from here to there. "We know it's a little confusing. But we like it that way," they claim.

The very first inhabitants to walk down that hill were Pequots; they had come to stay and to fish. To them "Nawyanque" (meaning Neck of Land) was a sanctuary for the few who had survived the slaughters of the late seventeenth century. A busy mainland tended to pass them by here. Not until 1705, long after Noank's neighboring points and harbors had been settled by the English Puritans, did this secluded peninsula catch the eye of some land-eager whitemen. They saw the paradox of a superb harbor with nothing on its shores but "tepees." It was then simply a matter of pushing the necessary legal buttons and the paradoxical place was theirs. To attract settlers they utilized that wonderful real estate gimmick, the lottery, open exclusively to the landed proprietors of New London and Groton, the two towns to the west. (Today Noank, a *village* as they name things in Connecticut, remains a part of the *town* of Groton.)

The once-haughty Pequots did what they could to defend their lovely and productive peninsula from this cultural usurpation. A protest was filed unto the authorities, with the aid of an interpreter—much as we, if threatened by a development on prized land, would call upon the Wetlands or EPA commissioner. The Pequots' plaint said in part:

> Since we are settled in a place called Nawyanque being convenient for fishing and hunting as well as planting, which is a great part of our subsistence and which we know not how to live without; there being no other place where we can come to salt water or to fish or hunt without trespassing on the rights or properties of the English. Beside this, there was one great reason, as we have always understood from the English as well as from our predecessors why Governor Winthrop placed us here, so that we might never be hindered from hunting and fishing as well as planting, it being all rocky land not fit to plow but only for the hoe. . . . Designing men, by cunning contrivances, are cheating us out of our just rights.

But this got them nowhere. The lottery went merrily forward. And as early as 1713 the colonists' houses began to appear.

A descendant of one of the first Noank settlers told me, however, that specters of the Indians remained; a partially comforting thought. One summer morning a man she knew, then a boy, woke up (in the mid-1800s) to find Indians camped in the front yard. They looked as if they had taken over, with their equipment and squaws. Terrified, he ran downstairs to warn his mother. But she calmed him, saying that the red men still had the right to come there and fish every now and again. He watched them all through the day as they tried their luck in the waters. By the next morning they were gone.

FISHING occupied the minds and the ambitions of the flocking settlers. Connecticut colonial histories sing of the increasingly magnificent catches, taken by means of artfully crafted shallops and by weirs stretched across the rivers and out in the bays. It was all rather primitive by modern industrial standards, yet inshore fishing in the eighteenth century was a sizable enterprise: The wealth of the so-called River Gods (the great families who dwelled along the banks of the Connecticut River in their elegantly furnished mansions) was based on the unfailing supply of seasonally prolific fish, salted and shipped abroad. By now the sounds of the shipbuilder's adze and the caulker's mallet could be heard along the Noank harborfront. The business and the site attracted more and more who would associate themselves with fishing, both the clever and the shiftless.

The preferred vessel for going out into ever deeper waters was a bluff-bowed sloop, the traditional shoal-draft coaster built with heavier and heavier spars. From a sharply cocked bowsprit she flew two jibs; the stubby mast carried a gaff-rigged mainsail, with small topsail. Back from the sea in such sturdy though leisurely craft, Connecticut fishermen brought to Noank and other ports in the pre-Revolutionary year of 1772 nearly 30 million pounds of dried fish (much of it cod) and nearly 25,000 barrels of pickled fish, mostly bound for distant lands. It's notable that the greatest portion of Connecticut's exported fish went then not to the mother country of Great Britain or to the fish-hungry Catholics of southern Europe but to the slave plantations of the West Indies; notable too that fish exports from the colony of Connecticut plus those from Rhode Island and New Hampshire did not equal those from mighty Massachusetts, where cod had long made rich men of fish shippers.

The Revolutionary fishermen—political radicals, sailors for the New England navies, attackers of Crown ships—challenged His Majesty's squadrons. And the British assaults on the Connecticut coast commenced. One raid stunned Stonington, just east of Noank; a spectacularly brutal raid on New London by the treasonous Benedict Arnold leveled the town. The village of Noank just about survived.

But the fishermen managed to bang a serviceable fleet of boats back together; as early as the 1790s the Palmer family's shipyard was in full operation. By then—and after the War of 1812 was fought and not quite lost—the market for fish was changing dramatically. Nineteenth-century Americans were asserting a continentally strong appetite, and they would pay cash. The old days when dried and salted cod was regarded both as the obligatory winter staple and as a kind of international currency—those days were passing as market centers in New London, New Haven, and of course New York flourished with fish stands and with transportation systems to the interior. Of Connecticut it had long been said that the state was like "a cask of good liquor, tapped at both ends—at one of which Boston draws, and New York the other." But in the case of the fisheries, the market was generally down Long Island Sound to the west; the supply out to sea to the east.

Enhancing that geographical advantage was a biological boon: Multiple, enormous schools of mackerel appeared out of the blue, within range of southeastern Connecticut. Boats built at Palmer's, then at Latham's yards could be out on the richly teeming Nantucket shoals and home to market again with full holds in but a few days' sailing. This fishy bounty is now no wonder to ichthyologists, their

Eighteenth-century fishing sloop: A time when awkward vessels, ancient techniques and war-troubled seas made for meager catches. Peabody Museum of Salem; watercolor attributed to M. F. Corne.

studies having confirmed that the waters south and east of Cape Cod are the prime spawning grounds of the mackerel. But in the days of the young republic, it seemed like a gift given from above.

Thus the species mackerel (*Scomber scombrus*), each weighing about two pounds and measuring about eighteen inches, came to be crowned King of the Sea—for its sweet taste, its sudden dominance over the other fisheries of southern New England, and its royal perversities. Fishermen occasionally reported "wild swarms" of mackerel that would snap at any hook and would churn the sea's surface, uncountable thousands roiling as a great silvery mass. Then at other times the mackerel would completely disappear, leaving the fishing boats to cross the empty waters in a vain quest. All that was really known about them was that they would usually appear off Block Island about April 1, slightly later farther east, staying for the summer season. Where they went in the winter, no one presumed to guess.

It was understood all too clearly, however, that the royal mackerel had one terribly common characteristic: when dead, the fish would quickly rot and stink. Pickling them in a salt solution (casks of brine) was the accepted solution. But the strengthening market for fresh fish suggested another answer—get them there *alive*.

There then came sailing upon the scene an evolved vessel, the "smack," which was designed specifically to help get the Connecticut fisherman's product to market fresh and snappy. And it was the sloop-rigged smack that Noank's yards excelled in turning out during the nineteenth century. As opposed to "tight bottomed vessels," smacks have special holds that admit water through holes bored in the bottom planks. These tightly sealed wells might be compared to extra-large centerboard boxes. (Well do I remember staring into the centerboard box on my father's sailing skiff when a boy and exclaiming in horror, "Hey there's green water in there!") But the smacks' compartments were generally built in the form of a pyramid whose top has been cut off to receive the deck hatch. So down through that hatch into the green, oxygen-rich water were dumped the just-caught fish from the fishermen's barrels, there to swim about till landed.

Best known and most admired of the Connecticut smacks is the *Emma C. Berry*, which was restored by Mystic Seaport in the early 1970s. She measures 38′ 6″ on deck, with a broadish beam of 14′ 7½″ and draft of only 5′ 3″. Though built at Noank's Palmer Yard after the Civil War (1866), she patently reflects and summarizes the design improvements that fishermen and builders had worked out together ever since the 1820s. Handsome of sheer, tall-rigged with mainsail and jib topsails strung from a lofty topmast that seems to bend eagerly forward, she looks as if she could hold her own against any competitor, yesterday or today.

It was the beauty of her lines that saved her. In 1924 she was observed abandoned on the mud flats of Beals Island, Maine, after having served as both a fishing vessel and a fish carrier for decades in Connecticut and Maine. The sight was pathetic, as the tide drained in and out of her planks. But having fallen in love with the vision of what she yet could be, a new owner patched her up and used her for several years as a coaster. She was saved from a second abandonment by another lover who sailed the *Emma C. Berry* as a repaired, repatched character yacht. In 1969 she was given to the Seaport—representing more than a hundred years of maritime history.

For seaman and landlubber alike, the beauty and the character of this mackerel hook-and-line sailing vessel are compelling. The *Emma C. Berry* seems to symbolize absolutely the heyday that Noank enjoyed in the mid-1800s: maritime technology at its most luminous. Yet I remembered a finger-wagging warning against putting all one's trust in material objects as palimpsests of history, a warning delivered by that grandfather figure of New England studies, Harvard's Percy Miller. He scorned those "who direct their researches to ships, trade routes, currency, property, agriculture, town government and military tactics." The secret, he believed, could only be found in the mind. In this case, the mind of the community.

The mind in historical Noank, one must admit, was quite directly linked to the fisherman's hand. And in those hands as the fishermen stood on the deck of the well smack were lengthy lines, lines that worked more productively because of another splendid bit of maritime technology. This specialized tool, studied and appreciated and used by the fishermen, was called a "mackerel jig" and had been invented about 1816 by Jacob Lurvey (species: *Ingenious Yankee*). His brainchild consisted of a lead casting which would embrace the mackerel hook. Each fisherman made his own jigs from one of Lurvey's specially designed molds. Having tied those newly cast jigs to his set of lines, he would bait the hooks, then fling the entire rig over the boat's side. Pulled by the jig's weight, the hooks would swiftly descend to the desired depth (about forty feet from the surface) "Jigging" a line in either hand, the fishermen would pray that at that very moment a hungry school of mackerel would sweep along beneath his boat and would lunge directly at his hooks (rather than at his neighbors). A chancy system perhaps, but vastly superior to the old line-and-pole fishing known as "drailing," which had meagerly served fishermen of sea and sound in previous generations.

Yet, even as I held the tools and walked on the planks of the creations that had brought an economic boom to this little town, I wondered why—why anyone had persevered at this risky, chancy calling. Why did this unprepossessing fishing center attract such newcomers as George Brown of 65 Front Street? He arrived at an expansive time in those United States, roads and canals stretching out to

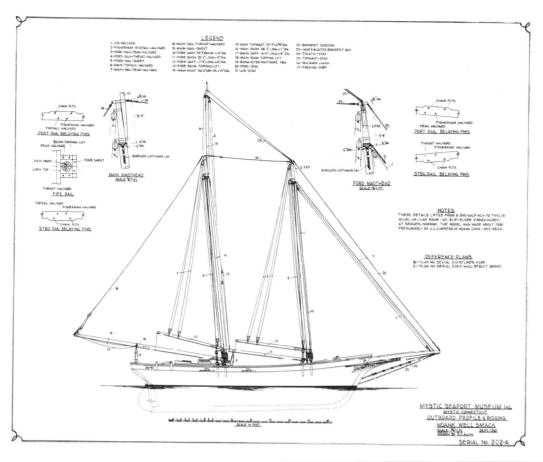

Mary Hoxie: *The typical Noank schooner stowed her catch in a midships well, or "smack"; note that the smack schooner in the photo has an added topmast not shown in the plan. Both, Mystic Seaport Museum; plan by R. C. Allyn; photo, Scholfield Collection.*

the newly opened West, river-powered factories offering steady employment to "mechanicks" and spinners, male and female workers of varying skills.

He could obviously make some money at fishing, if he brought any luck at all with him and if he grasped the new techniques. But how much money? The standard sources informed me that the customary process in the fisheries at this time was that upon sale of a fish cargo, the vessel's owners would keep half, and (after deducting a stated amount for equipment and supplies) the other half would be split by the men, according to how many barrels each had caught. This was the fundamental economic principle of the enterprise. But what I didn't appreciate at first was the accompanying phrase, "each on his own hook." I kept reading that each man was "fishing on his own hook" on board these smallish, hand-lining vessels. But what did that signify? Finally I figured out that it bespoke a situation not strictly economic, not wholly social, but some of both. This described a way in which George Brown or anyone else might relate to the others around him, and indeed to God and the Devil as well. You had your chance; you were working with your own strength, your own skill and luck (if you had any). You were competitive with the best of them. If this trip out, this "fare," was less rewarding for you than hoped, wait until the next one.

Drawings exist of what life was like for the band of men on board these hand-liners from Noank and other ports. The fisherman stood on the starboard side of the deck, in an assigned place (the "high-liner," or best catcher amidships—lucky fellow), while the sloop eased along under minimal sail. Working his lines with knowing jerks and rhythms, he would have his own barrel right beside him and into it would expertly flip the snagged mackerel. This assumes that he had spent the night before getting his bait (usually clams), and that the skipper had done an adequate job of locating the mackerel school and seeding the waters with chopped-up menhaden from the "bait mill" (another invention!). With all conditions favorable, the mackerel fisherman might bring in ten or fifteen barrels—some two thousand fish—in one day. After accounts were squared away, he might receive for that work coins totaling nearly $1.00. It sounds like not much, but this was at a time when a dollar a day was considered "white man's pay."

Furthermore, each man was fishing truly on his own hook, at a time when that independent working pattern was on its way out. It was in distinct contrast to the modus operandi in the new factories. There workers were obliged to take an "ironclad oath" promising to accept whatever regulations and pay scales the employer chose to dictate. The worker also had to keep his mouth shut; he vowed to abstain from entering into "any combination whereby the work may be impeded or the company's interest in any work injured." Hardly an acceptable condition for an opinionated Yankee.

In addition, fishing was kind of fun . . . mackerel being pursued generally during the balmy summer months. There's a vivid portrait of the typical scene, from the shipboard perspective, in that famous report on *The Fisheries of the U.S.* by the Smithsonian's George B. Goode:

> The confusion and excitement is increased by the frequent snarling of the lines. . . . Little is said while the fishing is going on; the men lean far over the rail in strange attitudes of expectancy with one or two lines in each hand, the hands moving up and down and constantly hauling in and throwing out one of the lines.

It was a great contest, physically demanding. But hell, I'm strong enough, and I'm a free man now, aren't I?

Handliners' heaven: At assigned places along the rail, fishermen bring their catch aboard an early nineteenth-century schooner. Peabody Museum of Salem; unsigned oil painting.

ADDED to the excitement of the catch and the cash reward after each voyage was the possibility of advancing from being the possessor of one fraction of a share in a relative's boat to being the owner of a full share; then owning shares in other boats as well. For some fishermen, constantly mounting debts and disappointments were too oppressive to attempt that capitalistic route. But as recalled by such Noankers as Captain Adrian Lane, there were plenty who did all right. "It came to the point where men owned shares in several different vessels at once. They'd buy shares in a boat before they'd buy a house," Captain Lane told me. "Each time a boat went out, they had a chance to pay all their debts back. Of course usually they didn't."

Samuel Eliot Morison puts it this way: "To save enough to acquire a fishing vessel, and live ashore on her earnings, was the fisherman's highest ambition." Goode confirms that in New England at this time most of the fishing boats were owned by the men themselves; Capitalism with a capital C and its massive industrial maneuvers and its class imprisonments was still a generation or two in the future.

Disasters swept through the fleet with dreadful regularity, however, wiping out all holdings. The little that one had gained—and promises beyond that—could be swept away by a single squall on the Nantucket shoals. Also, Noank's harbor is not sufficiently sheltered by the neighboring islands and bars to offer much resistance to the equinoctial storms that rage through in March and September. Harborside memory has it that, in one desperate attempt to preserve their fleet against such a storm in 1815, the skippers scuttled their vessels at anchor. Other times, the boats were hauled up river, up into the eel grass and mudflats, a stratagem that increased but by no means guaranteed one's chances of survival. Frequently all the stagings and shacks were blown apart; April and October were times of rebuilding.

They all went through it together, these "independent but cooperative" folk on Front Street. Theirs was a special kind of tight society, all the more inward-turned as a result of the village's location out on a bypassed peninsula. But this clannishness in Noank seemed not to have produced a suspicious, xenophobic community, from what I could hear of the old stories. The people had some education, went to church, I supposed. And did they have enlightened or obtuse leaders? It could make a difference.

ON CHRISTMAS EVE in 1959, a wild fire broke out within the church at Noank, the huge, white First Baptist Church on Main Street. Blazing out of control at first, the conflagration was eventually subdued, leaving the 1887 structure nothing more than four charred walls. Two years later a pseudo-Colonial version of the old building appeared, as if by the wave of an angel's wand—or so it seemed to impressed observers. "I'd always heard as a girl that the people in that church were 'sanctified,' " a nonmember told me. "Now I understood their power."

This "Baptist" is not, I soon learned, in the Southern tradition but in the tradition of Rhode Island's Roger Williams, the saint who was thrown out of Cotton Mather's Puritan Massachusetts in 1636. Williams could hardly be called a revolutionary, for he agreed with nearly all the tenets that tangled the brains of the Bay State's theologians. But, in contrast to those theocrats and the godly city founders of Massachusetts and Connecticut, Williams had one, vital, liberating social idea. Whether or not some strange fellow or woman (say, a Quaker or a Jew or an Anglican) might persist in those deviant religious beliefs after moving into a given community, Williams declared that he or she should be allowed to live alongside the true believers. For that idea and other radical proposals Williams had been banished, his concepts blocked in Massachusetts but allowed to spread up and down the waterways around Providence. Between Rhode Island and eastern Connecticut runs a little river that is more of a carrier than a barrier. From that river Noank is not even ten miles distant, closer as The Word flies.

Connecticut's first Baptist church was established in Old Mystic in 1705, its founders seeking to build a religious community totally independent from the colony's civil authority. In that same philosophical line, Noank's church was the third to follow. It was an open philosophy that welcomed the fishermen of variegated persuasions who moved to Noank at about the same time as George Brown. This broad faith appealed also to those workmen who came generations later, with saw and auger, to the thriving shipyards. Many of these originated from Canada's Maritime Provinces and from Europe—foreigners, people from well outside the clan. But in a remarkable way, both on shipboard and in the boat shed, they were signed on and accepted, few uncomfortable questions asked. They settled in the midst; there was never anything like a "Little Italy" in Noank.

"My father had already been working here for a couple of years by the time I arrived," a grizzled Noanker named Aldo Bacciocchi told me. "I was ten and a half, it was July 3, 1913. The next day they scared me out of my skin with all the fireworks and cannon fire. I hadn't heard anything about how they celebrated Independence Day in a village like this. But after that, I felt at home right away."

Presumably the tolerant teachings of Roger Williams had much to do with that easy acceptance of people from elsewhere. Skeptics may quibble with this patristical idea, saying that the immigrants' lot must have been just about as chilly and oppressive in Noank as it was other places in the country (where nativist mobs not infrequently burned newcomers' churches and homes). To those skeptics I can only point out the planting and flowering of immigrants' churches that occurred in the village as the century was changing. Catholic, Anglican, Methodist, these delightful wood and stone structures—modest of belfry, richly textured in siding—blossomed at various spots on either side of Main Street. They add much to the polyglot harmony of the place.

But, curiously, many of the newly arrived Italians became Baptists. The best explanation I could find for that phenomenon lay in the personality of Deacon Palmer, he who owned the shipyard and built the Victorian palazzo. Embodiment of the village's Baptist tradition, he (in the judgment of one of Noank's historians) "ran the whole thing as if it were an integrated operation—the church, the yard, the Sunday School. He got those families to go to his church as a part of the deal."

A woman who remembers the deacon personally agrees that he was, by all odds, the community's commanding spirit. "He was a great man . . . a very humble man. When I was a little girl, I heard him deliver a prayer in the church before a concert; he had a distinctive, quavery voice, and would drag out the final syllable of the words." The retired teacher who was giving me this verbal portrait, a sprightly ninety-year-old named Mary Virginia Goodman, paused as she recollected the scene, then went on with her story. "A relative of my first husband was in the Palmers' house often; he said that the deacon wouldn't let the hired girl eat in the kitchen. She ate in the dining room with the rest of the family, you may be sure of that."

Another pause. "We don't have any upper-crust here. Why should we?"

Mrs. Goodman had originally been a Morgan, one of the first families to enter upon the peninsula. They had sold the land to the Palmers for the shipyard. She and I stood on the porch of her Gothic Revival home, with its Belle Epoque busts and draperies. The view from the back ridge on which her house was poised, out over the harbor to the sea, was breathtaking. The house had been built as a present for her husband, whose parents had once dwelled in the handsome Greek Revival temple in front, on Main Street. Mrs. Goodman had taught school in Noank for twenty-odd years, beginning in the 1930s; now she admitted that a recent fall down the curving staircase in the front hall had slowed her down. "But did you see me on television when they showed our Memorial Day parade?"

Among the mottoes she had regularly put up above the schoolroom's black-board, her favorite was

ORDER IS HEAVEN'S FIRST LAW
—*Alexander Pope*

In her classes, disorder was not a problem; the same rules applied to immigrants and natives, boys and girls. This was, after all, a school with an ancient egalitarian tradition, the very school on the hill that had trained generations of New England fishermen and their sisters.

In the old days, boys went off to sea with their fathers and uncles at about the age of ten. They usually served as cooks in the primitive galleys on board, having learned in their mothers' kitchens how to keep a stove going, how to fry fish and boil water. When they returned from those exciting mackerel summers, they faced the schoolroom again, and maxims like those of Mrs. Goodman. As a slight deviation from the norm, navigation was taught to these young, returned sailors along with the classic fare of the three Rs. Girls had a tendency to remain in school longer, and to get better grades.

Dr. Goode, the official observer, opined that girls did profit from local education more than boys: "The intelligence and refinement of the women of the fishing towns seem to a stranger quite noteworthy. The excellent education of wives and mothers of fishermen cannot be without effect upon the intelligence of the class."

He might be right: religious and educational leadership surely helped nourish Noank. The fight against intolerance and Industrial Age pressures called for stout hearts, to use the language of the time. Exactly how Noank solved some of the particular problems of its day gives additional clues to the sustaining life quality of the place.

"IMMIGRATION into the United States should be Absolutely Prohibited" was the proposed Resolution. The date was 1894 and the debate among Noank citizens was to be held at the nearby Mystic Opera House. Elitist though the subject was, the methodology was thoroughly democratic. Wayland Morgan, a Noank lobsterman, headed the Committee on Decision. The Male Quartette and the Noank Instrumental Trio (both of which were manned by a diverse crew of seamen and shore men, Yankee and otherwise) provided the entertainment. After all that close-voiced harmony and striking of glockenspiels, it's remarkable that no record remains of the decision reached. But that wasn't the point, when you think about it. The point, clearly, was to let *everyone* sound off, then forget it. Let the voice of the people be heard (and, if nonsense, ignored).

Another factor in this get-it-off-your-chest-fellow tradition may have been the peculiar, rough kind of democracy that obtained on board a New England fishing vessel. There the captain was by no means a figure of aloof omnipotence and supreme authority (nor is he a Caesar today). He shared his cabin with the men, ate with them. In Goode's words, "He tried to make his orders sound like requests."

That equal-to-equal attitude carried over to life on shore. There a common conviction was forming that Front Street, particularly at night, was a muddy and dangerous disgrace. The street's nickname was "Bootjack" because so many fishermen, struggling home in the darkness after a full day at sea and to market, often lost a boot to the tenacious, persistent mud. Dawn would find the poor man hopping from stoop to stoop, looking to reclaim his treasured, red leather friend.

Well, who was going to do anything about it? As Claude M. Chester recounted the tale in his collected *Papers*, the village rallied, and

> a Village Improvement Society was formed which assumed the responsibility for furnishing some method of lighting the street. And through their efforts, about 25 street lights were installed at strategic points. They were simply glass cages, supported by iron posts, containing an ordinary kerosene lamp. Every morning the lamplighter visited each light, armed with a short ladder and a can of kerosene oil and a roll of polishing cloth. At night he retraced his steps, lighting each lamp in consecutive order.

It was pretty nifty. The institution of democracy gleamed, and the village gained even more charm.

BY THE TIME of surging immigration and civic improvements, Noank's fishery had changed considerably. By now many of the old well-smack sloops and hand-liners had disappeared; the harbor was crowded with some forty sharp-bowed schooners and other vessels of swift purpose. The competition was intense, but the supply of fish seemed to be never-ending. Captain Lane, in recalling his grandfather's stately, fifty-five-foot schooner *Redwing* (which drew about eight feet, maximum for the harbor's depth), described the new turn to "market fishing"—the business of supplying iced-down fish for markets in the major cities.

> They'd go up and down the coast, packing the fish into ice barrels; they'd get the fish into Fulton's the very same day they caught 'em. Or they'd take the fish in from the pounds at Martha's Vineyard or Block Island, sailing just as fast as they could against the others. When it blew, they'd reef the old way: by taking the "bonnet" off the bottom of the jib. One summer my grandfather made seven round trips to Fulton's in seven weeks. I don't know how they did it!"

They did it by driving themselves and their vessels hard, often beyond the point of physical and mental toleration that we would find endurable. And the losses were tremendous.

Claude Chester's *Papers* record a melancholy legend that goes a certain distance to dramatize Noank's continuing losses at sea:

There was a ship to be seen at rare intervals in the home waters. She was not a product of the craftsman's art—nor had she been fashioned by human hands. She always came in just as the shades of night were falling. Some of the older people remember seeing her as she came slowly and majestically through the winding channel into the harbor, not aided by either wind or tide. No word of command was ever issued from the lips of that wraith-like figure which stood at the wheel. Just a brief stop, and she was gone, lost to sight in the deepening shadows of the evening. She had come to bring back to the home port the soul of one whose body the sea had claimed. "Home is the sailor, home from the sea."

By this time, the 1880s and 1890s, Noank had been through two or three generations of prosperity—at the cost of many a sailor's life but without significant changes in the "independent but cooperative" way of living. The railroad had arrived in about 1870, but it skirted the village on the northern fringe; everyone still lived "on the water side of town." Summer people set about building their showy "cottages" on points and islands in this era, but they too seemed to respect the social fabric of Noank for what it was.

They bought the preserves put up by the fishermen's wives from fruit picked in the grape arbors and pear and apple orchards behind their houses. They cheered and took part in the concerts and pageants that the fisher families and yard workers were fond of staging in their grandly named clubs and halls. They enrolled in the Baptist Church, with its heterogeneous mixture of "brilliant and otherwise," and they joined in charitable activities to aid the Widows and Fatherless Children.

Oh, there were snobs and there were divisions. Minutes at the historical society indicate that the ladies of the Female Sewing Society of Noank, mostly shipyard owners' and managers' wives, were not joined by many of the fishermen's wives. And one woman of long memory told me that "the charity for the fisher families from the shipyard owners, through various societies, was very real but was carried out with some condescension." She thought back and sharpened her recollections: "Possibly it was carried out more for reasons of self-aggrandizement than for Christian or community reasons." Nonetheless, all took responsibility for the well-being of the indigent, and no one was too high and mighty.

BUT EVEN AS THE COMMUNITY continued to work together in its peculiarly harmonious way, the lamps were going out in Noank. There were negative trends in the fisheries against which a little fishing village on Block Island Sound could

OPPOSITE. *Main Street, South: Between the two-storied provision stores stands Noank's humble fish market. Mystic Seaport Museum, Scholfield Collection.*

not stand up. The most important was that the mysterious mackerel, father fish of the community, had begun to fade away. It wasn't just the fish's usual trickiness: in a pattern that residents and fishermen of the New England coast would see again with other types of fish, the mackerel was behaving as if too much of a good thing had gone on too long. The decline commenced, grew steeper, and then dove down to absolute bottom. By 1910 it was so bad that in neighboring Massachusetts Bay scarcely a mackerel was recorded as hooked.

Perhaps the decline had been accelerated by the invention and introduction in the 1870s of the purse seine—an immense net which the sharp-eyed crews of fast-sailing mackerel schooners would seek to string around a school of fish. Six men, straining at the oars of their thirty-foot longboat, and urged on by the steersmen almost as if they were after a whale, would at length succeed in getting the net around the school before a neighboring boat could achieve the same encirclement. Then a line would be pulled at the very bottom of the net, ensnaring the surface-schooling fish (which, fearing capture, struggled higher and higher to get away from an unknown terror in the depths). Thereafter it was merely a matter of bringing the schooner alongside and scooping the silvery fish into the hold with a long-handled net. It was very efficient. And, in fact, the method, with some refinements, is the same one used today.

Noankers declined at the beginning of the new century to go in that purse-seining direction. "We were the last stronghold of the hand-liners," Captain Lane said, not without pride. Robert Palmer, descendant of the famous boat builders, remembers that there were fishermen who took to dories, or who phased into dragnetting—or lobstering. But one way or another, the bounty of the sea began to seem each year a little less bounteous. The Spicer store, where so many fishermen had outfited themselves for the time at sea, added up the figures with increasing discouragement; they'd dismantled the wharf in 1894. The shipyards cut back.

Whereas the editor of the *Mystic Press* had noted with neighborly good cheer in February of 1877 that "we are glad to congratulate our Noank friends on their evident continued prosperity," there were different tidings in June of 1918. Then the editor noted: "None of the old-time boat shops are having any work done. A few boats which have been stored in winter quarters are being overhauled and painted but no new ones are built."

In fact, the Palmer Yard stopped operating in 1914. It was not just because of the mackerel—they would recur later (though never in so great numbers) and would tempt other generations of fishermen to come after them with new inventions. Nor was it the advent of the internal combustion engine that destroyed Noank's prominence as a fishing and boat-building port. The place of the sturdy

smacks and glamorous schooners in Noank's harbor would be taken by a variety of craft, including some steam launches designed by the eminent naval architect Frank Paine. Built by the Morses of Maine after Deacon Palmer and his son had died in 1913 and 1914, these power craft of the new era ranged farther and farther out to sea, pursuing menhaden, swordfish, bonefish, anything.

As late as 1928, when he built his big, bold *Baby II* (a diesel-engined sixty-footer), Aldo Bacciocchi thought that fishing in Noank still had a future. And in smaller craft, other members of the still striving Noank fishing community went out after lobsters, river fish, anything.

The point is that the Noank fishermen did not succumb easily to the wipeout of their special world—whoever or whatever triggered the destruction. They fought back with everything at their command, despite the allurements of other industries, the jobs and entertainments to be found in the cities, the call of Gay Paree. The boys kept coming home; the girls could not close up and leave behind the house on Front Street—the population remained almost constant through the low years of the 1920s and 1930s.

Captain Lane himself remembers going out lobstering with his brother then in their uncle's boat. "In the twenties, you could get two loads a day by paying attention to the slack water in the Race." Maybe this was the twilight of the fishing business in Noank, but to him the waterfront still looked immutable: the gear-packed shanties and boat houses, the old smacks pulled up on the shore (who might outfit them again?), and the large, somewhat decrepit rooming houses where the workers from the shipyards used to stay. People were still doing okay. It was not taken at all well when someone found a story written by Theodore Dreiser in the 1890s which had referred to Noank as "a little played out fishing village."

But the captain also remembers from those days the awful moment, out in the boat, when a bight of the lobster warp wrapped itself around his brother's head. Over the side the lad went as the weighted lobster pot dragged him down; he was nineteen. Unhesitatingly, the uncle unsheathed his knife and dove overboard. Feeling his way down the line in the darkness, he eventually came to the form of his nephew, hopelessly caught in the grip of the heavy line. The knife did its work, the boy and the uncle rose to the surface. It was an introduction for the boys, in depth, to what life at sea had meant for all those preceding generations of sailors.

And of course lobstering can be a pretty good business. For a while, Noankers were taking half of the lobsters caught in Connecticut. Old smacks like the *Emma C. Berry* could be resurrected to carry lobsters as well as fish. In this feverish business of the delectable crustaceans, there's still the chance to be your own boss; you work like hell, and you get another job to make ends meet (maybe as a carpenter). This is what's now called being self-employed, which is the category into which 10 percent of the resident Noankers put themselves today. And you can keep quite a lot of the proceeds in your own pocket—who knows how much? You're still on your own hook.

Fisherman's poverty as the route to American nobility may be nothing more than a romantic dream, my warp. But in Noank the collective experience of the people has added up to far more than Architecture or Boats or even Tradition. The cumulative episodes of courage, independence, tolerance, accommodation, and the prudently limited expectations have woven a communal fabric that continues to be unfolded before you like a tablecloth at a family feast. If you have trouble seeing it, you may nonetheless feel it or hear it.

Liberty seems to have flown into this place like an eagle along about 1815,

Catboat and lobsterpots: After the glory days of Noank fishing had passed, men in small boats still sailed out for the day's catch. Mystic Seaport Museum, Edward H. Newbury Collection.

never to leave. Yet in these postindustrial days eagles are endangered. So are the related ospreys which used to fly down the Mystic River scanning for fish. Aldo Bacciocchi wishes he could still be fishing but said that is impossible now: "You can't find anywhere to bring the fish in. The waterfront's all taken up with other kinds of places. Oh, I've had lots of offers for my property down there; but I wouldn't think of taking any of them. Good offers too. I know what it used to be like down there."

So. That will be the death of it—land values.

Noank, which I had been privileged to get to know (and which had ultimately yielded the answer that its architecture's harmony and balance *were* indeed expressions of a communal ethos) now inspired me to go on and explore other fishing communities. I'd see if there, too, in those towns where men fished on their own hook (and women made do until things got better) liberty still endured. Or had those communities been done in by exaggerated land values and a complexity of other modern forces? Of course I had to recognize that Noank was a funny kind of antisuccess story, in terms of its unpretentious leaders and small-scaled institutions. No Rockefellers happened to have been spawned here, hugely powerful personages who could endow the village with perpetuity; no senators or admirals who could stage press conferences for its preservation. Indeed, Noank's historic economic base, slippery as a mackerel, had obviously failed, failed to position the community securely in the counter-currents of the twentieth and twenty-first centuries.

"Well, maybe," John Beach counterposed. "But you should understand that we've had many distinguished people here; just nobody very prominent. Hey! Did I tell you about Amelia Earhardt's wedding? She wasn't from here herself, of course; her husband was, almost (his mother was a Palmer). It was such a big day the principal called a fire drill so the kids could watch the newlyweds go by."

Back at Carson's Sundries—where they make chocolate milkshakes the old fashioned way, as if waiting for William Least Heat Moon to slurp in—the stool two down from mine was taken by a young electrician. He was not amused by the remark I'd heard somewhere else, to the effect that Noank had started to "go to hell" when they put in the water and sewer systems—that being the time when real estate prices started to soar out of sight.

"No. That's not the damn problem," he maintained, putting down his cup of coffee. "It's the rich people themselves: they drive up the prices further by paying those unrealistic prices (for them it's a gamble, a fun risk). And then they never live here except in summer! They don't vote here, of course, but they've got the dollars behind the scene. And they shake the place up."

"I'm not worried, though," he added with a quick smile. "They're not going to change Noank. Lots of us work in Mystic and Groton, places like that, and we don't want those things here. I'm not talking zoning or laws that would turn Noank into a museum or something. I'm talking about what people are willing to get together and fight for . . . like if anyone wanted to put a McDonald's over there." He gestured across Main Street where an old man was raking the lawn. "Nossir, don't worry about Noank."

SO IF you're wondering whether there's a place where a quiet, deep-seated form of democracy once existed, where the social and economic goals of the American Revolution commenced and continue, I suggest that you look along the fishing waterfront, at a pleasantly obscure place like Noank. Daniel Boorstin is the historian who wrote that memorable judgment: "The Revolution itself was, in a sense, a by-product of the New England fisheries. For it was to serve her fishermen that New England colonists built their own ships and so had begun to justify English jealousy." Now I understood more completely what he meant about the fisheries' importance to the never-ending cause of revolution.

But for those of you who may be looking for a retirement place, a shingled cottage with a view, a place with congenial people, I suggest that you reconsider what that means. It means invasion and murder. Your residential investment and your Volvo wagon with extras may be the final straws, the ones that kill a place like Noank. The village is that fragile, and that important to the ongoing story.

MARBLEHEAD: ALL OF ONE ILK

MY COUSIN, a naval architect and customarily a bold navigator, despaired at first of directing me from Boston's Logan Airport to his house in Marblehead. There was the confusion of shifting route numbers, of intersections at which streets would suddenly change names, of blind lanes that would be impossible to find in the dark. But we persevered in the telephoned communications, and he finished his instructions with more hope: "Then, after the sign to the fish market and the hauled-out wooden sloop . . . if you find those . . . ours is the next lane to starboard."

It worked. I arrived safely in what had once been the capital of New England's fisheries.

The next day the navigator and his wife walked me around their part of Marblehead—the oldest part, the cluster of shorefront dwellings called Barnegat, which faces Little Harbor. But even after orientations and explanations, the place still seemed strangely confusing. Front Street used to be called Main Street; Orne Street had no real beginning. How much like Noank that seemed! Yet here there was so much flotsam and jetsam: the well at which the ankle of fisherman's daughter Agnes Surridge had caught the eye of an English nobleman in 1743 (she later became his lady); the cemetery whose close-anchored grave stones were etched with tragedies at sea; the ancient, tilted houses, many nicely restored, that had just sold in the high hundred thousands to professionals from Boston. The sites and episodes appeared to be piled on top of each other as in a rich but disorderly pirate's sea chest.

Of people asked, none could tell me how the curious name Barnegat had washed up on these shores. They did tell me repeatedly, however, that you pronounce it with stress on the last syllable (to rhyme with Krazy *Kat*), just as you must emphasize not the first but the final part of Marble*head*. Accents and speech patterns continue to remind one that this is a community used to speaking to itself, in its own way, at pain of strangers' embarrassment.

OPPOSITE. *Little Harbor: Launching a fishing boat; an early photographer's view of working Marblehead. Collections of Bowden G. Osborne.*

Nevertheless, the bulldozers, backhoes, and cement mixers grinding away on the grounds of the sold-out Hood Boatyard speak loudly in a quite different language. From a glance at the estate-sized houses rising at that site, it became clear that what had been a vital part of this pleasantly confused, still water-related neighborhood was now nothing but a real estate windfall. Ted Hood, one of the East Coast's most successful boat builders, had not been able to refuse the offer for his yard; off to Rhode Island he went, taking the profits and the name Little Harbor with him.

As I heard the situation discussed by Barnegat neighbors, the loss of the yard is a mortal blow to the spirit of the place. And I too regretted the out-of-scale, Brobdingnagian structures that were even now beginning to block the view of the harbor and to overshadow the former fishermen's dwellings. Yet perhaps this is none of my business? I felt forced to examine, more completely than in the innocent and obscure village of Noank, what had happened in this far more important place—where another part of the working waterfront had been peremptorily canceled.

Aesthetics have much to do with my ruefulness about the disruption. But

Marblehead's Front Street: At the end of the nineteenth century, a boat club sought to perk up the former fishing capital's decaying waterfront. Collections of Bowden G. Osborne.

there's also the matter of life quality for those who have chosen to live here, precisely here, because it is the way it is. That their rights are being violated by real estate takeovers is a fragile argument, yet one that can be made with passion, even in the face of economic-political realities. And then there's the issue of the community-as-document: We are looking here at an invaluable, original source for anyone interested in the social history of the American people, not the high and the mighty but the low and the scruffy, the people who did the necessary work. Their houses are veritable libraries of information.

These were the people who were called upon to conquer the first frontier—the treasure-rich lands that lay a couple of hundred miles to the east, underwater. Theirs was the earliest and most crucial of our national victories (or exploitations); it enabled the young, Colonial civilization of New England to survive and, along the way, to develop a certain, salty character. Thus it seems fair enough for me and other outsiders to be interested in these humble houses, these crooked and narrow lanes down which the sea breeze carries the stink of exposed mudflats. As stated in the Preface, there has been no social history of New England's fishing communities. And although I may never write it definitively (or prove the

Little Harbor: Boats preparing to sail to the fisheries beyond Marblehead's ledges and rock islands. Collections of Bowden G. Osborne.

value of the case), you can spit in the wind and take it in the eye if you don't share my belief that the prime sources for creating that history should be protected as vigorously as Williamsburg or the Vanderbilt mansions.

When walking through Barnegat, halfway along Orne Street, my cousins and I soon came to the house of Pastor John Barnard. Painted the authentic color of winter squash, the house is a comely, two-and-a-half-story Colonial that manages to combine two of New England's architectural inventions. The gambrel roof somehow gives way to a saltbox design in the back. Looking around, I realized that one could spend instructive days gaping at the distinctive gambrels of Marblehead. They are generally of a peculiar, short-peaked variety that in each case looks a bit different, just as repeated notes, when played by an artist, never sound exactly alike. One of the most memorable gambreled structures in Marblehead is the rear and oldest part of the "King" Hooper Mansion, Hooper being a member of Pastor Barnard's seafaring congregation who came to do well as a merchant. Even while inquisitive about the royal title of this house's owner, I was content for the moment to see that, though he had ultimately affixed a conventionally grand, eighteenth-century façade on the front, he let the old, raw-boned, naively crafted wing at the back say what it would about the monarch's origins.

Pastor Barnard's own house has been respectfully, beautifully restored, but the particular importance of its owner to this community is too little remembered. (Preservation all too often, unfortunately, gives the impression that a smoothly faced building must be the absolute reflection of an immaculate, original owner.) The young, community-minded cleric was called to the First Congregational

Church in Marblehead at a critical turning point in the growth of the town, namely, 1715. Though an intellectual, he was by no means removed from life; he rolled up his sleeves and turned this place around.

Barnard must have pondered as he traveled north from Cambridge and Harvard all the stories he'd heard about the radical difference between the brawling, disorderly community of Marblehead and the other, more normal and peaceable towns that characterized the Puritan Commonwealth of Massachusetts. He had turned down a call to Yarmouth, on the Cape, because the town was too rude—what would this place be like? Surely he'd heard the hoary joke (reported by Samuel Eliot Morison in his *Maritime History of Massachusetts*) about the retort from the irreverent lips of a Marblehead fisherman to an admonishing preacher. "Our ancestors came here *not* for religion," the man declared. "They came here to fish."

EVER SINCE the early 1500s, Europeans in perilously small vessels had sailed forth in the spring of the year for favorite fishing spots along the northeastern coast of North America, from Labrador to Cape Cod. There they had camped out, these Irish and French and Portuguese sailors; the English set up "flakes," or "stages," on which to dry a catch of codfish above the high-water line. Finally, their holds loaded with the delicious, full-bodied fish, they all sailed home again across the Atlantic, there to tell tales of the bountiful bays and rivers of the New World. But, following the successful establishment of the first Separatist and Puritan communities in Massachusetts, merchants in the southeast of England concluded it would be far wiser to implant hardworking, pietistic groups in godly communities along the coast, and to get them a-fishing, than to continue investing in the hazardous, seasonal voyages.

Alongside those communities with their transplanted English names (Hingham, Dorchester, Gloucester), unplanned Marblehead grew up as a kind of free-for-all aberration, philosophically speaking, and a specially favored haven, geographically speaking. In the words of a seventeenth-century explorer, it was "a convenient place for a plantation—especially for those as will set upon the trade of fishing—and where there is a good harbor for boats and safe riding for ships." The commodious harbor's natural shape (almost completely enclosed to seaward, like a lobster claw snapped in Neptune's face) includes many coves and secluded anchorages. Little Harbor is located near the tip of the lobster claw; Main Harbor is the gap between that claw and the lower clamp, called Marblehead Neck. Only fifteen miles from Boston, the rocky protuberance of Marblehead, no more than three miles in length, thrusts imputently out into Massachu-

Marblehead memories: BELOW, "King" Hooper's eighteenth-century mansion has an older wing out back; OPPOSITE, Pastor Barnard's house has an undisguisable gambrel roof. Both, Marblehead Historical Society.

setts Bay in much the same manner as its far larger neighbor to the north, Cape Ann.

Marblehead's first inhabitants, ancestors of the mixed crew who welcomed Pastor Barnard, were thus not backward people who struggled to advance from subsistence farming and fishing to a sturdier economy; they had brought their industry with them. And besides their fishing skills, they had brought a robust form of "Don't Tread on Me" democracy. More a collection of tough-minded individualists than a worshipful community, they faced entrenched enemies on land as well as the dangers on sea. Of the land enemies (i.e., the exploitative merchant princes of Boston and Salem, who sought to achieve total control of the fisheries), it's been said that "by dint of alcohol, high-priced supplies, and easy credit [they gradually] foreclosed on the fishermen's homes, farms, and boats." A kind of peonage that was not quite slavery had manifested itself in Marblehead in this early era of the late seventeenth and early eighteenth centuries.

Adding to the squeeze then was the difficulty of acquiring any property. The merchant princes had stacked the deck so that these free-lancing fishermen could never be diverted from the sea and could never win a holding on shore, with its diversity of opportunities: The landowners granted only the tiniest allotments to those who wandered into Marblehead looking for berths and home sites. Farming was out of the question; these people could only fish. And yet they came, from Devon, from Dorset and Cornwall, also from the Channel Islands and from Huguenot France. They were Anglicans, Quakers, even Roman Catholics, as well as Puritans. Many of them, having been cordwainers in the old country, banged away at the last during the cold, nonfishing winter, turning out seaboots for sale and for self. By pluck and hard work they would fight back as effectively as possible against anyone who would enslave them, but often they succeeded only in falling more deeply into debt.

The pastor was not favorably impressed by the Marbleheaders when he arrived in 1715. Of his new flock he later wrote: "They were as rude, drunken, swearing, and fighting a crew as they were poor." A commentator of some years later, Captain Francis Goelet, seconded the pastor's low opinion, calling the town a "Dirty, Irregular, Stincking Place." But something was about to happen here. In the not-too-distant future Marblehead, its economy energized and its people freely prospering, would be earning praises for elegant mansions and mid-nineteenth-century sophistication. A belle would recall that there was "a dance in some hall in town every night in the week during the season." Even later, painters and photographers would portray the bustling waterfront as close to Elysium, with its ritzy summer trade and its flag-snapping yacht clubs.

As I continued my walk beyond the pastor's house, I wondered all the more intently how this minister of the church had helped bring about such an economic miracle. Further, who had benefited most from this liberating upsurge—the fishermen themselves or the shoremen and shipowners?

IT TURNED OUT that John Barnard hadn't so much revolutionized the place politically and freed its people from their peonage to the lords of Salem as he had concentrated his intelligence on the economic process. He had figured out how the fisheries worked. He saw that there was no way Marblehead's fulminous, hardworking people could hold on to any profits until they gained control of the *distribution* of the fish. His visits to the wharves, his talking with the fishermen and the fisherwives as well as the fish vendors brought him to the point of secular enlightenment: only the merchants who sold the fish down along the line made any money. But why shouldn't his parishioners take up that business themselves, the pastor must have asked? Why did they need the aristocrats in Boston to handle the shipments? Didn't the men of Marblehead have the sense and the ships to sail for the West Indies themselves and to find there takers of their salt cod? And what about England and the rest of Europe? Come on now, lads!

The bold and the able responded to his call. Fishermen like Joseph Swett, Jr., entered upon coastwise trading in the 1720s, made shipping partnerships with other Marbleheaders, and embarked on a course of commercial autonomy that would severely challenge the Brahmins of Boston. Most remarkable of all, these fishermen-turned-shippers did not divorce themselves from the actual operations of the fishery; on the contrary, they dedicated themselves to the closest possible coordination of the catching and the merchandizing of the product.

Joseph Swett's partner was his energetic son-in-law Robert Hooper, Jr. The way in which that dynamic young Marbleheader (who would later build the renowned mansion with the gambreled wing) happened to win the title "King" proved to be even more interesting than I had suspected. It demonstrated the new modus operandi of the town at this time of change under Barnard's tutelage. Hooper's father had been one of a limited elite in the First Congregational Church; each had been called "Doctor" by the fishermen, in recognition not of any academic degree but of prowess at sea. Young Robert was of that lineage but needed to prove himself in his own way before any type of recognition would be accorded by the men on shipboard and along the wharves. He responded to the challenge by creating, with his partner, a system for the production and distribution of fish that is still notable for its efficiency *and* for the respect it accorded to the lifeways and traditions of the fishermen.

The Swett-Hooper system had three revealing features: (1) No setting sail from Marblehead on Friday (one of the seamen's oldest and strongest superstitions). (2) No sorting of the caught and barreled fish to determine value by size; the whole lot would be sold of a piece. (3) No signing on of skippers from beyond the Marblehead waterfront; the crews too would be Marblehead-born. Furthermore, Messrs. Swett and Hooper took it easy on the fishermen when debts accumulated and rents went unpaid. In the partners' own words, they "greased the wheels" so that the whole business might roll forward to the satisfaction of all. And in a gesture quite extraordinary for the time, Robert Hooper single-handedly underwrote the cost of the first free school in town (1746), as well as the town's premier fire engine.

For all this, he was given the new appelation *King* (a term related not to those Georges in Westminster but to the fishing "kings" of Newfoundland, mercantile entrepreneurs of far-flung fame). And he reigned with careful attention to the moods and mores of local society; there was nothing here of the brutal leader whom one might expect to command a peonage. Indeed, in Marblehead the historic, local worker, if he proved his stuff, became a partner of sorts—a situation related to but not exactly like that in other towns along the coast. The interchange between shore and sea was here far more fluid. Only local mariners were advanced to become masters; the newly successful members of the local gentry were repeatedly reelected to positions of power by a content people. Hooper recognized the exceptionality of this social contract himself, writing that he and his partner conducted a business that was "very different from other places in New England." He excoriated a Boston businessman for being inhumane and worldly.

In the words of Christine Heyrman, a witty and iconoclastic modern historian, King Hooper and his father-in-law were "concerned to prove themselves worthy of their social position by behaving in a manner consonant with their conception of a responsible elite." Paternalistic, God-fearing, and parochial, this king was surely the very model of a leader prayed for and nurtured by the good pastor.

But John Barnard must also have been aware that, even as the more capable fishermen and shoremen responded to urgings that they be Industrious and Frugal, so did other men of the waterfront take the lower road. One observer noted, "Many persons undesirable, and of noe estates butt rather Indebbted . . . [are becoming] burthensum to the place." Another commented on the growing numbers of men with no ambition to speak of, characterizing them as a "dull and heavy moulded sort of People that had not the skill or courage to kill anything but fish."

Sadly, some aspects of peonage did remain. That was driven home to me when I was shown a reproduction of the indenture certificate of young Moses Merry, a lad who had signed himself over to fishing boat owners John and Mary Oakes of Marblehead in 1769. To anyone today, the terms of that indenture sound cruelly restrictive—quite beyond the bounds of the free and democratic societies that are supposed to exist in fishing towns. But remember that this is the middle of the eighteenth century (a revolution was still to be fought) and that such indenture then represented a way for a property-less boy to get himself a profession and an education. The Oakeses promised to teach young Moses to "read and write and cipher." Finally, at the happy day of the indenture's expiration (eighteen years and seven months from its beginning!), the graduated fisherman would be given two suits of clothing. Considering that a man's suit in Colonial times was regarded as a lifelong inheritance, and that some workers' wives had to *weave* as well as sew their husbands' suits, this seemed like not too bad a deal.

Swelling with a populace of both upward-bound and down-beaten, Marblehead had become by the 1760s a tightly congested center at the heart of New England's fishing industry. It was the scale of its success (as well as the special character of its fisherman-centered ethos) that set Marblehead apart from Noank and a hundred-odd other fishing ports along the coast: this was the leader of Colonial America's most venerable business. In the view of Daniel Boorstin, this was the time "when New

The young fisherman: Moses Merry pledged his indenture to Marblehead's John Oakes by this 1769 document. Peabody Museum of Salem, Russell W. Knight Collection.

Englanders were catching more fish, and their catch was a larger part of their income, than it ever would be again." Marblehead—that "cultural barnacle on the hide of Massachusetts Puritanism"—then possessed more than a third of the Commonwealth's entire fishing fleet. Among all those ports, including mighty Boston and yet-to-rise Gloucester, Marblehead was the first in production and delivery. It is not surprising, then, that the feisty character of this community would profoundly affect the shape of the nation that even then yearned to be born.

AT THE very time when I was trying to imagine what Marblehead looked like and sounded like at its pre-Revolutionary peak, my cousins and I happened to reach Front Street. There stood two "half houses" dated, respectively, 1747 and 1753. So this was the face that Marblehead presented to the world as Pastor Barnard's preachments went into effect. These handsome structures expressed the taste and the self-esteem of the shoremen and fishermen who wished to demonstrate their prosperity upon the streets of Marblehead.

A plaque stating whether the original builder had been of the shore or of the sea appears on each waterfront house; that social distinction was apparently important but not divisive. Both of the "half-houses" we were looking at here were set with ridge-pole parallel to the street; their front stoops were immediately on the sidewalk. On the ground floor there were two windows plus the door, with three full-height windows on the second floor. Very solid and urbane (a realtor today might call them townhouses).

Of the two houses before us, one had its door on the left, the other on the right, as if to say "Good morning, sir—you go your way and I'll go mine." Also, one of the houses was marked with the family name of Knight, its neighbor with the name Russell. How fortunate: the Marbleheader with whom I was to have an appointment that afternoon was Russell Knight; obviously he would be genetically equipped to answer questions about how life had been organized in old Marblehead.

But as is often the case with a spokesman who knows his subject intimately, many of Mr. Knight's stories were a bit shocking, deviations from any prettified preservation job. "To tell the truth, it's always been a rather bleak and unattractive place," he said. "George Washington took a look at Marblehead soon after the Revolution and left post-haste. He said it had 'the appearance of antiquity; the houses are old; the streets are dirty; and the common people not very clean.'

"There was no real wealth running the show. Oh, there was a handful of rich folks—the Hoopers and the Lees—but they didn't get in anyone's way. This was *not* an oligarchy or anything like that. The secret was that the people were all of one ilk. They sailed with each other, only did business with each other, and married each other. What's the word? Endogamous, that's what they were. I prefer that to *inbred*, don't you? Hard-boiled, kind to their own, hostile to outsiders. And of course fishing was at the heart of it. Marbleheaders were the first out to Georges Bank, you know.

"Not everyone liked it when things started to boom in Marblehead, of course. There's one crowd, I've discovered, who began to get itchy when the population got up to around 1,500, packed into some 300 houses. They felt that it was much too crowded—we're talking about 1730 now—and that they were losing their freedom. So they up and left for Maine. They founded 'New Marblehead' up along the coast. Today it's called Windham. Ever heard of it?"

AS THE eighteenth century matured, Great Britain seemed to take a perverse delight in imposing exactions on New England's merchants and seafarers. But the Crown's regulations were fought at every turn. Typical of this combatative era was an enterprising patriot named John Glover. Born in 1732 in Salem, he had come to Marblehead as a young boy, had hung around the wharves and learned what he could about fishing, had also paid attention to the family craft of making boots. Finding his way on land and water, he became, among other things, a fish vendor. And, by shipping the fish in vessels that he owned in part or in whole, he gradually acquired enough wealth to be emplaced as a member of the town's new gentry. A daughter from his happy marriage became one of King Hooper's four wives. When Lord North's Parliament banned American vessels from the Grand Banks in an effort to assert the principle of British mercantilism, the livelihood of Glover and his fellows was threatened. He became increasingly active in work for the revolutionary Committee for Public Safety. He had a score to settle.

Subsequently, when the newly appointed General Washington came to Boston to free that city from the occupying British, Glover was made a colonel and transferred to the general's staff. The story of Colonel Glover and his Marblehead mariners ferrying Washington across the Delaware at Christmastime, 1776—thus achieving the first victory for American field forces in the Revolution—is told in a number of delightfully naive and inaccurate depictions. These need no correcting, myth having its own importance. But the story of another Glover maneuver does need to be put more fully on the record, if only for its reminder of what Marbleheaders gave to all Americans at that time in history.

This event occurred a few months earlier, after Boston's liberation, when the American Continentals were reeling from the impact of the British invasion of

Long Island. Washington desperately sought a way to escape from Brooklyn and naturally turned to Glover for aid. The Marblehead colonel and his "amphibians," accompanied by men from Salem, Lynn, and Danvers, were able to round up a number of craft from Long Island harbors and to start the task of freighting the men and horses across to Manhattan by night. But in the midst of this suspenseful operation, both the wind and the tide turned contrary. It looked as if the remaining troops would fall captive to the rapidly approaching British forces. After hours of agonized waiting, however, Glover's weather-sharp nose detected a shift; he commanded the sails to be set again. The freshening breeze filled the unfurled canvas and the boats surged across the ebbing current. Before dawn broke, some nine thousand soldiers were transported to fight another day; they would go on to win the Revolution.

In the matter of the war for independence, the fisheries had been a central issue. "The fisheries or no treaty!" John Adams demanded when negotiators finally sat down in Paris in 1783. Thanks to Adams and to Marblehead diplomat Eldridge Gerry, the Banks and the Labrador coasts were opened up again to American fishermen. Yet the cost of the war had been terrific. Samuel Eliot Morison reckons that few waterfront communities were more devastated, in terms of men lost and ships destroyed, than those in the Marblehead area (where, of course, most of the attackable wealth had been located). But with their accustomed doggedness, the fishermen rebuilt what boats they had, mended their nets, and went off to sea again. They even had the heart to initiate a lottery for the relief of war widows.

So Marblehead resumed its distinctive ways, though the War of 1812 and the accompanying struggles with both French and British marauders continued to plague fishing and shipping interests. What followed was the grand era of the splendid Federalist mansions and of Jacksonian romanticism, which the visitor to Marblehead assumes (not quite correctly) to be the glory of this fishing community. The glory remains the fisherman's shared society and the recollection that shippers and fishers, though in different houses, were all of the same ilk.

WHEN looked at from the perspective of the fishermen, the essential accomplishment underlying the prosperity of the new century was the opening of the fisheries on Georges Bank. This victory by Massachusetts fishermen, this regular harvest of salt cod and halibut in great quantities, was clearly the "agricultural base" for the industrial expansion that ensued for the Commonwealth. Fish shipping fortunes capitalized mills and railroads; here lay a contribution to the growth of the nation that may even have been greater than the tenacity of Glover's amphibians.

Constantly foggy, swept with confused currents, and shoaling in places to barely one and two fathoms, Georges Bank had ever loomed as a formidable barrier to those who worked the sea. It lies but a hundred miles east of Cape Cod and, even more importantly, it lies where the blue waters of the Gulf Stream, richly burdened with protoplasms from the Caribbean tropics, meet the cold and green waters of the Labrador Current, with wondrous effect.

The beauty of the northern waters is that, chemically, they can contain far more oxygen than can warm waters; they energize and feed the breath of life into the mighty fish that swim in the boreal seas. No wonder that gigantic fish were reported by early explorers out in the madly intermixing, dangerously shoaling waters on Georges Bank, or that in 1838 a codfish was caught there that weighed 180 pounds (big ones normally are in the 25-pound range).

Seasonally, the cod (*Gadus callarias*) spawn on the eastern slopes of Georges Bank—as well as on the Banks farther east—as winter turns to spring. These are essentially ground fish, choosing, when mature, to hover close to the bottom, hunting, probing, digging. In this proclivity, the big "bottom fish" are quite different ethologically from surface-swarming fish like the mackerel. Some cod have taken the matter to extremes, cruising down to the awesome depth of 250 fathoms.

It's all for food, of course; to assuage their monstrous appetites. Near the bottom or in the sand and pebbles they find quantities of crustaceans, squid, and smaller finfish. The cod have even been known to ingest the seemingly inedible, spikelike alligator fish and the seahorse. They also rise to the surface to snag wild ducks and shearwaters. Mighty hunters, they find Georges Bank to be less a congenial community than a great sporting ground—just as do those who hunt them.

Many vessels from the Marblehead and Cape Ann fleets had been out to Georges before the Revolution. There the fishermen had earned the name *Georgesmen*—regarded as peculiar types who plied their trade in the old-fashioned, hand-lining way even after new techniques came in. They fished from the decks of "heel-tappers," antique schooners equipped with higher quarterdecks and more substantial gunwhales. (Russell Knight shared a laugh with me that these eighteenth-century vessels had acquired their name from the fact that they looked like the bottoms of upside-down boots. No one forgot that the Marblehead skippers who sailed these vessels were, when ashore, often heel-tappers and bootmakers themselves.)

The fear and excitement of those early voyages out to Georges live on in a variety of accounts: they call it our most dangerous fishing ground. Dr. Goode writes:

The first vessels that went out to Georges never anchored. The fishermen had an idea that it was not safe to do so, for when the tide began to run, the eddies were as great as those of another Maelstrom. One man came into port with a story that he had come to anchor on the shoal ground of Georges and the tide ran so fast that the water began rushing into both hawse-pipes of his vessel, which frightened him so that he cut his cable and came home.

It was not until later (1837) that a younger generation of better-equipped fishermen, specifically those out after the deep-dwelling halibut, solved the riddles of anchoring in those vexatious waters without being "drored under," and succeeded in bringing back prize-winning catches.

FOR a fisherman aboard one of the bulky, sixty-foot schooners of 150 years ago, and for the same man and his family ashore, life was almost unimaginably different from that in our world of push buttons and union wages. What a man risked, what he hoped for and hated, what he came home for—those questions can only be partially answered from such clues as what he wore and how he carried out his work and whether he or his wife were frequently hauled before the judge. To empathize with him and her and their condition is a subtler process than to applaud the splendid ambitions of a Joseph Swett, Jr., or to admire the public benevolence of a Robert Hooper (both of whose grand gestures we can identify with comfortably).

Along Front Street in Barnegat, the pride and the polish of the half-houses may very well speak accurately of the respectability of their first, proud owners. But what of the other-than-respectable, the I-don't-give-a-damn fishermen? Their shanties are generally gone. (My cousin pointed out with some amusement one such humble, remaining structure which had been mockingly labeled as the waterfront community's Republican party headquarters during the 1930s.) Gone completely are the roominghouses and rented "digs" where the fishermen and their families had lived in poverty. These structures are simply not in the reconstruction picture, mostly because we have never wanted to see them or to hear the stories they would tell. Thus other kinds of evidence beyond residential architecture must be considered before we conclude much about daily life in Marblehead. Pastor Barnard's upwardly mobile parishioners notwithstanding, New England traveler Timothy Dwight (president of Yale) generally characterized the citizenry as "indebted." Further: "The fishermen are less industrial, economical, and moral, unless I am misinformed than their neighbors. . . . In the summer, they labour hard in a very toilsome occupation; and frolic away the remembrance of their hardships during the winter." Frolicsome, were they really?

In search of the particular question, how women of the waterfront got along, the historian Christine Heyrman has found fresh answers in the court records. There and elsewhere she's found that Marblehead women succeeded in achieving a perfectly dreadful, collective reputation. They were constantly in legal imbroglios—for promiscuity, for nonpayment of debts, for church-related offenses—especially in the time before Pastor Barnard's arrival. It was then that they earned the name *fishwives* in the opprobrious sense; their loud and litigious personalities were to be immortalized in that word. Yet this characterization should be understood in quite a different way.

Of course the women were loud: how else to defend their pathetically small holdings when their men were away? Of course they were sexually unconventional: in the town's early stages, the ratio of men to women was something like ten to one. Under those frontier circumstances does not another type of behavior usually come into play? To make the sexual situation all the more disruptive, it happened that summertime in Marblehead was the time when husbands and lovers were at sea *and* foreign fleets of fishermen dropped anchor in the harbor. Well, now.

As the town grew under John Barnard's enlightened encouragement, the sexual

Fisherwives: Hanging the wash, feeding the hens, the women cling to their marginal holdings on rocky, landlord-owned Marblehead. Collections of Bowden G. Osborne.

imbalance was evened out by the sheer growth of the population. The fisher families enjoyed at least a part of the new affluence, and coincidentally the women chose to control their lung power (or at least their voices were heard less in the courts). Nonetheless, the reputation of the "fishwives" remains, not to their discredit really, but to that of the merchants who tried to put them down so that more could be taken from them.

Despite these rather besmirched beginnings, the women of Marblehead eventually (in the late eighteenth and early nineteenth centuries) became sedate and respected members of the church community, docilely dressed in ruffled bonnet and clean skirt. Yet some of them retained a distinctive role: Whereas they had often served as *agents* for their at-sea husbands, actually getting promised moneys from the fishhandlers and arranging loans for clothing and food, they remained active in the business world even after their husbands' deaths or wave-swept disappearances. They went on to become owners of fishing vessels themselves, managers of other enterprises. Theirs, it turns out, is an unusual and bright page in the often shadowy history of American commercial women.

FOR the men of the community at sea, the main thing of course was the catch—and perhaps these toilers can be best understood by focusing on how they worked. What the fisherman wanted most of all was to "wet down" all the salt that had been brought along in the hold—that meant to use it up in the process of packing and pickling a maximum number of fish. Then, after this day-and-night business of baiting the hooks and hefting the fish up over the rail and packing them into the briny barrels (which usually took about six weeks), he and his six or seven mates (to most of whom he was related) could sail home. So, having begun his year in March, our Marblehead fisherman, out there on Georges hand-lining for the hungry cod, could usually manage three "fares" a season. Returned to port and wharfside, he spent his days handling the fish, repairing tackle, obtaining more salt, and rerigging for the next voyage. There was also the matter of taking the girl of one's choice out for a buggy ride. What with one thing and another, the weeks passed. the voyages proved lengthy disasters or brief triumphs, and soon it was November, the season's end.

To get from the harbor out to a favored position on Georges took four or five days, given the calms, currents, and contrary winds. About a week was needed to reach another oft-visited location, Browns Bank, the next of the offshore shoals that stretch east from Georges along the continental shelf to the Grand

Bank, southeast of Newfoundland (see map). At one or another of these grounds, the vessel hovered under shortened sail until the men's task was accomplished—one of watery earth's most physically demanding, most "labor intensive," and most necessary occupations.

The salt whose level the men kept watching until it finally reached zero and they could go home—about 125 hogsheads of it on each vessel—had been bought by the vessel's manager from a European contact (Spain, Sicily, or England) at upwards of three dollars a head. This cost was but one of the deductions to be subtracted from the total yield of the fish at market, other costs ranging from bait to medical equipment. Only after these had all been met would the remainder be divided between the ship's owners and shareholders on the one hand and the men on the other. Thus had it ever been.

The "high hand" often got a bonus—for him the trip might be worthwhile. For the other men, a full season might come to not much more than $100, paid at season's end. For the lowest-ranked of the men and boys on board, the "cut tail," there would be extra pennies earned on each voyage from those fish he'd been able to catch when not involved in other duties (mostly cooking and baiting and gutting); he'd make a particular notch in the tail of his fish to show that they were his.

To protect themselves from the spray and the drizzle (not to speak of the blood and the slime), the men and boys wore garments that now seem stranger than those of the space travelers or of medieval knights. The customary outergarment was something called "petticoat trousers," a kind of skirt (possibly sewn in the middle) made of much-oiled, coarse canvas. Over that was— the famous "barvel," a leather apron that hung from shoulders to knees. On the feet were worn thick cowhide boots (usually of a distinctive russet, that is to say, *red*, color), their tops coming up over the hips. A kind of tarpaulin hat, ancestor of the later sou'westers, covered the head and shoulders. To protect the hands from the cold and the abraiding edges of the tarred twine lines, "nippers" were invented and universally used. These were digitless gloves that protected the palm and thumb while also allowing their wearers to feed onto the hooks the indescribably wiggly squid and clams that the cod so admire.

On Sunday there was no fishing, of that the men assured church members, upon return. The cook—often the twelve-year-old son or nephew of the skipper—served up molasses-rich "duff" on that day, or a buttery, sugarless shortcake called fatcake. The word *pig* was never uttered on board; seagulls' droppings on one's hat or sleeves were a curse that required exorcising. Luck, after all, not Pastor Barnard ruled the day at sea.

Even with the vast distances pursued and the lives cruelly lost, it was a natural, comprehensible world for these interrelated people by the sea in Marblehead. The town's senior historian, Samuel Roads, Jr., wrote of Bankers "sailing into the harbor and unloading their salt cod near Barnegat at Fort Sewall; there the fish were put in a 'pound' and washed sufficiently of brine so they could be dried on specially constructed flakes that could be turned toward the sun." He went on to itemize the "garney," the special part of the catch that was retained by the fishermen themselves: the cods' tongues and sounds (air bladders); the halibut fins, and indeed some smoked halibut, too; then one or two "hagdons," or shearwaters, a sea fowl regarded as "strong in its odor but sweet and toothsome to the taste." Historian Roads also painted a vivid picture of the skippers, home from the sea, walking up and down along the wharves, "fore and aft as if on shipboard," discussing earnest questions of public interest. The salt-flavored democracy of the ancient Greeks.

Appleton's Wharf: With "heeltappers" tied up between voyagings, the fisheries' business is carried out by a variety of shoremen. Peabody Museum of Salem, unsigned watercolor.

ALL of this classic harmony came to a halt, according to some observers, with the great maritime disaster of 1846. Then the prosperity and splendor of the successful Marblehead families, the small-scale survival of others, and the uncontrolled squalor of yet others ran communally up on the reef of overcommitment to one fragile industry. The business and the society came to an end, Marblehead thereafter overshadowed by other ports.

The tragedy was caused by a sixty-knot gale on the Grand Bank southeast of Newfoundland, to which the Marblehead and other fleets had advanced on the nineteenth day of September in 1846. In all more than fifty vessels were lost. Contemporary accounts tell how the seamen on this vessel would watch with helpless horror as that other vessel, after pitching and tossing at anchor in the mountainous seas, would charge away, the cable having parted or the anchors broken out; then the defenseless vessel would be swept off to destruction on the reefs to leeward. On that dreadful day thirty-four vessels from Marblehead Harbor had anchored on the shoal. Eleven of them were lost; on board were sixty-five men and boys. The men left behind forty-three widows and more than a hundred fatherless children.

Some of the vessels from Marblehead and other ports that survived the storm elected the desperate option of raising anchor and trying to sail clear of the reefs with minimum canvas, even while being swept downwind. Russell Knight showed me his primitive but compelling fireboard painting of the episode (see page 82), in which the free-running squarerigger on the right, the *Samuel Knight*, has chosen that risky route to survival. The little schooner struggling at anchor in the foreground of the painting, with jib and foresail tightly furled, is a typical Marblehead "heel-tapper." (Note the very old-fashioned-looking, cocked angle of the bowsprit. A reason for this oddity is that the sprit is supported not by the foundation of machine-cut sections but by the curved chunk of a tree branch known as a "gammon knee," crude but effective over the ages.)

In the face of the disaster, the town was defeated and demoralized. Therefore, most historians tend to date Marblehead's decline as a power in the fishing industry from this event, and certain statistics seem to justify that conclusion. But Samuel Roads points out that 1839, not 1846, was in fact the zenith of the Marblehead fishing fleet; then there were ninety-eight vessels (including those under thirty tons) sailing out of this harbor, the greatest number since the depressed time of Jefferson's embargo before the War of 1812. Never again would there be here a first-ranked fleet: in terms of tonnage, Marblehead's started a two-decade fall in 1840 (from 12.5 to 7.9), whereas that of most other Massachusetts fishing ports went up. It becomes evident that Marblehead, even before 1846, had begun to run into heavy weather.

What plagued Marblehead, as so often happens with classic heroes, was an inherent, ingrown flaw. The people were, after all, of one ilk: they did not attract or welcome the new adventurers, the new technicians with larger and better-designed vessels that could power the evolution of the central industry. A half-century before, George Washington had called them and their town "antique"; it would determinedly remain so, with its "heel-tappers" at sea and its inbred society at home.

BEYOND that, there were threats to the town's ethos. A defeatist faction reared its head during the dedication ceremonies for the monument to the memory of the Grand Bank victims, staged on Old Burying Hill in 1848. The address by the Reverend E. A. Lawrence dealt with ultimate realities, of course, for a healthy dose of doom was always expected. Throughout New England's generations, seaside Protestant churches had seemed to revel in the damnation and the associated sinfulness of the fishing industry. A veteran of the last century named

LEFT. *The Great Storm of 1846: A fireboard screen captures the horror of that gale. Peabody Museum of Salem, Russell W. Knight Collection (fireboard by W. T. Bartoll).* ABOVE, *an Old Burying Hill postcard shows the monument to sixty-five fishermen lost in the storm. Collections of Bowden G. Osborne.*

Albert Morris recalled this theme when an old man: "There was only one ray of hope held out to the sinful sailor—that he might Make Jesus His Friend. Otherwise 'Your vessel and your cargo will sink to Hell.' " Mr. Morris emphasized his point by quoting a remembered hymn:

> His standard unfurl'd see it wave through the air,
> And volunteers coming from far off and near.
> Now's the time, brother sailor, no longer delay.
> Embark now with Jesus; good wages he'll pay.

Along with its broad-sweeping condemnations, the sermon on that commemorative day in 1848 delivered a particular blast against the fisheries. The preacher's "argument," as they called it then, consisted of two basic points: (1) No Marbleheader had ever become rich from going out to sea and fishing; (2) What little profit came from fishing was in no way commensurate with the risks. For its own salvation, Marblehead should abandon its maritime calling.

Although the preacher's points were and are difficult to contest, what a backdown they represent from the Protestant moral imperative of up-and-at-'em! And what a departure from the sensible message of Pastor Barnard: "We can figure this industry out and learn to do it better." Not to speak of how they contradict the courage of John Glover, ready to fight against all odds for his people's destiny.

As if to recall that heritage and to reject Mr. Lawrence's defeatist message (realistic as it might have been), the people of the waterfront gathered in great and gay numbers for a big event in the next year, 1849: the launching of the deep and powerful fishing schooner *Robert Hooper*. She was owned by Edward Kimball, one of the local businessmen who trusted that their investments would justify the community's straight-ahead course. During the next nine years, he followed this public launching with six others, for a total of twenty schooners of some 87 to 112 tons, in the whistling-in-the-dark hope that the family-binding business of fishing would never disappear.

Marching in step with these undiscouraged smalltown capitalists went a number of fishermen and other Marbleheaders, high and low, and of course of the same ilk. One of them came to my attention through the reports of a sharp-eyed waterfront newspaperman of the 1920s named Frank Damon. He had been intrigued by the question, Why Did These People Keep Fishing? Weren't they supposed to have been doomed by the disaster of 1846? In search of answers he interviewed an ancient Banksman, Thomas Jefferson Peach. That gentleman's father had skippered a vessel through the disastrous gale; young Tom grew up right in the midst of families who had been "sadly bereft" by the loss. "There was a sailor in about every house, you see."

"I was initiated into the mysteries of the forecastle of a fishing schooner later—in 1855. Father took me, much against Mother's wishes." Tom remembered his father fondly, admiringly. The old man in winter made "the great fishing boots" in a little shop on home premises; he turned out stock sizes for sale, keeping a little money coming in until fishing recommenced in the spring.

"No, he didn't get rich. Did you ever hear of a Marblehead skipper who did? Captain Josiah Green . . . came the nearest of any skipper I ever knew. He laid enough by to invest in some land enterprises—and nearly lost all of it. Not only did life on the Banks in those days fail to produce a competence for families but it *unfitted* the heads of families for general business."

Tom agreed with the interviewing reporter that he would have been better off if he had not, himself, followed in his father's trade. "But you couldn't tell a boy of sixteen anything then, any more than you can today. They know it all." Yes, Tom and his peers along the waterfront understood all that was to be known then, including the phony allurements of the land in towns and cities to the west as well as the very real perils of the sea to the east. "But, as to those perils, I think that rather than deterring us, this knowledge urged us on. Marbleheaders are nothing if not courageous, and I think we young fellows instinctively looked up to a returning fisherman in his red shirt and 'gansey' frock as he strode homeward from the wharf, with his smoked halibut and his hagdons, as a different species of man than what you might call 'the shore variety.' And we longed to emulate them. I know I did. And after I had spent ten years or so in fishing vessels, it was too late for me to try to take up another calling."

Nonetheless, undaunted Tom Peach was aware that the industry was both *changing* and declining. (Indeed, was it not declining because of the intensified fishing which had been brought on by technological changes—the grounds gradually being stripped of fish?) There were only forty-three sail in the harbor in 1859. On the Banks, though not on Georges, hand-lining was giving way to fishing from dories, those awkward double-enders that are so miserable to row until they are deep-laden with fish (and then they're risky because of the low freeboard). "All right, boys, now we'll do it in dories," you can hear Tom Peach saying, even as he wondered about the innovation.

Conservative to the core, all Massachusetts fishermen were undoubtedly puzzling over this new step, wondering whether it really did deliver a full fare in half the time. The Barnstable *Patriot*'s views on the issue (May 10, 1859) must have been read by an attentive audience:

It is becoming a custom quite general among the Grand Bank cod fishermen to take dories with them upon the fishing grounds, and fish in them at a short distance from their vessels. Cod fish will often take a hook from a dory while they will not notice a hook from a vessel anchored within a rod from the boat. . . . The motion of the boat, giving quicker movement to the hook, renders it more attractive to the fish than that from the vessel. It is a change of habit in fish, thus to desert the vessel for the dory.

Strangely unscientific to our ears. But sufficient unto that day.

Soon that newfangled idea was followed by another, the introduction of "trawls," or long-lines, which comprised a system for laying down miles of buoyed and anchored lines from which other lines with baited hooks depended. The dory-borne fisherman would reel in the buoyed lines, making several sweeps of the total territory in the course of one day. The operation, it was said, had been introduced from Ireland, via the immigrant fishermen in Boston; and perhaps it should have been observed that the cod and similar ground fish in the reachable seas north of Ireland had been greatly diminished thereby.

During these years of innovation and augmentation—what might be called the long-expected modernizing of the quaint old fishing business—Tom Peach experienced no doubts about where his future lay. He struggled to keep up with the competition, even though Marblehead boasted but few of the larger, sharper new vessels.

> I sailed out of the harbor as the holder of three-quarters of a share in the old schooner *Boys*, William Standley master. And for the next 20 years, except for the time I spent in the Union Army during the Civil War, I followed the calling of my father.

By 1866, the war for the Union having been won, he had become a "full sharesman." Of these vested fishermen there were usually four on a given vessel in the mid-1800s, plus six hands paid variously and a cook.

The men would be dropped off in the five dories as the vessel sailed along under riding sail on a certain azimuth. There were two men per dory, one hauling in the line and snagging the fish, the other baiting a new set. As the early summer fogs obscured the scene, the men constantly kept one eye on the location of the mother ship, the other on the weather. When the horn blew at midmorning, they rowed over for a "cup up" of coffee before returning to their back-breaking, finger-numbing work. Their day finished about four in the afternoon, by which time they would have delivered several dories' full of fresh fish to the mother ship. The captain noted carefully in his records which dories had come alongside with how many loads.

By 1876 Tom Peach had become skipper of a vessel himself, the *Henry West*; he functioned as both master and navigator, his father having taught him the secrets of the sextant years before. In the interview with Damon, he recalled one incident that demonstrates the responsibilities of the skipper:

> Two dories were gone all night. It blowed like thunder. I gave them up as lost, and displayed the flag at half mast. But the next morning, while we were all below salting the dressed fish, we heard them come alongside. One dory had developed a serious leak. They abandoned her and got into the good dory. They managed to make out a Cape Ann schooner late in the evening, and were taken aboard and cared for.

But that was the same year when one of Tom's cousins, often the mate on a fishing voyage, wrote home in a letter: "There ain't *no fish* on the Bank . . . I hope there'll be plenty of shoe making when I get home."

No fish and the never diminishing perils of the sea (as well as the increased temptation of fulltime employment in the booming mills of a nearby city) were certainly strong reasons for Tom and his cousins and their descendants to abandon the fishing business, despite romantic images of what a real man was supposed to be and to do. (Tom admitted that one friend quit "because his girl wanted him to.") But certain men persisted against "the inevitable," no matter what the defeatists and the purveyors of common sense had to say. And the greatest reason for the industry's ultimate collapse in Marblehead was not that the blood thinned or the spirit failed but that in 1846—the same year as the great disaster on the Bank—the railway line between Boston and Gloucester had been completed. With its prominent harbor out on Cape Ann and its technologically superior fleet of Bankers then effectively linked to the marketing centers, Gloucester emerged as the unbeatable champion of the industry. By Tom's later years, Marblehead's competitive position had been totally destroyed. The large-scale capitalists of Cape Ann—quite a different breed from the aristocratic merchants of Salem (who had abandoned fishing as not worth their time) and from the smalltown investors of Marblehead—these new tycoons went after the modernization of the industry with a zeal that proved quite terrifying.

Still the die-hard fishermen of Marblehead held on, many of them. Lobstermen, seiners, on-shore fishermen, they could not cease going down to the sea, leaving their homes on Front Street, when the new season blew in. And a colorful, unique crew they remained even as their numbers dwindled. Russell Knight remembers a particularly impressive character named "Mutcho" Frost:

> He stood six-foot seven, a big, gangling fellow. When he had to stop lobstering for the season, he'd get work over at the tannery in Peabody, and he'd come back from that work stinkin' like anything. He liked to tell the story of himself during the Spanish-American War. The big guy walked down out of the hills with some other soldiers

Fishermen departed: In an early twentieth-century view, Marblehead's waterfront blossoms with cottages and yachts. Mystic Seaport Museum, Henry David Fisher Collection.

into a town somewhere in Cuba. When the little people there saw him, they said, "Mucho Alto!" And he was asking himself ever since how they'd known his name.

Russell Knight recalls that during his own youth the Marblehead waterfront, though falling apart, remained fascinating. He showed me that in those days there had been more meadows to play in and ponds to skate on, much for a boy to do even if the men had to go elsewhere for work. His family had retired from the fishing business at the time of the Civil War: the Knights sold out when it became difficult to man the era's larger vessels; though many fishermen from elsewhere may have known of open berths in Marblehead, few cared to risk the antagonism of this family-dominated harbor.

Today "Marblehead is fast going the way of the cute, old fishing villages," Russell Knight went on to say. "Oh, it's fine that the folks at City Hall won't let the motels get started here now. . . . They're smart enough not to turn it into a place like Rockport or Provincetown right away, with all those crowds. You wait and see, though; it'll happen one way or another."

But isn't it possible to believe that, just as Marblehead once fought off the "inevitability" of its industrial decline, and persevered in the face of its smalltown limitations, so today it might find a creative way to preserve its character? Other fishing communities, I later learned, have successfully fought along this route—couldn't Marblehead take strength from its own history?

I asked the question of Russell Knight. And he at length replied: "They gave us a treasure greater than gold."

PROVINCETOWN: FISHING AT THEIR OWN DOORS

"A MAN may stand there and put all America behind him." Henry David Thoreau once wrote that of Provincetown—a phrase pleasant to quote but difficult to execute. For when you stand there looking out across the harbor, as I did on a September day, America is not behind you at all. It tends to be on your *right*, for some reason. The landlady says that's west. My wife and I had come in from the left, I remembered, and we were told that was east. (As if we'd driven across the Atlantic!)

But in another sense, Provincetown is a place to put America before you rather than behind. Here's all the glitz of an artsy tourist town removed by distance and desire from the real world; and here's all the history and architecture of our nation's oldest, continuing fishing community. Thus it's a meeting place for two combatants who seem to need each other—fishing and tourism. If you care to know how a mixed populace can be both antagonistic and supportive unto itself, you're here at the right place, U.S.A.

I gradually learned that in Provincetown, before fishing and tourism had joined in combat, fishing had been struggling with other, successive alien forces. What's remarkable is that the fishermen still go to sea from here—it's the third biggest port in New England after New Bedford and Gloucester—and that their continuing survival seems to feed new vitality to the entire town, including even the art galleries and the leather boutiques. In the words of Josephine Del Deo, chairman until recently of the Historic District Study Committee: "As long as the fleet remains, Provincetown's character as we know it will remain."

Josephine is a gracious, dramatic brunette with flashing eyes, long red finger-nails, and a robust memory of who's done what to whom in Provincetown's history. As I watched, the nail of her forefinger traveled down the page of a ledger at the Heritage Museum, of which she is now president. The nineteenth-century ledger, kept in a display case at the museum, was once the record book of

OPPOSITE. *Across the harbor from Provincetown: Other fishing vessels wait for the sloop in the foreground to finish unloading its catch from the hold. Collection of Diana Worthington.*

Provincetown's druggist. "You see all these first and last names of the men who bought medicine here?" Josephine asked. I nodded. "What does this one say?"

" 'Portuguese,' " I answered. "No name."

"That's right," she replied, closing the ledger. "No name. His place of origin was all that he was. Then suddenly, two generations ago, they were running the town."

The reason Josephine is no longer head of the Historic District Study Committee is that the committee is out of business. Its proposition failed, by a maddeningly thin margin. The committee's objective had been to establish preservation regulations for the town, regulations with teeth. But the progress-minded voters decided that they should not give away their right to put up aluminum sidings here, glass storefronts there, no matter how lovely the buildings may have been back when fishermen were kings. Concentrating on her museum, with its half-scale model of the fishing/racing schooner *Rose Dorothea* and its lifelike period rooms, Josephine almost succeeds in not being bitter about the defeat. But her repressed anger gave us a first hint about what stirs at the heart of this community.

When my wife and I confessed our confusion about the geography of this nautilus-like, final part of Cape Cod, Josephine suggested that we go back to basics and visit the Pilgrim Monument up at the top of the hill. "There you'll be able to see 360 degrees—the whole world. That will help put what we've got here into perspective."

You would think so. But a Pilgrim jotting that we found at the monument's museum, written by *Mayflower* passenger Robert Cushman, sounded more like a complaint to the AAA Tour Guide office than a "Thank God We've Arrived!" He groused: "The bay is so rounded and circling, that before we could come to anchor, we went round all the points of the compass."

Yes, that is the true story of the shape of the place. We could see that it's positively vertiginous for any vessel coming in from the sea; the mariners must go round and round until they find the innermost chamber of the land-fingers forming the fist beyond the wrist at the end of the arm of Cape Cod. For the driver, it's no simpler: from the Cape Cod Canal, which severs the Cape from the mainland and makes it an island in fact as well as in spirit, to the tip is some sixty miles of driving, mostly east and north and eventually west in order to face south back toward the beginning. The car rocks with the unceasing wind that sweeps across from the Atlantic on the right to Cape Cod Bay on the left; dunes threaten to block the way, insinuating themselves across the pavement. From the Pilgrim Monument, the view—such as it is before wind-lashed tears completely blot it all out—is breathtaking but not particularly reassuring. There's no reason at all why Boston should be over *there*.

Though turned about a bit, the Pilgrims were grateful for the shelter of the Cape's hook. William Bradford noted that the harbor was commodious enough to hold a thousand ships. Because their landing had been made in November, they caught none of the expected cod in the vicinity. (Explorer Batholomew Gosnold, he who had named the Cape, claimed that earlier in the season he and his men had been "pestered" there by the fish.) The Pilgrims did, however, spy many whales; it was clear that these were waters where the big fish swam— and pursued the lesser orders. That argued for the Pilgrims to stay at "Cape Cod," as they called Provincetown. But the arguments for the more sheltered mainland won the day, and off to Plymouth they sailed.

Not completely straightened out, my wife and I tried to get ourselves organized for an assault on the town that evening. Having but recently been in New Orleans, we thought we could handle Provincetown's main drag, which is named Com-

Rose Dorothea: Provincetown's proudest crosses the finish line of 1907 fisherman's race in first place, although with broken fore topmast. Peabody Museum of Salem; Henry G. Peabody photo.

mercial Street (though, as you may be sure, it used to be called Front Street and then something else before that). Today the street is a hurly-burly of shops, churches, inns, pizza parlors, outdoor-indoor restaurants, facial and hair and foot salons, discos, and old houses. It runs three miles from east ("down along") to west ("up along"), more or less in a straight line parallel to the beach—except for a zigzag around an eighteenth-century house whose owner had refused to move his salt works out of the way. As you proceed west, in daytime, you are teased by tempting views of the harbor between the jewelry shops and the T-shirt basements; at the end of a pier, fishing boats in harsh-bright colors rock together at a remove, gulls wheeling over the hoisted nets.

Our evening foray was moderately successful. By slalom-style pivotings of hips and shoulders, we avoided actionable collisions with the stream of boys and girls, men and women, boys and boys. Everyone seemed extraordinarily happy; the evening was golden lights upon black, salt-air velvet. But suddenly a yell cut through the genial hum: a woman or something else in wig and long skirt was running around the parking lot in front of an inn, hollering at potential customers that they had better come into his *outrageous* show now because it was starting in "Just five minutes!" To get more attention, he executed a horizontal arm stand on a stanchion of the inn's marquee. But for the crowd none of this was worth more than a pause and a chuckle.

Then, as we passed down along—no, I mean up along—the street and encountered a brightly lit patch of pavement in front of an interesting-looking theater, a dark figure stormed through the crowd. A cigarette hung from his lips, hands thrust into soiled windbreaker. But it was the boots that gave him away: he was a fisherman. The crowd closed not immediately behind him, there was a wake of troubled space. Whose town was this, anyway?

WAY OUT here in the middle of the sea, Provincetown is quite as much the plaything of the sand as of the waves. The gritty grains are everywhere; lasses of the last century would be recognized as Provincetowners by the deft way they could flick the sand out of their slippers without losing a stride. Timothy Dwight, the long-nosed president of Yale who dutifully kept diaries of his travels through New England in the 1840s, ventured the opinion that, what with the sea wind and the shifting sands, the town would have been swept away long ago if it weren't for the beach grass. Yet after finally getting oriented and used to the peculiar society there, he found himself rather liking it: "Nothing was perceived of the roughness which I had expected from a mere collection of fishermen and sailors."

Caught up in the excitement of the town, he sensed a cosmopolitan flavor.

"There is hardly any spot [on earth] except the trading cities which is more frequented by vessels of all descriptions than this," he exclaimed. He was aware, of course, that neither London nor Constantinople had been built there and never would be; that, in fact, the populace was poor. But he rallied from that disquieting discovery with a remarkable insight, saying that in its own way Provincetown was rich: "all other riches are by comparison."

What wealth there was came in as a gift from the sea. True to their knowledge that there were quantities of great fish to be caught off the tip of the Cape, Pilgrims became constant visitors in the earliest years. They came under well-defined terms: Plymouth Colony, in an effort to make up for poor harvests and unsatisfactory economies, had determined that the leasing of shore stations to bass fishermen could bring in needed funds; the revenue would finance schools in such colony towns as Barnstable and Duxbury.

Cod they found as well as bass, in the season. The fish, cleaned and cured on the beach, were taken home for sale abroad. Captain John Smith himself is credited with a profit equal to $7,500 from the lot of salt cod he sold to Spain.

Prey of the voracious cod and the surf-sporting bass are the skittery, little, gray-green alewives (*Pomolobus pseudoharengus*). The Pilgrims soon learned that the upriver run of these fresh-water-spawning fish is a magnificent vernal event that stimulates all the wildlife, the hunters and the hunted. A contemporary wrote of the Pilgrim fishermen:

> Experience hath taught them that in April there is a fish much like a herring that comes up into the small brooks to spawn, and when the water is not knee deep they will presse up through your hands, yea, thow you beat at them with cudgels, and in such abundance as is incredible.

The scientific categorization for alewives and similar species is *anadromous*, from the Greek *ana* (upward) and *dromo* (to run); they and their kind must find a freshwater brook or pond up above tidewater, possibly their ancestral water source, for the depositing of their eggs. Exhausted, they return down the river, searching for shrimp and other food at its mouth. More often, they are found themselves.

For the two centuries before Timothy Dwight's arrival, Provincetown grew little by little as fishermen in search of the precipitant alewives, the bass and cod, the herring, and of course the mackerel (to name but a few of the many) came to settle with their families. With names like Snow, Cook, Mayo, Rich, Nickerson, Smith, and Dyer, they came in increasing numbers, leaving behind their birthplaces in Sandwich, Barnstable, Yarmouth, Harwich, Eastham, and Truro. By 1727, the isolated little community ventured to become a town within the Puritanical embrace of Massachusetts. But whereas the citizens had chosen the name Herringtown for themselves, the lords of the Commonwealth told them that they were *Provincetown* (after the "Province Lands" of the Cape) and that they should mind their peace.

In these early times, wood and the struggle for it was one of the place's unpeaceable problems. A limited variety of trees had succeeded in withstanding the ocean blast, among them "shrubby pines, sassafras, and juniper." But those and anything else that passed for wood were soon requisitioned for fires and for shelters; you struggled to get the wood before others found it.

The would-be homebuilder's other challenge at Provincetown, after the lack of wood and the merciless wind, was the pressing, ever-invading sand. A carpenter by the name of Seth Nickerson, whose house still stands "up along" Commercial Street, figured out how to become master of the situation. In 1746 he laid down a foundation that was, in the local manner, so circular that the sand could push right around it and not through it. He built a central chimney structure, to serve three immense fireplaces and a beehive-shaped oven, that was so heavy (16 tons) that no wind could ever overpower it. Then, the structure well anchored, he scrounged down the coast and found enough odd lumber to build a house that would hunker down low out of storm's way.

The main supporting beams of Seth Nickerson's house are 8" x 8" oak members. The random-length floor boards immediately reveal themselves as having been taken from one shipwreck or another. But the beautiful windowpanes of Sandwich glass (six over six in this full Cape) and the handsome door hinges and hardware throughout show that Seth had an eye for both that which would please forever as well as that which resolved local difficulties.

Evacuated, occupied, and humiliated during both the Revolution and the War of 1812, Provincetown remained one of the Cape's smaller towns—a couple of hundred pertinacious families. But then the fishing picked up, along with inventive ways of doing it better. And by the end of the century the population had magnified to more than five thousand souls, the harbor crowded with hundreds of fishing vessels. Having started life as the birthplace of American fishing, it went on to become the industry's home port, possessed of seven successive (and occasionally overlapping) fisheries.

When Thoreau, that journalist of grand and possibly transcendant ideas, walked the Cape with a friend in the early 1850s, he found Provincetown to be "the most completely maritime town that we were ever in." He also made the witty point that far from being an isolated or out-of-the-way place, this Atlantic port was "directly in the way of the navigator." He watched the in-shore cod fishermen and the hovering mackerelers with fascination, the boats' sails catching the sun differently as the fishermen followed this or that course. Arms locking his knees together, seated in the warm sand out of the breeze, he marveled at this essentially agricultural scene. "A village seems thus, where its able-bodied men are all ploughing the ocean. . . . But the sound of no dinner horn can reach the fisherman's ears." He had begun this reverie by musing that what was happening here could only be called "fishing before your doors." And, after taking a cheap shot at Provincetown as merely an "inhabited beach," he ended by pondering what might be the evolving destiny of such an industry, such a people, such a community in changing America.

AS THE TOWN grew to something more than a collection of fishing shacks, increased traffic suggested that there should be a better road than merely across the beach. Carts with extra-large tires had been devised that could be pulled by oxen over the sands and pebbles. But, even so, was there not a way for vehicles to avoid the twice daily inundation of the tides and the washouts and the on-shore clutter of the fishermen's business?

Besides the fishermen's stolid disinclination to do anything differently from before, there was another industry standing in the way of the new road building: salt making. Invented by a Cape Codder named John Sears, the complex facilities that produced salt for the codfishermen's barrels consisted of windmill-driven pumps that brought water up through hollow logs to twenty-foot-square vats and a series of drying pans. When Timothy Dwight came to town, there were seventy-eight of these complexities; room for them had been made by leveling the hills, pushing aside the houses. They employed scores of older men and younger boys during the summer months when the manpower was at sea. To produce one bushel of salt for the Bankers required 350 gallons of sea water. At their operational peak, Provincetown's salt works were producing nearly 50,000 bushels of salt (that's 1.75 billion gallons pumped by the windmills).

Then, of course, there were the all-important drying stands called fish flakes, an industry of themselves. Also there were the important boat yards and the other necessary waterfront buildings—plus the central idea that the community had always pushed right upon the beach and harbor. The connection between the men who fished at their own doors and the community was intimate and binding. In wintertime, the little schooners were hauled up into depressions that had been dug in the beach, their bowsprits thrusting here and there between the houses. A proposal to orient the community differently, that is, along a road running in back of the houses, seemed subversive, as well as a damn waste o' money.

Nonetheless, $1,273 was expended by improvement-minded people in 1835 to construct the twenty-two-foot-wide "Town Rode." Houses were turned front end around to back in order to face it. As my wife and I discovered on our walk, the street's only real deviation from a straightline course is where salt maker Benjamin Lancy had declined to move his salt works. We will deal with Mr. Lancy and his heirs later. Finally, a federal-state subsidy came through and more money was available to build a wood-plank sidewalk; regulations were passed prohibiting spitting on said civic structure. Still, the improvement seemed anti-Provincetown to some. In protest, the discontented minority refused to tread on the sidewalk, preferring to trudge along the sandy road. I thought of the fisherman who had stormed through the crowd; he walked in company with others who had walked in the sand and the shadows.

But with the establishment of this road, followed by another parallel throughway called Bradford Street, connected by a myriad of side streets, the pattern of Provincetown was set, between the harbor and the ever-encroaching sand dunes. Now domesticity and religion could find their ways in, too.

That is not to say that Provincetown houses or life styles settled down. Probably the most eloquent commentator on these eighteenth- and nineteenth-century residential structures was Mary Heaton Vorse. She lived in the town for some sixty years and is much honored today as first hostess of the famous Provincetown Players at her wharf fishhouse. She wrote:

> It is, of course, a matter of individual tase, but personally I like to live in an old house. I like the careful, leisurely workmanship of a former day. I like the quiet patina which is purchased only with time, the golden dimness that the years lay across a well-constructed dwelling. For, above all, give me a house with doors, rooms and not enlarged hallways. Give me a house whose work I can do myself if need be—then I am no man's debtor. In a house of a shape and size where I can do my own work I am insured against fate.

She was fortunate to have arrived in the town when many of the ancient dwellings were still standing and were available. She bought the house Ephraim Cook had built in 1795—he being the founder of the Cook fishing dynasty and his sons having gone on to construct more elaborate mansions than this full cape. Like many another Provincetown house, this one has gracefully endured many haphazard additions, as if to say that life can last if you're basically beautiful.

Yet another aspect of Provincetown houses caught the eye of observant Mrs. Vorse: their strange mobility. She explained the matter with her usual charm:

I didn't understand [at first] this peculiar flexibility of Provincetown houses or why they did not stay upon their foundations after the fashion of houses in other towns, but picked up their skirts in their old age and went wandering up roadways or sandy dunes—not until some out-of-town people bought a piece of property near me and wanted to build on it. What to do with the old house? The carpenter was a Provincetown man and he was not for a moment perplexed. He shoved the house out into the bay and there he anchored it. Unfortunately a storm came up and for two days the distracted house rocked and courtseyed. Its shutters and door blew open. The blank windows and the yawning door looked like frightened eyes and a doleful screaming mouth. Then I realized why it was that our houses are more flexible than houses in other towns. Provincetown men are not landsmen at all. Almost without exception they have at one time or another followed the sea. . . . They look upon houses as a sort of landship or a species of houseboat, and therefore not subject to the laws of houses.

Apprised of this flexibility, no one should have been overly surprised to see a number of houses rafting their way across Provincetown harbor one day in 1847. The exodus from the stretch of sickle beach across the harbor called Long Point had occurred because of a typical, endemic Provincetown battle—which had been lost. In this case the struggle of the townspeople out at the settlement of Long Point was not against other human factions; it was against a monster fish.

Long Point had been established in 1818 when the Atwood family moved there, followed by a few scores of other families who wanted to be as close as possible to the fishing process. The men fished for cod in small boats or for mackerel, scup, and other in-shore fish by sweep seines that were pulled into the beach. Word was that the bass were "too clever" to be caught in weirs but might be brought in this way. Women wove the nets and helped haul the seines. Children helped, too, when not caught themselves in the schoolhouse; they also shoveled and sluiced alongside their grandfathers in the six salt works. Of fresh drinking water there was none, except what fell from the skies and was collected in plank cisterns. It was a productive community, turning out sizable harvests of fresh and salted fish, as well as 600 hogsheads of salt annually. Then the monster struck, the bluefish.

Captain Nathaniel Ellis Atwood was a young man in those disruptive years of the 1840s. He recalled that in the years of his youth no one had ever seen one of the savage bluefish until 1838; then their numbers began to swell. The effect of their raids was devastating. Captain Atwood had been accustomed to fishing with his father; he led a hard-working but pleasant life. The family was so poor that they owned no clock; but that didn't seem to be an impediment since time could be told by the tides. Undeterred by poverty, or by the terror that would envelop his and the other Long Point families, the young man went on subsequently to fish in more distant waters, then to become noted as an ichthyologist, the friend and associate of Harvard's Louis Agassiz, and ultimately a state representative and senator.

Bluefish (*Potatomus saltatrix*) are hailed for their taste and as trophies of the chase but deplored as "the most ferocious and blood-thirsty fish in the sea." When they discover a school of mackerel or alewives, they decimate it as if in a lustful rage. Goode, deploring their rapaciousness, wrote:

> [The bluefish], not content with what they eat, which is itself of enormous quantity, rush ravenously through the closely crowded schools, cutting and tearing the living flesh as they go, and leaving in their wake the mangled fragments. It is not only the schooling fish that fall prey to them, but scup, squeteague, hake, butterfish, cunners, and small fish of all kinds, besides squid.

Another authority estimated that when the bluefish were at their height, they destroyed 12 trillion millions of fish annually off southern New England.

Thus did the monster destroy the happy family scene at Long Point. But what were the people to do if they could no longer fish at their own doors? First there was the practical business of where and wherein they should live. The little houses—including even the schoolhouse—were put on rollers and push-pulled down to the water's edge, then trundled onto cask-buoyed rafts and floated across to Provincetown. One report claims that the housewives continued to go about their daily chores as the armada crossed the harbor. By the time of the Civil War, the settlement of Long Point had been completely abandoned.

That was the era when many other changes came to Provincetown. Salt works were being dismantled (a great dome of the stuff having been discovered in New York State); mackerel fishing was revolutionized by the purse seine; the lure of and profits from salt cod fishing on the Banks and in certain well-known Canadian waters proved irresistible. Captain Atwood was but one of the hundreds who set sail for the Bay of St. Lawrence—where he was shipwrecked twice in the course of two weeks in 1851.

Others were off to long-lining on the Banks. By 1866, some seventy-two of Provincetown's ninety-one salt cod fishing vessels were Bankers. They brought back a huge harvest in that good and lucky year, 10.5 million pounds of fish (93,663 quintals), using up in the process 4,098 barrels of salt clam bait. The disaster of the 1840s might therefore be seen as having helped impell the change of habits that brought on the boom of the 1860s. There certainly was a shift in the dispositions of men and ships, a shift which Marblehead had not had the flexibility to pull off.

EVEN before the changes of the 1850s and the boom of the 1860s, the schooners that sailed north and east from Provincetown were nothing like the old, sparsely crewed Marblehead "heeltappers." Larger and sleeker, between forty-five and one hundred tons burden, these vessels carried as many as twelve men to a prized territory known as The Labrador, at the northern jaw of the St. Lawrence River's mouth, a beautiful, cliff-edged coastline to which American fishermen had been granted special rights in the Treaty of 1818 after the War of 1812. It was as much "home" to the fishermen from Provincetown as Cape Cod Bay; and here they engaged in exactly the same type of in-shore dory fishing as they were used to while within sight of Cape Race. They were still fishing in company with their friends and neighbors. And so in a certain sense they were still fishing on their own shores, even a thousand miles from Provincetown.

These waters too teemed with cod. The fish had come in pursuit of the marvelous capelin (*Mallotus villosus*), another salmon cousin. It shares certain habits with the shad and the alewives but spawns on the graveled or pebbled bottom near tide line rather than upriver. In July along the Arctic and sub-Arctic coasts, the capelin come ashore in vast numbers, executing an intriguing sexual maneuver. Laden with eggs, the female swims in through the surf, accompanied usually by *two* males. They crowd her between them, intent it seems on squeezing the eggs from her body. However that friendly game works biologically, it is astonishingly effective. One observer reports that the beach is so littered with eggs that it is "springy to the step, like a mattress."

The capelin is the chief bait fish of the northern seas, sought by whales and every predaceous fish, but particularly by the cod. Those great hunters of the depths have been seen swiftly pursuing the capelin at the very surface of the waters—especially when the cucumberlike odor of the ripe capelin eggs hangs on the sea air. And the catch is worth the quest: the capelin makes one of the sea's best meals, for man or beast. Once the fishermen from Provincetown had used up the bait they'd brought with them (usually mussels or clams, preserved by pickling), they well knew that the proper move was to sail into a Labrador harbor and get a load of capelin. The cod would love it.

My knowledge of this primary phase of Provincetown's fishing life comes directly from its most understanding chronicler, George Bryant. George, one of those rare and fortunate men who can combine a ring fighter's physique with a sensitive disposition, is originator and keeper of the Grand Banks Archives, a formidable collection (by which I mean boxes and boxes and boxes) of documents and pictures concerning the northern fisheries. He is also a butcher, in charge of the family store at the ground level of his massively timbered building at 467

Commercial Street. This used to be the "store" (meaning warehouse) of E. & E.K. Cook & Co., a variegated, multistoried, nineteenth-century industrial complex, with trap door over trap door so that materials could be hauled up or lowered down at will. Outside was a salt works, whose windmill and underpinnings George is in the process of restoring. But because he's a real estate surveyor, concentrating on the validity of older structures, he has little time for his salt works reclamation—or, regrettably, for writings from his archives. As gratified as I was to be introduced to George's clippings and documents (including the little red books in which each fisherman kept his own tally), the introduction to his friendship and to his family's story was even more valuable.

As George has pieced the picture together, the fisherman's day on The Labrador in the 1820s began at 3 A.M. when the captain shouted, "All hands, ho!" Then, after the men had set out in their twenty-foot-long "Hampton boats," the routine for these hand-liners went as follows (assuming no untoward interruptions by drifting ice or sleet squalls):

> The boats anchored and fished inshore waters whose depth varied from ten to twenty feet. The three or so boats from each schooner tended to travel together and were usually close enough so the men could pass a comment or a joke from one to the other. . . . During the morning aboard the vessel the captain, cook, and four men who were not fishing prepared for the return of the boats at noon by erecting gutting and salting tables and carrying materials and green salted fish to shore. After the midday meal, the small boat crews returned to the grounds for the balance of the daylight hours while the six aboard the vessel processed the fish for drying on the rocks ashore.

Though not without risks, it was a beneficial business for all. In the 1830s, the fishermen, who seem to have signed on with a definite and predetermined contract, earned between sixteen and thirty dollars a month, depending on performance. And skippers, at least those who brought back good fares, had chances to buy into the ownership of vessels. For the profits were considerable. Yet both the men and the vessels wore out fast: schooners more than ten to twenty years old were judged no longer fit for service.

Certainly sailing to The Labrador was preferable to cruising fruitlessly through the impoverished waters of Cape Cod Bay. There, after the scourge of the bluefish had eased somewhat, fishermen asked themselves and the experts what had happened. Why had the cod disappeared? Was it simply because they were as fickle as the mischievous mackerel I remembered from Noank? Not at all; the answer was related to the development of the entire New England region. Industries were gearing up; dams were being built; effluvients were staining the once-clear rivers up which the alewives no longer could run. One by one the rivers were either closed or diseased beyond repair; the cod stayed away, finding better hunting along the Banks or the Canadian coasts. The salt cod fishery, once everyone's game, would now flourish only in major ports where men and capital came daringly together for the mounting of long-distance enterprises. In the smaller ports fishermen turned to the tamer pursuits of lobstering and weir tending. Men of the Cape regarded smack skippers like those from Noank as "pirates" for the way they would take a local product (i.e. lobster) away with them to New York City and make a fortune from it.

IN PROVINCETOWN, with its diminished in-shore fishery and its strengthened link to The Labrador, the lives of the people continued to build as before—tensely, argumentatively, creatively. Back in the opening decades of the 1800s, when all New England had thrilled to the socioreligious messages of the Great Awakening, this town too had been visited by Methodism. It called to the people in a releasing, spiritual way that was quite at odds with the static, orthodox preachments of the state-supported Congregational church. Inevitably, a confrontation occurred. Focus of this local battle was a load of Maine-purchased lumber which had been delivered to Provincetown and with which the Methodists intended to build a house of worship. The boards were seized at the beach by the Congregationalists and carried to the top of one of the town's seven hills. There they made a spectacular bonfire—which delivered a message to all who would pay attention. But the Methodists chose not to heed it. Having obtained another load of wood and positioned armed men to protect it, they proceeded to build their deviationist church.

Yet the Methodists' victory was still to be won. In the words of a church historian:

> Persecution continued for thirty years, so that it was far from safe, not to say respectable, to be a Methodist. Men piled up fish heads on the shore for boys to throw at Methodists as they went to church. Many a woman crawled on her hands and knees under fish flakes in order to avoid the insults sure to be heaped upon her. So great were these abuses that, at one time, thirty or forty members of the early church removed in a company to the state of Maine.

Finally there was a kind of triumph for Methodism: the new church structure they built in 1860 boasted the highest spire in town. Indeed, it was higher than any Methodist church's in the United States, a towering 162 feet. And although the topmost pinnacle had to be taken down after the punishing Portland Gale of

1898, the building is still a magnificent assertion of spiritual determination, architecture rising from the fish flakes. For sailors approaching Cape Race the spire has remained a constant signal that they are within reach of their doorways. Also, given the way structures in Provincetown change hands as well as locations, it's not surprising that the former church building now gives shelter to Josephine Del Deo's Heritage Museum.

Methodists in Provincetown: Center Methodist Episcopal Church 1860–1958; now Heritage Museum. Provincetown Heritage Museum.

GEORGE BRYANT helped me understand the changes ashore and at sea that occurred coincidentally with the technological advances of the 1850s. Mackerel schooners—some of them "sharpshooters" (that is, with clipperlike bows), and most of them outfitted for purse seining—were lively additions to the Provincetown scene, constituting a second, and quite separate fishery. At times during the century's latter decades, there were 300 mackerelers in the harbor; the dram shops were full of money-flush hands. Many of the vessels were actually owned by firms in other Cape towns—owners whose fortunes soared and crashed at the mackerels' whim. The fishermen on board commuted to the harbor from their home villages, a migration made all the more possible when the railroad came out the Cape to Provincetown in 1873. Along with the migrant fishermen came the first generation of summer people, carrying paints and parasols. Also thanks to the railroad, the business of shipping fresh, iced fish to market ballooned in volume and men employed, becoming a rival to the salt cod fishery. A rival but not the chief.

For in those years directly after the Civil War, the striving capitalists of Provincetown (some of whose families had initially done well in whaling) perceived the Banks as the grounds where the smart money went. This intensification of fishing on the Banks was the third phase, after in-shore fishing and mackereling, of the town's industrial growth.

From the Cape to the Banks and home with a hold-full of salted codfish was then a three-month expedition, usually commencing in May and ending in late August, though some tried to get in two voyages a season. That was quite a departure, in terms of financial and human commitment, from the in-shore fishing (whether near home shores or on The Labrador) and the swift forays for mackerel in their seasonal locations. Skippers and owners agreed that for these lengthy expeditions the vessels had to be sturdier and more burdensome. So, to get the best, they went to the headquarters of fishing-schooner construction—the heavy-production yards at Essex on Cape Ann. In a move that was also a direct challenge to Gloucester (whose firms had long ordered their schooners from Essex), the Provincetown owners presumed to order a *series* of vessels. These had the capacity and the up-to-snuff technology to command fishing on the Banks.

The first of them was the *Lizzie W. Matheson*, built at Essex in 1875 by the John James yard, for a cost approaching $10,000. Along with her 108-foot length and capacious hull shape, she revealed something unique about Provincetown inclinations: she was a three-master. Few fishing skippers in other towns favored this rig; it became the unmistakable silhouette of a Provincetown schooner as she sailed along the horizon line. Many two-masters were also sailed out of

Provincetown, but it was the three-masters (occasionally called terns) that told this town's tale.

Because of the *Lizzie W. Matheson*'s immediate profitability, and because she sailed so masterfully, three other, quite similar three-masters were soon under construction at the James yard. We know of the even greater success of one of these, the *William A. McKay*. In 1882, her second year of sailing, and skippered by Captain Angus McKay of Provincetown, she brought back the largest share of codfish ever known, having been on the Banks for three months. When the fish were dried and prepared for market, they amounted to half a million pounds (4,062 quintals), sold for $22,000. Crew members were paid an average of $300.

By 1885, the peak of Provincetown's salt cod prosperity, there was close to a million dollars tied up in this fishery. When the Bankers, mackerelers, and residual whalers came in to harbor, they were warped alongside fifty-odd wharves that now jutted out from the beach. What a shift that represented from the time, exactly sixty years before, when a young woman from the Boston area had arrived and complained that there was "not a wharf in the place!" Congeries of subindustries also flourished around the wharves: cod liver oil tryworks, net makers and sail makers, boat builders and hardware forges.

The mega-industry took over the town. In charge of it was a tightly organized group of Yankee families whose basic strategy was to manage all by a balanced system of investment and insurance. This dynamic but prudent strategy gave Provincetown a fighting chance against Gloucester and other modern-era cities in the penultimate decade of the nineteenth century, an era when Progress was achieved by a single-minded (or is the word *ruthless*?) concentration of effort. Industrial specialization in the 1880s and 1890s was generally accompanied by exploitation of a labor force which had been imported for that special purpose.

In the case of Provincetown, the handsome profits of the ship owners were but one side of the coin; the other side saw a number of human-diminishing concomitants. A fisherman was paid now in wages, not in shares of the take (which had been the practice of old in most New England communities); furthermore, though he might succeed in becoming a skipper, he could never become a partner along with the town's privileged, owning families. This was particularly true if he happened to be foreign-born. George Bryant told me that in the counting houses, you would hear this sentiment: "Why should a good-for-nothing crew member get as much as some one who's put real money into the venture?" The Yankee Fishing Establishment ruled the day, and no one else need apply.

The powerful fishing firms were usually organized as partnerships which owned a wharf and a fleet of vessels. Ownership of a particular vessel was divided into sixty-four shares, with most owned by a group not exceeding ten people. Each owner insured his shares personally; the vessel itself was not insured. As some of the newly sprung mutual insurance companies prospered by this fractional system, others were wiped out, sometimes as a result of a single storm.

Members of the ruling consortia had roots that stretched back into the town's simpler days. The Lancy family, which had distinguished itself when Commercial Street was under construction by refusing to move its salt works, had done well in association with the Nickerson family (on whose vessels they had originally sailed). Under the leadership of Benjamin Lancy, Jr., who became a wealthy merchant as well as ship owner, the family now aspired to all the external grandeur that was then associated with richness. Those ambitions were expressed in the mansion he built in 1874, the year after the Old Colony Railroad came to town.

It was an elegant, mansard-roofed, Victorian four-square castle that had a peculiarly brooding air about it. It still stands on Commercial Street, but don't be discouraged if you can't spot it right away: it's almost blotted out by cheap stores and shops whose glass and metal sidings encircle its lower floors. No longer visible are the twin bay windows that once glowered out at the street, nor the Carnegie-style balcony above the front entryway, nor the overall mass of power and pride. You can, however, see the raised eyebrows over the third-floor windows and the grotesquely pretentious tower, if you wish.

The feature that best expressed the Lancy house was the "sandstone" blocks that seemed to be what gave it strength. These were phony, as phony as the pretensions. They were cleverly beveled and processed pieces of wood, the process having been invented by the grand Mr. Lancy himself. After his death (not greatly grieved, one gathers), his son frantically searched through the mansion, through all the paneled rooms, to find the make-rich formula for his father's alchemistic wood-into-stone secret. He literally tore the place apart, but found nothing. He and his sister retired to the basement and lived out their years, as the local saying goes, in miserly frugality.

THE HEYDAY of the Yankee Establishment gradually turned into a lingering sunset. The power was passing to others. As early as Captain Atwood's day, it was clear that something grossly inequitable had happened to the conduct of the cod fishery. In 1876 he reported that of the forty-eight Provincetown vessels on the Banks, only six were skippered by native-born citizens of the United States; nine of the captains were Portuguese and thirty-three were natives of Nova Scotia. That imbalance of foreigners was repeated in the fo'c's'le. The crew list of the schooner *Addie Osborne* (which was sunk by an English liner) shows that at the most two or three were Americans. George Bryant, surveying the list, estimates that the rest were either Cape Bretoners, Irish (possibly from Newfoundland), or Portuguese. George goes on to conclude that the ownership of the vessels was still in the hands of the native-born, though the operatives were immigrants; it had been trending that way since about 1860. The Yankees were getting the money and taking none of the life-threatening risks of the game.

George speaks of this exploitation of nonnatives with spirit, in part because his own family came from Cape Breton—whose natives were called Herring Chokers by the established Provincetowners. They were invited down by the fleet owners when they were needed for the season, George explained. And a number of them stayed, like his grandfather and his two brothers. One of the brothers drowned. But George's sympathy for the immigrants is by no means limited to his own kind. He gives full credit to the Portuguese for contributing both the brains and the muscle to man the various fisheries at a time when the original settlers were tiring of it. . . . The fishing industry of Provincetown would have died in the 1880s if the Portuguese hadn't come here. George's comments made me remember Marblehead, where such newcomers were neither recruited nor desired, however much needed.

A clipping from the *Cape Cod Times* quoted surviving Banks skipper Captain Alex Kemp:

> The inducement for us Nova Scotia fellows was that the Provincetown vessels paid off in *gold* at a time when the [post-Civil War] "greenback" was worth 72 cents. Back in Canada, company store scrip was the reward. . . . You wouldn't be here for six months when the townspeople would have your weight and measure. If they found you a right man, they didn't care where you hailed from and they'd kick you to the front as fast as they could.

So there were advancements and advantages, but of course the system wouldn't let you into the tight circle of owners and merchants. And the drownings continued.

In the Grand Banks Archives, my wife found an even earlier clipping. "Hope Abandoned," the headline read. The story told how the schooner *Cora S. McKay* was now presumed lost. Her skipper had been Cape Bretoner Roderick Matheson, thirty-six years old, father of two children. The schooner went down at Virgin Rocks on the Grand Bank in the great disaster of the American coast that came to be called the Galveston Gale. A subhead in the yellowed newspaper account said, "Crew Mostly from Here," and narrated that they were Portuguese except for nine Nova Scotians and a Frenchman and Scotsman; they left behind fifteen wives and forty-nine children.

A related story began with the headline "A Sad Christmas," and went on to quote Father Terra, the pastor of Provincetown's St. Peter's Church: "Once again the angel of death [has visited us.] One after another the poor wives put their little toddlers into black clothes . . . [and] applied for assistance." This and the other clippings about the much-grieved loss of the *Cora S. McKay* had been pasted into an album kept by the skipper's wife, Mary Matheson Murchison. She had come to Provincetown from Grand River, Cape Breton; Gaelic was spoken in the home. One suspected that an account at which she gazed often was the one about how the captain had been "deeply esteemed by the town's people." (Deeply esteemed, but replaceable by other immigrants.) It seems curiously appropriate that the widow's second husband was superintendant of the Second Life Saving District.

George could tell me less about the precise origins of the Portuguese who had come to Provincetown, only that many of them were, in fact, from the Azores. It's said, however, that the very first Portuguese settler was Manuel Caton from Lisbon. Unlike others of his fellow countrymen who had sought out Provincetown as refugees from New Bedford and the whaling industry, Caton came on a pirate ship. His story, reported in a 1931 history of the town, has all the drama of a silent film clip:

Caton went to sea after running away from home. His ship was captured by pirates. Every man on board was compelled to walk the plank, the story goes, but Caton survived and was put into service as the pirates' slavey. Subsequently the pirate captain fell ill. The ship anchored off Provincetown and Caton was sent ashore to get attention for his master. The pirate was nursed back to health here. He went his pirating ways, but Caton remained here and made his living here until his death.

Provincetown's Portuguese fishermen were indeed the backbone of the town's Banks fishery. Manuel, the Portuguese fisherman in *Captains Courageous* (played in the movie by Spencer Tracy, as I recall fondly) could be limned so accurately because author Rudyard Kipling had so well picked the brains of a Provincetown sailor who had served with these men. The extraordinary courage and patience of the Portuguese fishermen deserves to be remembered. But they also had the wit to see the worm in the apple; they knew as well as anyone that ownership was the name of the game. And, declining to be peons for ever, they developed over the years a fishery of their own. This was the in-shore, dory-conducted, fresh fish business which again could be pursued now that the bluefish's depredations had ceased and the buying public had developed a taste for whiting and other small, schooling fish. It was a business that allowed them to fish in the ancient manner, at their own doors.

Initially the fresh fish landed in Provincetown—comprising the fourth of the town's fisheries—reached the mainland markets via smacks or fast-sailing packet boats. But, with the arrival of the railroad, the fish could be shipped to Boston or New York packed in ice. Whereas making salt had once been a major subindustry for landsmen, now natives and newcomers worked the ice ponds, praying that the cold weather would last. By 1874, newly constructed icehouses had a capacity of nearly 5,000 tons. And those who supplied the fresh fish throughout the seasons were doing very well.

But it should be pointed out that this business was productive because of the extra zeal with which it was pursued. An astonished Yankee wrote of that zealousness in the *Provincetown Advocate* on February 22, 1871: "Our Portuguese fishermen are very restless. They go out in all kinds of weather and upon all days. It is quite strange that no more are lost. Many fish upon the Sabbath, as do some of the Irish fishing vessels of Boston, we learn." Better to fish dangerously, in freedom, than under the exclusive rules of the Establishment.

And no strangers to Provincetown were the Irish. They had come in the middle of the nineteenth century to labor in the salt works and shipyards. According to Captain Atwood, they had introduced trawl fishing (long-lining) to the Banks. And they had had the audacity to introduce the first Roman Catholic Society to Provincetown, in 1851.

By 1887 there were 1,730 Catholics in town, mostly Irish and Portuguese. They had put up their own church in 1874, at a cost of $8,000. It was named St. Peter's, in recognition of the fisherman's patron saint. But, far from rattling the cages of the Protestant Yankees, the Catholics (particularly the Portuguese) tended to stay by themselves. It would take some impulse as stark as the bluefish incursion to jolt them out of that posture; that shock came when the KKK burned crosses at St. Peter's on Monument Hill in the mid-1920s.

To the challenge of blazing crosses the Portuguese reacted decisively. They recognized that the time had come to assert themselves in politics and in business. By then they had the numbers, the fishery, the bank accounts, and the conviction that—if only in terms of those who had lost their lives for it—Provincetown was as much theirs as anyone's. Their individual names began to appear, on drug store lists and directorships. Yet George Bryant sees the recognition of their leadership as a long time in the coming: there was no mention of a Portuguese fishing vessel *captain* in the local press until 1874.

AS THE old Yankee oligarchy endured its own *Götterdämmerung*, the solid salt cod schooners of the 1870s and 1880s were replaced by leaner, more multipurpose vessels, and Provincetown's Banks fishery faced a time of change. Yet there was something about the town's business chiefs that prevented them from seeing that the market was doing strange and interesting things. No longer did American housewives want to put up with all the awkward messiness of unprocessed fish; they preferred an easily packaged product, easily flipped into the pan or the oven. Possibly the reason for the blindness of the local entrepreneurs to this new opportunity lay in a fear that they could not get factory hands to work in a bone-picking, processing plant at adequately low wages to make the economic formula work. So at the same time as the port of Provincetown went ahead with increasing shipments of fresh fish, it continued to send the hard-dried fish of yesteryear to an increasingly reluctant market. Meanwhile, Gloucester delivered handsome, wooden boxes of skinned and boned fish to m'lady's pantry shelves.

Meanwhile, there was a threat of another kind. Canadian authorities, ever unhappy with the Americans' free ways upon the Labrador, sought to arrange a new, more restrictive treaty. And to make their position of power more obvious, they cut off access to the bait our fishermen along the coasts and on the Banks had always obtained in the Maritimes—those wondrous capelin. Yet Province-town's fishermen in the eastern seas were not defeated; they found they could get their bait in the form of leftovers from the newly initiated fresh-fish business. The town began to function together again in many of its parts.

Then a rather ungainly structure at the foot of Johnson Street (not far from the Old Colony Railroad wharf) made the bait supply business all the more efficient. The building contained an anhydrous ammonia absorption system; its sign iden-tified it as the Provincetown Cold Storage Plant (1893). And this plant, along with others, revolutionized the industry. Although Gloucester had pioneered in freezing facilities, Provincetown countered with six more plants upon the success of its first. Any fears of lack of workmen eased as men flocked to the year-round jobs and as former sailors proved themselves capable plumbers and mechanics. Now the bait fish caught by the in-shore fishermen could go right off, in freezer compartments, to the Banks; the long-line trawlers would have enough for the season. And Canada could go hang.

Another source of supply had also opened up, offering both bait fish and fresh fish. These were the traps, the salty, colorful traps which many painters and regional writers portrayed at the turn of the century—and which developed into the fifth phase of Provincetown's fisheries. But they were not really all that new; Captain Atwood recalled that the first deep-water stake-and-net weirs were pounded into place by the Solomon Bangs family as far back as 1851. Soon thereafter the immutable design of the trap was set; it worked, no one knew quite why.

Overall, the trap looked something like a cello: the "neck" of the instrument (a very long, staked net, usually 900–1200 feet) first blocked the fish as they swam along one of the Cape's beaches; then the fish would find themselves swept into the "heart" of the trap, which was about 200 feet in diameter; then there seemed to be no place to go but into the "bowl," which at 320 feet in diameter was large enough to hold thousands of captives. There was all hell to play if seals or tuna or sharks got in there, too, but generally the tenders—who worked from specially designed, thirty-foot trap boats driven by two-cycle engines—could scoop out the ensnared fish before disaster followed. In lucky years, when the herring and the mackerel were schooling well, the traps were so loaded that two and sometimes three draws could be made a day.

But it was not until the need for bait became acute and the freezing plants

Trap fishing: LEFT AND BELOW, *After the horses assist in setting up the trap's structure and the tide rises, fishermen move in to haul bagged fish into a trap boat.*

A marauding tuna is removed from a trap by gaffers. All, Collection of Diana Worthington.

made the product all the more useful that the traps assumed a major position in the Provincetown fisheries. It was a wonderfully happy coming-together of Provincetown's resources, its personnel and their persistence; it appeared that the people had hung in there and won. George Bryant summed up that era by pointing out that, as a result of the trap and freezer development here, Provincetown was still landing the same poundage of fish in 1935 as it was in 1887, whereas Gloucester had declined by half.

YET this proved to be a goal scored in the twilight. The end of fishing as an essentially man-against-fish (or do I mean man-*with*-fish?) endeavor was upon every town of New England. Henceforth the industry would take off in an entirely different, mechanized direction.

For all its picturesque appeal to the painters and the summer people, who saw the muscled men of the traps working out their destinies against the excitement of the silvery catch and the harmony of the background seas and sands, this was a factory-style operation. Most everything here was owned by the freezer companies. They encouraged output. So at the height of the trap fishing era, there were one hundred traps between Race Point and Wellfleet; about one quarter of all the fresh fish sold on the Eastern seaboard had come from traps. The Cape Cod Storage Company alone hired two hundred workers on a year-round basis.

To maintain their operations, the freezer plant managers took the first 50 percent of profits from a haul; the remainder was divided among the crew, with the captain getting a double portion. But the trick was that the plant decided what the weight and the worth of the catch might be—individual managers earned wicked reputations among the fishermen as cheaters and withholders. Nonetheless, it was a "healthy, invigorating life," as one of the trap fishermen recalled.

Meanwhile the salt Bankers were disappearing. The men of the Cape saw the long haul out to the Grand Bank as not worth the brutality, the lack of stake in it, the time away from home. For example, the miniscule community of Truro, next door to Provincetown, had lost over the years 352 fishermen to the high seas. Along the storm-damaged wharves of Provincetown—where one of the sheds still was marked by a roof-line notch which had been cut out to allow the great bowsprit of a Banker to rest there when in port—one searched in vain for towering topmasts at the turn of the century. The last big schooners had been sold off to Gloucester. With few regrets for the generation past, the men seized upon the alternative of trap fishing, adaptable as ever.

It's the nature of the diverse fisheries, however, that immediately when men become most dependent on one of them, most trusting of it, the fish make a decision to the contrary. Or so it seems. Often imbalances caused by man lie behind the perversity of the fish. Whatever the cause, the summer fish faded away; within a few years of its peak in the 1920s and 1930s, trap fishing was dead. Dead as a smelt.

Whereas the supply of fish in these mixed south-north waters had once seemed unending—the whiting said to be so thick "you couldn't see the ocean bottom" through the schools—now weeks went by with no catch in the traps for either fishing schooners or freezer plants and their newly ravenous buyers. An oft-glimpsed, summertime scene in the Provincetown area had been a schooner coasting up alongside the trap, sails a-flutter, with an American flag flying upside down from the gaff peak, indicating that she had a desperate need for bait and that the trap boat should come out to shovel it aboard. But now the schooners stayed away, knowing that the visit would be in vain. On the wharves, on the beaches, the fishermen glumly discussed what monster had struck them this time.

One school pointed to the Cape Cod Canal. This Yankee version of the Suez, connecting Massachusetts Bay and Buzzards Bay, had first been dug in 1910, then widened in the early 1930s. Environmentally, it had had an uproarious effect on the waters at Provincetown's doors, warming them and bringing in new species. Perhaps that was the reason for the fishes' disappearance.

Also in 1910, the practice of dragging had been introduced, the sixth of Provincetown's fisheries. In dragging, great harrows were towed by heavily engined craft across the fishing grounds, scooping up every living thing into wire nets that were then hauled aboard with immensely powerful winches. It was all the work of a new age of mechanical might; the approach to fishing was so efficient that it destroyed some of the very areas the fish held most dear. It became increasing difficult for mere men, in their traps or in their dories, to compete commercially against the mechanical giants of this new age. In the words of Provincetown fisherman Louis Cordeiro, "If fishermen had stuck with [long-line] trawling, we'd still have fish today. The ocean is just like your garden at home. You have to take care of the ground. The draggers put us out of business."

AS A KIND of elegy, Mary Heaton Vorse wrote:

Every year sees another of the old houses passing into the hands of "summer people." The newcomers have treated the old houses tenderly. And as yet "summer folks," as they are known, play but little part in the town's prosperity. But the old days are passing. Last summer for the first time the Town Crier cried no more. . . . There are more flowers, more trees than there used to be when I first came. There are fewer sailing dories.

With the economy of the town turned more toward the tourist than toward the sea, the tensions and disruptions of the place tended to change character. The biggest hassle of the 1920s was between the conservative and the modernist wings of the local art fraternity; it was only resolved by staging two separate summer exhibitions. The theaters flourished as the fisheries declined.

But as recently as 1986, the *New Yorker* had a major story on the fishermen of Provincetown. It explained the relatively modern and expensive and moderately successful business of otter trawling. (Now we have arrived at the seventh stage of the fisheries—the "seventh age" of the fisherman?) In the otter trawling process, two barn-sized doors are lowered and pulled along at a certain depth as the trawler advances through the offshore seas. The doors widen the mouth of a huge net into which fall a great variety of fish (many of them whiting), not all of which are marketable. And in looking at and listening to these men of the new age who continue to bring in a big annual catch to Provincetown, the writer captured the ages-old argument of the fisherman: "When he comes to the wharf, the fisherman doesn't *sell* his fish. He gives it away. I got thirty cents a pound for a fish that you go to the store and they sell it for six dollars."

When it came to interviewing a man who had been forced to give up his boat, another voice was heard: the total—one could almost say the *religious*—despair at being removed from the sea. "As soon as a man gets away from the sea, he's lost. It's because God meant his disciples to be fishermen."

It's the same way with the community. As Josephine Del Deo pointed out, Provincetown needs to keep one foot in the sea for its own well-being. Even though the fisherman, when returned home to harbor, tends to busy himself at the end of the pier and to be only an elusive shade in the garish walks of Town Along Provincetown, he is still the essential character of the place. The *genius loci*.

He's quite used to being put in the shadows. As long ago as Captain Atwood's day, the world was trying to tell the fisherman that he could not be what he was and still be respectable and in charge of his own destiny. When the captain himself arrived in Boston, having been elected state representative by the good people of Provincetown, he was asked by the statehouse doorkeeper what his profession might be. Captain Atwood naturally answered, "Fisherman." But the official wrote it down as "Master Mariner." So much for American democracy, remarked Thoreau, who originally reported this reverse insult; so much for the men who continue to epitomize the American democratic spirit.

They and their families gave to Provincetown its scale and its punch and its endurability. Perhaps those qualities are even more of a gift than dead History. Castles never belonged here.

I was pondering that contribution on the morning of our departure from the town, when I should have been paying more attention to finding a restaurant for our breakfast. The cold wind hit the face like a snapped cod line. My wife and I scurried along seemingly abandoned Commercial Street, spying only snazzy eateries that had no intention of opening for the emptiness of a morning-after in Provincetown. Then there it was: on the glass front of what used to be a residence was the magic word *Donuts*; inside, up front, there was a bakery activity on one side and a one-dish-at-a-time cookery activity on the other. Beyond, there were little tables and benches and big people having breakfast with their kids. Leaving the coat at the table, one walked over and waited, leaning on the counter as the news of the day was exchanged among the coffee-flavored aromas, and soon enough got a mugful and a heavy, warm plate. The blueberry muffins steamed purple on the inside.

We left town with the satisfied feeling that the people of Provincetown would never let the essence get away from them. Yet what of other fishing communities and other fisheries? For example, whaling: Did its fish-induced dynamics make for continuation and mobility among the people or for restriction and decay? Nantucket and New Bedford would together tell the tale.

NANTUCKET: THIS SOCIETY OF FISHERMEN & MERCHANTS

HER breasts, housed in the carefully engineered upper part of a two-piece bathing suit, seemed to be functioning as a radar set, sensitively aimed to bring in Nantucket. She stood on the frontmost settee of the top deck as the car ferry surged across the Sound from Hyannis. Behind her, supportive arm around her waist, hulked the shorts-clad husband, face sprinkled with one-day beard in the manner of contemporary twenty-year-olds.

But who was I to deplore their public intimacy? A wee speck of time ago (if you don't mind counting in decades) my wife and I had honeymooned out in this direction, too, on that horizon-down island whose higher spires we could just now discern. White beaches, worlds away; the ideal banishment for lovers.

Another young couple—but in a small sloop, with five children and two helpers aboard—sailed across these choppy, green waters in the teeth of a gale in 1659. When the gale blew up to dangerous heights, the wife-mother rather sensibly suggested that they turn back. But the husband-father, in the eternal way of skippers, demurred. He's alleged to have cried, "Woman: go below and seek thy God. I fear not witches on earth or devils in hell!"

These were Thomas and Sarah Macy, for whom life on the Puritan-ruled mainland had become intolerable. They had committed the offense in Salisbury, Massachusetts, of admitting four Quakers to their house during a rainstorm. For that act of kindness—which was regarded as a punishable misdemeanor, Quakers being the wildest and most radical of the sects that had sprung up in England and the colonies during the Cromwellian revolution—the Macys were fined thirty shillings. Seeking now to put all that theological contention behind them, they yearned merely to raise sheep and farm on this little scrap of glaciation out in Nantucket Sound. The last thing they intended was to found a community devoted to Quakerism and to whaling and to monopolistic wealth.

Yet unto the Macys and the ten families who followed them to Nantucket

OPPOSITE. *Orange Street, Nantucket: Halfway up the cobblestone street, a broad brick house with roof walk is addressed by sideways front steps. Mystic Seaport Museum.*

("farmers, fishermen, and mechanics" all) came missionaries of that compelling faith which encouraged every woman and man to feel there was "that of God" in her or him. There was an "inner light" which enabled one to understand God's will; by living simply and prudently and by nurturing this light among other Friends, one could reflect Christ's message. Following the example of England's founding Quaker George Fox, one should never doff one's hat to authority. Many of the Nantucket settlers converted, following the example of Mary Starbuck who was known for her common sense and recognized as "the Great Woman . . . the chosen instrument for the firm establishment of the Quaker faith on this island." But many others (about half the population) chose to continue as Baptists or Presbyterians—or to become "Nothingarians." Tolerance was the order of the day; church buildings blossomed like the wild beach rose.

By that time (1673), the island had been formally purchased from its former owners—the Mayhew family of Martha's Vineyard—and a village named Sherburne established on the northwest corner. But the harbor there proved inadequate; more and more of the inhabitants turned their interests toward the sea. Gradually the settlement shifted eastward to the Great Harbor. Following the trend, but wood being scarce for new home building, several of the residents simply upped anchor à la Provincetown and moved their houses across the sand to the new location. In 1710 a substantial landing was built on the Great Harbor, the harbor into which the ferry was now taking us. And eventually the name Nantucket was applied to all, the town, the county, and the internationally inclined island.

We found our lodgings on India Street all too easily. When landed in a new place, I like to buttonhole a local in an innocent way and pretend deaf-blindness as his flood of quaint nativisms finally floats me along to the desired destination. My wife is of the far more upstanding belief that you should position yourself at a street corner with map in hand and turn round and round until the routes on the map align themselves with the features of the landscape. Then you stride off confidently in the wrong direction. I could nab but one passerby (an ignorant gentleman in pink trousers and blue blazer, reptile on shirt) before my wife reached the obvious conclusion that the house we sought was right over there.

The island is now totally given over to pleasure, a play place for the rich. I mused on that, beer in hand, and antiplutocratic thoughts foaming, as we waited for our comely waitress to bring us lunch on the sunny porch of a big, sprawling, stained-wood restaurant at the foot of the restored wharf area. Here was the kind of waterfront which Provincetown's Josephine Del Deo would deplore, an upscale pseudo-village of galleries on pilings, which had lost any connection with the honest-to-God fisheries. Marblehead's Russell Knight, too, would probably laugh this ersatz harborfront to scorn. The messy old reality is nowhere to be seen, and hasn't been for ages. Front Street has disappeared, along with its raffish denizens.

For almost a century and a half, that is, since the decline of long-distance whaling and the wipeout of the town center in the conflagration of 1846, Nantucket has existed pretty much for summer fun. In 1855 steamboat connections with the mainland were secured and members of Thorstein Veblen's new Leisure Class trooped hither. Whereas at its peak as a sea-working community the island's population topped 10,000, that year-round total is no longer approached. But summertime visitations range over 40,000 (not counting poor chumps who just ferry across for the day).

A brief effort was made to hold back the tide of summer folks at the turn of this century. Symbol of that crusade is the slightly battered, antique fountain near the bottom of the cobblestoned Main Street (which used to go by another name, of course: State Street). The fountain was set there to demonstrate to all that these streets were designed for slow-paced walkers and for horseback riders, not for whizzing autos; the automobile was banned in 1900, outlawed. But that legislation was repealed in 1918 by a fair margin, 336 to 296; and unrestrainedly the Buicks rolled in, with crossed yacht-club flags on their side panels. Another destiny that had never been intended by the founders was foisted upon the island.

Lost forever were the important, working-waterfront times between founding and tourism, the heroic times of the eighteenth century described so eloquently by Nantucket historian Obed Macy:

> In those olden days, the town was a social paradise, and Quakerism, relieved so largely from the interference of the outside world, put on its most beautiful form . . . the people were comparatively wealthy, while retaining great simplicity in their tastes and habits.

I'm reminded also of the comments at this time of that great, early American traveler, Hector St. John de Crèvecoeur (he who in writing the *Letters from an American Farmer* asked that still-debated question, What is an American?). He observed: "Here, happily unopposed with any civil bondage, this society of fishermen and merchants live, without any military establishments, without governors or any masters but the laws; and their civil code is so light, that it is never felt." That Paradise now lost, pink trousers call the tune.

Yet, enjoying the sun and the beer and the waitress as I was, and remembering the joys of a leisurely honeymoon a while back, did I have any right to rue this swarming of the Leisure Class? I looked about me. These incorrigible collegians, these women carrying scrimshaw-topped "lighthouse" baskets, these men with eyes glazed from having been dragged through two boutiques too many—there was nothing vicious about them, nothing for a fellow hedonist to criticize. Except that, recalling the quietly elegant Starbuck mansions at the top of Main Street, the modulated beauty and restraint of such institutions as the Atheneum, one might retain a vision of an elite that's different. If ever there could have been a responsible, contributory elite, it seems to have been here. A fishing community in the fullest flower of style.

"He who hastens to be rich will not be innocent," reads an inscription on the lintel of an eighteenth-century house on Academy Lane which I was to visit later. This tugs the conscience but has the leaden ring of a middle-class bromide. The oldtime Nantucketers didn't hasten to get rich; they never hastened about anything, as one can still feel in these gentle and deliberate streets. Christian innocence certainly existed at the early time when, for example, settlers taught Indians how to plow the land; it remained during the life of one Zacheus Macy, he who set bones for free for fifty years.

Yet can innocence endure for long?

THE MAN who impelled Nantucket toward riches, Joseph Rotch, arrived here alone and poor and twenty-one. Like John Glover of Marblehead, Joseph had begun life in a Salem cordwainer's family, perhaps Huguenot by extraction. Already the idea was in the sea wind that, given the gulping market for whale oil and the many barrels that could be boiled out of one fortunate catch, there might be smarter things to do than fish in the summer and bang out boots in the winter. Nantucket was beginning to ship quantities of whale oil to the world; the business looked good to Joseph. He set forth from the mainland in 1725 and soon found his love on the island, a daughter of the Macy clan. Together they created a dynasty as remarkable for its principles as for its success.

Some Nantucketers sniffed that Joseph was too "mirthful" to be a Quaker; nonetheless he became one before his marriage to Love Macy. And, as well as joining the increasingly dominant Society of Friends, he entered the elect circle of "landed proprietors" who, to put it simply, owned everything. Their major stake was now in the whale fishery. Already a dozen and more whalers sailed in and out of the harbor on missions along the coast; two years before, in 1723, the Straight Wharf had been built out from the bustling waterfront, ready to take in and ship out the precious barrels of whale oil. Additionally, the business had just swung through a profoundly important reorientation. They'd figured out how to make the whale fishery work as a business.

Since the time of the community's founding, Nantucketers had viewed whaling as a lively and attractive alternative to the initial, profitless pursuits of farming and sheepherding. In the words of historian Macy:

> The sight of whales playing near the shores led the inhabitants to contemplate the advantages which would arise, could they become possessed of the proper means of taking them. Those means were gradually attained, consisting partly of information derived from Cape Cod, but principally drawn from their own enterprising disposition and indefatigable industry.

In another charming account, one gray-clad Quaker standing on a hill in 1690 and spotting whales spouting off shore is reported to have exclaimed: *"There* is a green pasture where our children's grandchildren will go for bread."

To go a-whaling, to tangle with those gigantic beasts, obviously involved more risks, financially and physically, than did the tested business of finfishing. It called for large-scaled problem solving. Here there would be nothing like a humble fisherman owning his own little boat. This called for big money from single-minded investors, for qualities of mind and body that only the most daring culture would presume to put on the line. The Quakers presumed. In the words of de Crèvecoeur, "they [went] to hunt and catch that huge fish which by its strength and velocity one would imagine ought to be beyond the reach of man."

Legend has it that the Nantucketers learned the art of whaling from the Indians, having observed the "bold savages" going after the "scrag" in birchbark canoes. But, in fact, the presumptuous Quakers wanted to do it in nothing but the most advanced way. So they sent to the mainland for a succession of teachers. First came a noted whaler from the eastern tip of Long Island, James Loper, a former resident of New Amsterdam who had fled that gabled city when the British occupied it. He agreed to "carry on a design of Whale Citching on the Island of Nantuckket." For him the Quakers wrote a two-year contract sufficiently generous to belie their supposed stinginess: he would receive ten acres of land (except for woodland—*no one* would be given that) and "commonage" for three cows and twenty sheep and one horse. Yet, for reasons apparently not known in Nantucket, Loper decided to depart at the end of his contract.

By chance, I recently discovered the reason why he sailed away. Romance, or rather the lack of it. On reading Peter Matthiessen's admirable book *Men's Lives*, I re-encountered our friend Mr. Loper; he had returned to Long Island, having not found *his* love on Nantucket, and had married the daughter of Lion Gardiner, Gardiner Island's laird. Interestingly, Loper's state-of-the-art whaling system, employed wherever he went, was to engage Indians (at three shillings a day) to charge out through the surf in light craft after the whales which he and other emplaced spotters would spy from the shore. That became the approved pattern of the first phase of Nantucket whaling; it continued so even after the departed Loper was replaced by Ichapod Paddock, a Cape Codder who had been invited to continue the tutelage. De Crèvecoeur claimed that so intimate were the settlers and the Indians at this time in their endeavors that they both spoke in Nattick, the Indians' tongue.

At four points on the south and east coasts of the island, cleated spars were erected from which sharp-eyed watchmen would scan the seas for whales. When one was sighted, six men from that station would launch their boat into the waves and row or paddle in frantic pursuit of the unfortunate leviathan. On successfully harpooning one, they would let it exhaust itself as it charged away, dragging behind a weighted "drogue" attached by line to the deep-sunk harpoon. Then, the exhausted whale having been killed with lances, the hunters would tow the body back into the beach. And after the bloody and slippery work of making critical cuts in the hide had been completed, the great carpet of blubber would be peeled off by a capstanlike hoist and winch called a crab. Ultimately, the carved up blubber would be heaved into wagons and trundled townward for "trying out"

Unwrapping the beast: Flensers devised strategies for cutting blubber from various types of whales—even when the whale lay chained alongside the ship. Mystic Seaport Museum; John F. Leavitt diagram.

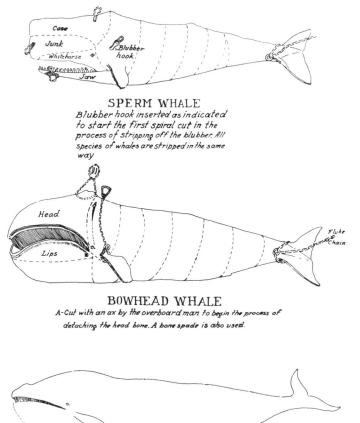

SPERM WHALE
Blubber hook inserted as indicated to start the first spiral cut in the process of stripping off the blubber. All species of whales are stripped in the same way

BOWHEAD WHALE
A-Cut with an ax by the overboard man to begin the process of detaching the head bone. A bone spade is also used.

RIGHT WHALE
Cut in the same as a bowhead whale

the oil—until townspeople complained that the stench from the boiling vats was too disgusting.

Critical to the process was the gradually evolving whaleboat, which emerged from its primitive forms when the eighteenth century was still young. This is both a boat and an art object. Taking issue with those who claim that the epitome of New England design in this era was possibly the Windsor chair with one-piece bow-and-arm, or surely the Bullfinch church with Revere bell, I will uphold the anonymously crafted, white cedar whaleboat as our most memorable work of art. Like many of the world's most inspired creations, this is primarily a tool, the perfect tool for its moment. With deep sources in prehistory (the Native American canoe), it also spoke to the future; it fulfilled the eternal human desire to take off and strike at a creature in another element. The Nantucketers had the perfect pursuit craft in their grasp.

In the very year of Joseph Rotch's arrival on the island, the chief justice of Massachusetts took note of this ingenious, indigenous craft. He wrote that the whaleboats were made of Cedar Clapboards, and so very light that two Men can conveniently carry them, yet they are twenty feet long, and carry Six Men, viz. the Harpooner . . . four Oar-men, and the Steersman. These boats by reason of their lightness can be brought on and off, and so keep out of danger. Our people formerly used to kill the Whale near the Shore; but now they go off to Sea in Sloops and Whale boats, in the months of May, June, and July, between Cape Cod and Bermudas.

Though wrong about how very light the boat was (surely all six men were needed to carry it), he was quite right about the industry: it was changing. Now that the Quaker hunters had the perfect missile to launch at their targets, the obviously more efficient system was to take these craft out to sea via a larger vessel and to seek the seasonal and diminishing whales in deeper waters.

But I have the feeling that the revolutionary whaleboats have not yet been described adequately here. They were designed to be as swift-cutting in the stern as in the bow, because of the sudden need to reverse away from the whale immediately after the harpoon had been driven home. Also, they were built both easily and inexpensively; the straight cedar planks were formed into gentle curves over a mold; then other planks were overlaid; finally the ribs were sprung into place. Whereas the heavy, costly whaleboats of the English had broad and flat

Loaded for action: Besides its carefully placed hunting gear, the twenty-eight-foot whaleboat has room for its mate and five oarsmen. Mystic Seaport Museum; John F. Leavitt diagram.

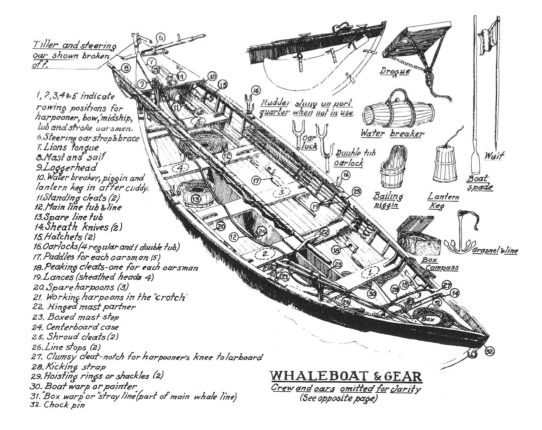

Tiller and steering oar shown broken off.

1, 2, 3, 4 & 5 indicate rowing positions for harpooner, bow, midship, tub and stroke oarsmen.
6. Steering oar strap & brace
7. Lions tongue
8. Mast and sail
9. Loggerhead
10. Water breaker, piggin and lantern keg in after cuddy.
11. Standing cleats (2)
12. Main line tub & line
13. Spare line tub
14. Sheath knives (2)
15. Hatchets (2)
16. Oarlocks (4 regular and 1 double tub)
17. Paddles for each oarsman (5)
18. Peaking cleats-one for each oarsman
19. Lances (sheathed heads 4)
20. Spare harpoons (3)
21. Working harpoons in the "crotch"
22. Hinged mast partner
23. Boxed mast step
24. Centerboard case
25. Shroud cleats (2)
26. Line stops (2)
27. Clumsy cleat-notch for harpooner's knee to larboard
28. Kicking strap
29. Hoisting rings or shackles (2)
30. Boat warp or painter
31. Box warp or "stray line (part of main whale line)
32. Chock pin

Drogue
Rudder slung on port quarter when not in use.
Water breaker
Oar lock
Double tub oarlock
Bailing piggin
Lantern Keg
Boat spade
Waif
Grapnel & line
Box Compass
Box

WHALEBOAT & GEAR
Crew and oars omitted for clarity
(See opposite page)

midsections, with two rowers seated side-by-each on equal-lengthed thwarts, New England whaleboats were as slim and as continually curved as a bent bow. And each rower had the whole thwart to himself; he sat on the side opposite from where his oar was hinged on the gunwale (two to port, three to starboard). Furthermore—and this is what made our design distinctive—the oars were of differing lengths, depending on where the rower was seated, for the fulcrums were at differing distances from each man.

By subtle improvements and augmentations, the whaleboat continued to evolve. The best description of the final, nineteenth-century model was written by whaling captain William M. Davis:

> This paragon of a boat is twenty-eight feet long, sharp and clean cut as a dolphin, bow and stern swelling amidships to six feet, with a bottom round and buoyant. The gunwale amidships, twenty-two inches above the keel, rises with an accelerated curve to thirty-seven inches at each end, and this rise of bow and stern, with the clipper-like upper form, gives it a duck-like capacity to top the oncoming waves, so that it will dryly ride when ordinary boats would fill.

So beautiful. So lethal.

Along with figuring out the best weapons, Nantucketers had to figure out the nature of the beast they hunted. Ever since the discovery that substantial revenues in sterling could be earned in trade with the mother country (by way of Boston) when whale oil was the product, the whale had advanced in popularity to semi-divine status. The most available whale was called the "right whale," primarily for its endearing habit of not sinking on having been killed—it could easily be floated into shore. But taxononomically speaking, the "right whale" is not a whale at all; it's a collective term for two or three species. These include the Biscayan whale, the Greenland whale, and the pigmy whale (which is quite rare).

The first of these, known to scientists as *Eubalaena glacialis*, had a long and productive history under the lances of Old World and New World hunters before the Nantucket Quakers began to investigate the business. In the primitive days of subsistence fishing, before the Quakers and others organized the industry (with the eventual result of near extermination for the species), the Biscayan whales were so numerous they seemed to wash themselves on the sands as offerings from a benign Nature. Even when attacked at sea, the right whale has little equipment with which to fight back, except a flailing tail. The right whale, indeed.

It's about as big as a good sea boat—fifty feet. When it surfaces, whale watchers see a sleek black back, preceded by a bumpy and irregular snout; whalers focus on the deep and capacious body that may yield up to 200 barrels of oil. In the manner of all baleen whales, it has a curious grill system in its mouth rather than teeth; out through these hairy slats of whalebone it strains the plankton-rich water that has washed into its immense oral cavity, retaining the tiny marine organisms for its food.

In the words of Nantucket whaleman Peleg Folger, the right whale looms up on you "very large, hollowing on the back, all slick and smooth, having no hump at all as other Whales." He caught enough of them to know. Then, speaking of the whale's other characteristics: "The tongue is monstrous large and will commonly make a ton of oyl. He has two spout holes and makes a forked spout."

True enough, but it was a creature with only one spout hole which would become the most important natural character on the Nantucket whaling scene: the sperm whale. This extraordinary mammal, larger by ten feet than the right whale, is notably different in the way it breathes and discharges its vapor. Peleg Folger observed this difference, reporting that the sperm can be readily identified by its single spout; this emission slants forward like a shower, not upward and back like a gusher.

Furthermore, the sperm whale (*Physeter catadon*) inhabits warm-weather oceans, as opposed to the right, which prefers Arctic seas and currents. Also, the sperm has teeth, a whole long, lean lower jawful of them—twenty-three on each side—for eating meat. When I was a lad, these gleaming, ivory, six-inch-high teeth graced the mantels of my grandparents' New Bedford parlors, dental mementoes of long-ago encounters with the largest of the toothed whales. I would be told countless times that, in life, the teeth's purpose was to grip the body of a succulent squid or octopus down at the awesome depths where the sperm whale chooses to cruise for food. Then, the prey secured, the whale would rocket up to the surface, subjecting the victim to more pressure changes than normal creatures can bear. The battle of the titans won, the sperm whale munches and digests its catch, ever seeking more.

Colored not black but bluish gray, the sperm whale reveals a lighter underside as it turns away. It can be vicious when attacked; but to Nantucket whalemen that battle seemed worth the struggle, particularly when they comprehended the parlayable value of the beast. That knowledge began to dawn about a generation before the arrival of Joseph Rotch. The islanders discovered one day on their beach a vast and unfamiliar-looking whale, dead and washed to shore. Was it a denizen of distant (southern?) seas, they asked each other? And they marveled at the noble and squarish head as well as the humpy backbone and powerful flukes. But it was not until they opened the head that they glimpsed for the first time the sperm's treasure chest of marketable products. Here was not only a store of wondrously pure oil but a waxy substance (later called spermaceti), which would prove to be prime material for candles, ointments, and perfume. It was the spermaceti most of all which lit up a new world of opportunity for the would-be merchants of Nantucket.

But the questions remained, How and Where to find these superior beasts when they did not happen to be cast up on the beach? And clearly the answer was to launch mightier boats, probe more distant seas, be more diligent, Friends.

A Captain Christopher Hussey heeded the injunction and headed out to sea in search of this rare beast, the sperm whale, in 1712. But as the day faded with no whale spotted, the captain turned back toward shore only to be confronted with a gale that drove his tender sloop further to sea. Just then as the storm peaked, a crewman saw a line of humpy-backed creatures on the horizon. Even while struggling to keep his craft from foundering, the captain urged his harpooner to go forward and prepare to strike at a whale from the bowsprit.

And strike the harpooner did, releasing, too, the drogue that the wounded whale then had to drag behind him. When the great beast surfaced again, wearied from the chase, the captain was able to work the sloop around into the lee, where the waters were smoothed by oil and blood; from that vantage point he could approach for the ultimate killing. Then the long sail home commenced, climaxed by the triumphant entrance into the harbor. This was the first sperm whale brought into Nantucket, however valid the details of the story may be.

In Captain Hussey's wake sailed other sperm whalers, ever in search of the whale which frolicked in sunny seas. Initially the technology of the off-shore hunt remained quite primitive. Herman Melville's character Ishmael, who loved a good sea story as much as any sailor, claimed that it was from Nantucket that "the first adventurous, little sloop [had] put forth, partly laden down with cobble-stones—so goes the story—to throw at the whales, in order to discover when they were nigh enough to risk a harpoon from the bowsprit."

Nor was the quest for the right whale abandoned. But whereas Newfoundland used to be the most distant coast reached by the right whalers, now they pressed on to the Arctic Ocean. And numbers of whaleboats were taken aboard, compelling the building of larger vessels. The entire fishery was becoming more intense, inviting bigger gambles. In 1726, the year after Joseph Rotch's arrival, no less than eighty-six whales were claimed by Nantucketers, both right and sperm.

Joseph set about managing a fleet of whalers in the name of his and his wife's families. He recognized that, even with all the maritime advances that had been made toward more productive whaling, the most important improvement had been to move the tryworks from shore to shipboard. Now the vats of whale blubber of all kinds would be tried atop brick fireplaces situated on the forward deck and fueled by wood and whale scraps. No longer would the whaler have to break for home immediately after spearing its prey, hoping that winds would sweep him there swiftly enough so the blubber would not turn rancid before trying (a problem that plagued whalers particularly in southern seas). The new system liberated the vessel so that it almost became a little Nantucket itself, farther off to sea.

The world opened even wider to the adventurous Nantucketers with the fall of Montreal in 1760. Across the now peaceful seas Joseph Rotch continued to push his captains farther and farther, longer voyages producing more oil per vessel. And because of his active and successful leadership, Joseph was the one designated chief when the senior member of the Starbuck-Macy clan died. Perhaps his most revealing act, upon that ascendancy, was to stop sending his firm's oil to London by way of Boston; now he ordered the ships to sail directly across the Atlantic, up the Thames. This he did with total confidence in the firm's capacity to handle the business and in Nantucket's ability to deliver all the desired oil. He also took the step with the religious conviction that he should not defer to such an authoritarian merchant prince as Boston's John Hancock (with whom a lengthy and ultimately victorious struggle thereupon commenced).

Indeed, Joseph's shipment of sperm oil to London was the opening step of the campaign for Nantucket's preeminence in the international business of sperm oil supplying and shipping. As the campaign succeeded, the colonies' clocks and mills functioned smoothly because of Nantucket oil; the nighttime streets of London glowed merrily because of the sperm oil from Nantucket; and soon the coasts of the nations would be safer because of lighthouses that shone winter and summer thanks to the noncongealing, clear-burning oil from Nantucket. With the competition from other New England ports falling behind, the Nantucket Quakers— without ceasing their daring at sea or their diligence at the ledgers—could concentrate without interference on their Society and the inner light. Or so it seemed.

Little of the original simplicity of the Quaker community was lost as capital accumulated; the business of increasing that capital did not become the point of living, nor the ethos of the place. The style that had been established in the final decades of the seventeenth century endured, strengthened by codifications and enforced traditions. Our understanding of this life—this life with the homespun suits and square-toed shoes and the "thee" and "thou" language, this life that made them so different from New Englanders elsewhere—can almost begin and end with a look at one powerfully typical house. Built for Jethro and Mary Coffin back in 1686 (a wedding present for another of these young couples who seem to crowd into the Nantucket story), the house was still representing the architectural norm well into the next century.

At first glance, it's just a modest, shingled saltbox, the prescribed "lean-to" of the early Quakers. But while from the front it appears to be humble and low-lying, offering only two tiny windows and narrow door to the outside world, I urge you to step around to the side. You'll see the impressive mass of the house (*two* full stories plus loft), and you'll nod with an appreciative smile. Some lean-to! The windows that poke through the high side wall may only be mouse-sized, crossed with dividers that make diamond-shaped panes in the Jacobean manner, but there are quite a few of these little peep-holes. They bring hints of the secular, daylit world into the interior gloom. And look up: the bricks of the massive, central chimney are laid in a handsome pattern that might almost be considered decorative.

This secretive house—the oldest still standing in Nantucket, and thus more isolated and farther to the west than the houses in the center of town—did continue to represent the norm as the decades advanced and wealth began to

Oldest house: Seventeenth-century Nantucket austerity dictated that this commodious, shingled dwelling retain the style of a one-story "lean-to." Mystic Seaport Museum.

accumulate as a result of the international trade. To de Crèvecoeur's eye they were totally plain, "entirely devoid of exterior or interior ornament." Only gradually did silver-gray shingles give way to white clapboards. As late as 1800, no fancy hangings or curtains were to be seen at the windows; one's mattress rested on a "sail," that is a piece of handwoven canvas stretched between rollers with ratchets. The houses in town crowded close together, pushed up to the very sidewalk so that in back secluded gardens might be cultivated. The Quaker families, many of them related, cultivated privacy as well as flowers; theirs was a very compact community "in the English style," as a visitor remarked. Daniel Webster called it a "city in the sea."

Because the main floor of the typical in-town house is raised up above a full basement (foundation stones brought from the mainland and emplaced in the sand), steps are needed to get up to the front door. But how to build the steps without blocking the narrow sidewalk? The problem was solved by devising a marvelous sideways staircase that snuggled against the house and invited the sidewalk-stroller to gain entrance by simply walking straight ahead. Whether coming from up-street or down, he could climb up the steps to the landing and execute a right-angle turn, where the knocker was readily at hand. There you were, tipping your hat, as the door opened.

Another solution was to put the front door at the side of the house, permitting entrance through an alley. That's the way it was at our lodgings in exotic India Street. The only difficulty was that while walking back there into the realm of private gardens and fenced courtyards and gated passageways, I was tempted to keep gawking into these removed, residential worlds, rather than continue with my business, on into the house. I felt a tug at the elbow, taking care of that.

A peculiar extravagance allowed here, even among the most modest houses, was the highly visible "roof-top walk." This platform of storklike legs and waist-high railings is reached from within by means of a "scuttle," or hatch in the roof's slope, and a ladder up from the attic. The out-in-the-open structure conveys a lot of implicit information to the street-level gazer about the people who lived here and climbed to those lofty aeries. From the dimness of their interior rooms and contemplation of the "inner light," they would mount the three flights of stairs and the ladder to the roof walk, there to squint seaward into the sun, straining to see the home-coming, tall-masted, white-canvased profit. The vertical house and steps stimulated the thought flow, up and down, like adding columns of figures.

One late afternoon my wife and I wandered through the narrow streets of the town; the fragrance of flowers, the mellow redolence of warm sun on old wood,

ABOVE. *Nantucket cityscape: An 1880 view from South Tower shows moors and a windmill beyond the tightly packed city;* RIGHT, *on Vestal Street, cows pass Maria Mitchell's house. Both, Nantucket Historical Association.*

the tidy peacefulness were so entire that we felt welcomed to this small-scaled and intimate society. We had read that throughout this network of streets there are some 400 houses more than a hundred fifty years old, mostly on their original foundations—the largest concentration of such treasures anywhere in the country. Having walked along Pleasant Street, we soon found ourselves on Mill Street, where stands a house Job Macy built for himself and bride (another bride!) in 1750. It boldly rises up from the street, two full stories with full-sized windows. Job's father was appalled at this arrogant breakaway from the established norms; he refused to enter the place and, reportedly, never did. But Mr. Macy's protest was too late; as the eighteenth century climaxed, most of the houses climbed to these proud heights. Nonetheless, a simplicity of detailing remained, the beauty of a tall, lithe girl in a plain dress. The ostentation of the very rich would be left to others.

Coming around the corner here, at this hour before the day had ended, we might have seen such a modest girl, possibly wearing a Quaker bonnet. If a "boat-steerer" or mate from a whaler had approached then along the sidewalk from the opposite direction, she would have cast an immediate glance at his lapel, to see if he wore the chock pin that indicated he had killed a whale. If so, the conversation might begin. Certain Nantucket girls set up a society, vowing that none of the members would wed a man who had not yet dispatched a whale. Merchants often gave their daughter a whale for a wedding present. If she chose to marry outside the Society of Friends, however, the daughter would be disowned.

But what a blow it would be to lose such a woman, de Crèvecoeur remembered.

> The richest person in the island owes all his present prosperity and success to the ingenuity of his wife: this is a known fact which is well recorded; for while he was performing his first cruises, she traded with pins and needles, and kept school. Afterward, she purchased more considerable articles, which she sold with so much judgment that she laid the foundation of a system of business, that she has even since prosecuted with equal dexterity and success. She wrote to London, formed connections, and, in short, became the only ostensible instrument of that house, both at home and abroad.

The whole community was embarked on the prudent enterprise together. Melville called them sea hermits. Because Nantucket's own captains were encouraged by Joseph Rotch and the other merchants to buy shares in their vessels, and because the "lay" system was at this early point quite generous, every voyage was a true investment for each man who sailed on it. A wealthy and congenial hermitage it was. The only thing de Crèvecoeur didn't quite understand about it was why the women tended to take a sniff of specially imported opium every morning. And the sheriff, too. He remarked that he needed three grains immediately after breakfast, "without the effects of which . . . he was not able to transact any business."

Maybe that was a bit decadent, but the lapel pin of the boat-steerer spoke honestly: the man was the right stuff. Admiration of him was quite proper on the girl's part. For he was a trained athlete, a combatant of nerve and poise whose moves embodied years of tradition. He served as a *specialist* on board one of the whaling sloops or schooners that sailed out of Nantucket harbor before the Revolution on months-long voyages to the newly opened sperm whaling grounds near the Azores or down to the Brazil banks. As a specialist, he was entitled to a berth in one of the miniscule cabins in the after part of the ship and to slightly better fare than the hands in the fo'c's'le had to eat. But he did the bidding of captain and mates (for mates there were on whalers, as opposed to the cod and mackerel fishing vessels), and their bidding was that he risk his life for the kill.

The whalers of this era tended to be 50-ton brigs; each would carry three smallish whaleboats and a total complement of nineteen: the captain, three mates, and fifteen men (at least five of them Indians). The boat-steerer began each dash after a whale as one of the five rowers, his position being on the forwardmost thwart. He and the others were allowed to look only aft—not at the dangerous beast they pursued but at the mate, or "headsman," who stood elevated on a small platform in the stern. It was the mate who first steered the whaleboat, with long oar and muscle and exhortations, urging the men to break their backs, drive their oars deeper that they might pull up to the targeted whale before any other boat. It was the mate, only the mate at this point, who focused on the whale, driving them right up alongside the great bulking monster; the first indication the men had of being near was a heady, seaweed-like smell, and the raging of the waters. Then the mate commanded the boat-steerer to rise from his thwart, to pick up the heavy harpoon, and to heave it into the whale's hide. As all hell broke loose, the two men, boat-steerer and mate, changed places.

This incredible bit of athleticism occurred even as the wounded whale plunged to the depths or took off for the horizon. Wherever he went, the whaleboat went with him, tethered by the line attached to the harpoon. The length of the line whirred out of its containing tubs in the bottom of the boat as the whale charged ahead; the mate had flipped a few loops of it around a post in the stern immediately when he saw that the harpoon had hit home. The post ("loggerhead") smoked with friction-heat as the tow line turned around it (only because water was splashed on it from a crewman's hat did the loggerhead not burst into flame). Then, during this wild, "Nantucket sleigh ride," the boat-steerer coolly walked aft to seize the oar.

Only when the whale had surfaced and begun to show signs of tiring, did the mate—who had been kneeling in the bow amid the spray and the tumult of the mad passage through the sea—only then did he order the men to start pulling in the line. The boat-steerer maneuvered the whaleboat up alongside the thrashing, heaving gray mass of flukes and jaw and flippers. Then the mate stood, braced by a special cleat-notch on the port side, ready to deliver the final death blows to the beast's heart or lungs.

I've never read a better description of the excitement, the terror of the time before the big kill than in *Moby Dick*. Ishmael speaks with special passion of the unreeling line after the first strike:

> For, when the line is darting out, to be seated then in the boat, is like being seated in the midst of the manifold whizzings of a steam-engine in full play, when every flying beam, and shaft, and wheel, is grazing you. It is worse; for you cannot sit motionless in the heart of these perils, because the boat is rocking like a cradle, and you are pitching one way and the other, without the slightest warning, and only by certain self-adjusting buoyancy and simultaneousness of volition and action, can you escape being made a Mazeppa of, and run away with where the all-seeing sun himself could never pierce you out.

Then the kill itself:

> [The mate], firmly planting his knee in the clumsy cleat, darted dart after dart into the flying fish; at the word of command, the boat alternately sterning out of the way of the whale's horrible wallow, and then ranging up for another fling. The red tide now poured from all sides of the monster like brooks down a hill. His tormented body rolled not in brine but in blood, which bubbled and seethed for furlongs behind in their wake. The slanting sun playing upon this crimson pond in the sea, sent back its reflection into every face, so that they all glowed to each other like red men.

Some of the crew were indeed redmen, carrying on that tradition from the days of shore-whaling. Melville makes the point that many of the others came also from islands—the Azores and later the South Seas—men for whom life riding across the middle of the ocean was perfectly natural. In this fishery, the peak of attainment for these dusky-skinned foreigners was to be a harpooner/boat-steerer; they could never, however, expect to marry the girl on Pleasant Street. Nor on shore could they rise above a certain station or move into the better streets. Elites don't work that way. Joseph Rotch and the Friends were noted for their tolerance of all kinds, but the mates and the captains and the owners were only to be of one kind.

OPPOSITE, ABOVE, AND OVERLEAF. *"Whale ho!": After a spotter raises the signal, the whaleboat sets off, harpoon at the ready; after the whale is harpooned, the boat gets a "Nantucket sleighride." All, Nantucket Historical Association.*

By now Joseph and Love Rotch had three capable sons . . . and immense ambitions for them all. Yet, when one had a sublime view of the world, how could familial or economic plans be restricted to merely Nantucket? As Joseph's creative mind moved up and down the ladders of thought, he commenced a search for a place on the mainland that would allow him to secure his hold on the spermaceti industry and to position his sons advantageously—even though permission from the Meeting had to be obtained, should a Quaker choose to break away from Nantucket.

"Follow the money!" That was the advice given to me by bright, young Bruce Courson at the Nantucket Whaling Museum when I asked for his interpretation of the Rotch family's next move. That took place in 1765, when Joseph purchased ten acres of land at a new community on the northwest shore of Buzzard's Bay, an industrial development planned by a mainland Quaker named Joseph Russell within the town of Dartmouth. So, exactly forty years after leaving the mainland, Joseph was to return to it. Strangely disloyal, I thought. Perhaps these people were not sea hermits but hermit crabs. Like the ever-moving hermit crab, they would scurry from a whelk shell they'd outgrown to another, larger one. Was the pressure of tightened Quakerism becoming too restrictive? I recalled the advice of Harvard humanist Irving Babbitt that not in material causes but in the nature of specific religions lies the answer to all such cultural disruptions.

But Bruce Courson urged me not to get too philosophical about this retreat across the waters; I should simply follow the money. It was clear enough that Joseph Rotch, accompanied by his sons Joseph, Jr., and Francis, intended to establish a spermaceti factory at New Bedford (as the mainland community came to be called). And not long after that the third son, William, opened another factory at Nantucket, where he had remained. As a result of these careful steps, the Rotches could then produce candles aplenty and distribute them right into the heart of the market, to the consternation of rivals in Newport or Providence or anywhere else. The firm now had a three-cornered monopoly: the "citching" of the whales, the shipping of the raw material, and the manufacturing and distribution of the product. From all three corners, money flowed.

The very building in which I was then standing, the Nantucket Whaling Museum, was originally built as a spermaceti factory. Bruce could therefore give me an on-site demonstration of how one corner of the monopoly worked. Here, spanning the whole central portion of the building, is a gigantic press—I mean a press so big you'd think it could only be used by a giant. Worked in fact by weights and pulleys and chains, it handled the "head matter" from the sperm whale. That waxy stuff having been separated from the oil, the material was "pressed, fluxed, and chrystalized" in order to produce the world's best candles. Lustrous and almost transparent, the candles were wrapped in special blue paper; they looked custom-made for the finest of homes.

Simultaneously with the pressing, the oil itself was going through various phases of heating and refining. The purity of the resultant product was designated by color gradations, from brown (not-so-good) to white (excellent). And many were the complaints from London that insufficient care had been taken by the suppliers in that vital matter of gradation. But, knowing the sensitivity of the Quakers, an interested New England merchant warned the English purchasers:

> I must caution you against being too nice and critical with the Nantucket men, for I can assure you nothing can be done with them in that case. . . . The only way is to make the best terms you can with them, whenever you have occasion to purchase; but 'tis vain to attempt to tye them down to any measures they don't like.

They were tough, they were independent, and they knew their business exactly, from the technology of the oil lamps (which should have *two* wicks, one to warm the oil, the other to draw and burn it), to how many pence for each piece of blue paper, to the best whaling ships to match with which captains (and should the ships themselves be bought or chartered?).

Ships, however, may not be quite the right word. In the peak pre-Revolutionary whaling year of 1770, when all the Rotches' systems were in place, Nantucket set out 125 different vessels on whaling voyages. And, if maritime historian Alexander Laing is right in surmising their rigs by looking at comparable Boston sailings at the same time, these were not ships at all but simple sloops, schooners, and more sophisticated brigs or brigantines (meaning vessels with two masts carrying combinations of fore-and-aft sails and squaresails). Ships (meaning vessels with three square-rigged masts) were apparently used only for transporting the oil barrels overseas. Whatever the individual rigs, the tonnage of the whalers' hulls was increasing, the average burden now being ninety-three tons (as opposed to forty-five a generation earlier). And the size of the fleet was swelling to an extraordinary degree as Nantucket asserted her preeminence in all corners of the sea. By 1775, that critical year, the total had reached 150 vessels; how many of these were under the Rotches' control we cannot be sure.

BUT we do know the dire destiny of two of the Rotch vessels, one from Nantucket, the brig *Beaver*, and the other from New Bedford, the ship *Dartmouth*. In 1773, having carried cargoes of whale oil to London, they were chartered from the Rotches by the East India Company to transport tea from the company's bulging warehouses to Boston. On board as "supercargo" was twenty-three-year-old Francis Rotch. It was he who, after unsuccessful negotiations with the authorities on the vexatious subject of the tax to be paid on the tea, faced the jeering rabble under the leadership of Sam Adams. As he watched the self-made "Indians" crack open the casks and hurl the tea into Boston harbor, Francis must have wondered what his father would think of this. He himself sailed back to London as soon as possible, those being his sympathies.

Quakers are deeply pacifistic. To their religious way of thinking, war is but one of the un-Christian activities which states get themselves into for the very fact of being states. It was because of the Quakers' desire to do away with stately and churchly authority that they were so abused (hangings, whippings, banishment) back when the Commonwealth of Massachusetts was young. Now other authorities in Boston and elsewhere were raising hob, dressing themselves up as Committees of Public Safety, talking up the possibility of war, interfering with the sensible business of making money. Old Joseph Rotch must have looked at the impending revolution in a profoundly distrustful way; he wanted no part of it. The closing of the port of Boston in response to the Tea Party probably confirmed his gravest misgivings. Nantucket, on the other hand, was independent—and always had been.

The Crown recognized that fact; indeed, the King's ministers were gratified to learn that on this little island, as in certain other New England and New York communities, the spirit of common sense prevailed (that is, the desire to keep fishing and to go along with the Crown's new rules, whatever they were). When Lord North clamped the notorious New England Restraining Act down on the region in 1775, Nantucket was specifically exempted, as were the neutralist towns of Marshfield and Scituate.

But when the cannons of war roar forth, there is little respect for pacifists or neutralists; they are swept up in the storm along with everyone else. Immediately after Concord and Lexington, when the cause of patriotism ignited in the rebels' breasts and the need for war supplies sent the new warriors up and down the coast on sorties of requisition, a vessel flying their bold flag berthed one day at the Straight Wharf. A hundred patriot soldiers stormed ashore, marched up Main Street, and ransacked the town. Rumors had reached them that flour had been cached on the island for General Gage, British commandant in Boston. Finding no flour, the soldiers regrouped around the bar in Pease's Tavern; disgruntled, they finally seized a number of whaleboats and took them back to the mainland as confiscated property.

A few years later another armed party stormed the island from seven cannon-bristling warships. But this assault, in 1779, was led by a pack of Tory raiders. They posted guards throughout the town and sent squads of soldiers to break open the doors of warehouses along the waterfront. There they found hidden casks of whale oil and quantities or iron, tobacco, and coffee. The helpless islanders could do nothing but watch as the warships sailed away with more than $50,000 worth of goods. Already reduced to starvation and misery by the seemingly endless war, the Nantucketers must have viewed this assault as the final, unbearable blow, presaging doom. Many moved away to locations in Nova Scotia, in England and France, to colonies that seemed peaceful.

If found at sea, Nantucketers were accused of smuggling by the patriots and of treason by the Crown. William Rotch showed how he felt about the struggle when, returning home to Nantucket from England, he dumped a cargo of bayonets overboard rather than deliver them to patriot soldiers—he was "obedient to his principles," he said, "not to the state." Whalemen caught by British ships were usually given a choice of arms for the King or manacles on a prison ship. One of these sailors, Nathan Folger, is remembered for different sentiments: "Hang me if you will to the yard arm of your ship, but do not ask me to be a traitor to my country!" Altogether, more than 1,200 men were captured or killed; 134 vessels were seized.

JUST as it was a pair of Rotch vessels that saw the opening of the conflict in Boston, so it was a Rotch vessel that saw the recommencement of overseas whale oil shipping after the Revolution. In February of 1783, even before the signing of the peace treaty, the ship *Bedford* dropped anchor below London Bridge. In her hold were 350 butts of sperm oil. From the peak of her gaff flew the American flag. She led the way back.

Though the Nantucketers had been able to preserve some capital and still possessed limited barrels of oil for trading, they had but *two* viable whalers. All things considered, they were desperate for a more secure location, the Revolution having revealed just how exposed and violable their island was. Negotiations began with foreign governments, the objective being to gain recognition of Nantucket as a free port. Emigration continued; plans abounded for relocating the island's industry. Possibly it would go to England (where Joseph's Tory son Francis continued to live), or to France (Dunkirk being the considered port), or to sunny Portugal.

Islanders even contemplated forsaking whaling for one of the "fin fisheries." They had noted, historian Macy relates, that the Marbleheaders and Cape Codders had been able to get back on their feet and to bring in welcome profits by actively pursuing the cod fishery. But No, not that, most Nantucketers decided (though some took off for the cod-rich waters of Maine). They felt that fishing would "not be suited to the genius and inclinations of the people." There was neither the thrilling challenge nor the vast promise of wealth.

Meanwhile, more vessels were being scrounged; voyages to the ends of the world opened up new whaling territories. Even before Cornwallis's arms were stacked at Yorktown, the *Penelope* pushed further north than would any other vessel for a century. State authorities scratched their whiskered chins and admitted that on that strange island of Nantucket in the middle of the sea valuable talents existed; it would be a gigantic loss to the Commonwealth if those whalers went elsewhere. So the authorities in Boston, having at first balked at the idea of a subsidy, ultimately turned themselves around and voted to help support the whalers by means of bounty payments.

With that boost, Nantucket and the entire New England whaling industry began to recover. By 1788, the total number of whalers from the several Commonwealth ports totaled over a hundred; several of them were capacious factory ships, in the new manner. And by 1789 the first Nantucket harpoon to spear a whale in the Pacific did its crucial job. (It must be admitted that the owner of said harpoon, one Archilaus Hammond, was serving aboard the British ship *Amelia*—yes, the British got around Cape Horn into the warm, whale-frolicking waters of the Pacific before we did—but the *Amelia* had a Nantucket skipper and a Nantucket harpooner; they found and killed the whale.) Immediately thereafter, the Rotches' *Beaver* was around the Horn, the first American whaler to sail to the Pacific and return heavily burdened with the world's best oil. When Joseph Rotch died in 1784 in New Bedford (having suffered deep losses during the British raid on that city in 1778), he must have shipped off to Quaker heaven with the comfortable belief that the industry he'd fostered would survive for the ages. Before departing, he put the cloak of responsibility for the family's interest in the whale fishery upon the broad shoulders of his son William.

MOST tours of Nantucket begin, for understandable reasons, at the very prominent, very whale-blood-red Rotch Building, which is also called the Pacific Club. Nearby is the Pacific Bank—that ocean's name continues to have weight here. Standing on the cobblestones of the square, I concentrated on the bank's roofwalk. Why would a bank have one of those essentially domestic superstructures? Well, one of the bank's officers was interested not only in spotting the homeward-bound whalers but also in scanning the heavens. His precocious daughter, Maria Mitchell, discovered a comet on that platform in 1847. My wife and I had admired her family home on Vestal Street above Pleasant, a trim house that's of no pretension but carries a rather large roofwalk. The area between that residential street and where we now stood was the sector most heavily hit by the great fire that destroyed Nantucket's downtown and commonplace buildings just the year before Maria's discovery. The brick bank survived.

At the time of Maria's birth in 1818, Nantucket was about to enter its second "golden age," the first having blessed the island between the recovery from the Revolution and the almost equally disastrous War of 1812. So as I gazed up at Maria's bank-top observation post, I wondered what the two golden ages added up to. Much elegance, of course—including the extraordinarily fine houses on upper Main Street. Much wealth banked and invested, much more wealth than in the other fishing communities I'd visited. (For whaling, whatever its greasy nature and base conditions on board might be, did generate greater gross revenues for New England than did the other fisheries.) But what else, of substance, came forth from all this? In Nantucket one was certainly not aware of the strong democratic tradition, the voice of the fishwives, that gave life and strength to the other communities. So what was there that proved the quality of this elite?

The down-to-earth historian Samuel Eliot Morison (who considered the Rotches misguided for concentrating so exclusively on sperm oil) rudely pointed out that, as compared with those equally elitist cities Boston and Philadelphia, Nantucket never made much of a contribution intellectually or socially. Falling in step behind Morison, other historians concur that here, in this city in the sea, a dismissable and unto-itself kind of elite had flowered, suffering from its own aloofness and its restrictions of others.

In an effort to rebut the critics, I ran back over pertinent facts. Item: Nantucket offered good and ample employment to workers for scores of years; in the 1840s the whale fishery engaged some 25,000 sailors, and (in the words of an exhibit at the Whaling Museum) it gave "rich employment to three times that number of citizens" on shore. Counter-item: increasingly, native-born Americans declined to serve in the fo'c's'le and desertions increased; to take their places, more islanders were picked up in the distant seas. Item: Quakerism continued to provide a spiritual base for the society. Counter-item: whereas in 1795 there had been 1,700 practioners of this serene religion, by 1845 there were only 300, mostly older folks. I pondered the grim possibility that the sailors' disinclination to serve before the mast on Nantucket whalers was related to the crass and careless mates and skippers who had fallen from the faith.

At first the "lay system" in Nantucket had been a true reflection of the community spirit; *all Nantucketers were in the enterprise together*, as noted before. At that time, three-fifths of the oilcask-laden whaler's take went to the owner—only a bit more than the one-half taken by the owners in the other fisheries. (But consider the greater risks of whaling!) Then, by whaling's profit-sharing lay system, the master got $\frac{1}{18}$, with $\frac{1}{48}$ to "endsmen" or mates, and $\frac{1}{75}$ to each able-bodied seaman; the cabin boy got $\frac{1}{120}$. Not bad. That was in the early eighteenth century, when whaling vessels carried crews of eighteen.

Whaleman's art: Though delightfully sketched in pen, this nineteenth-century sailor's view shows the dangers and smokiness of Nantucket's at-sea community. Mystic Seaport Museum.

But by the "golden age," the larger ships sailed with some thirty-six men—twice as many as before (enough to crew four or five whaleboats plus the cooper and other specialists). You'd think, therefore, that the mate would then get something like 1/90 and the seamen would sign on for 1/150. Yet this was the era when Melville's Ishmael was looking for a berth out of Nantucket . . . and what a mockery the lay system had then become! Worthy Ishmael, having been threatened with a 777th lay by the harsher of the Pequod's two Quaker owners, was finally given a 300th by the more generous partner.

A prosperous voyage of some three or four years during these halcyon years might bring in something like $200 to a foremast hand. But, when charges for clothes and tobacco were subtracted, the fellow was often more deeply in debt after the voyage than before. Meanwhile, a quarter of a million barrels of magnificent sperm oil was being brought in annually, selling for never less than a dollar a barrel! On considering this munificent flow and the human consequences, I had to remember the cautionary advice of a prominent analyst of the Quaker ethos. He advised that, though the Friends believed in the equality of all men and women before God, that said nothing about their belief in the equality of all economic conditions.

De Crèvecoeur had pointed out that there was an understandable distinction to be made between the rich, not so rich, and poor in the whaling society of Nantucket: "This difference will always be more remarkable among people who live by the sea . . . [because with them as opposed to farmers,] there is greater hazard, more adventure; hence profit and misfortunes are more . . . a greater disparity."

What's fair? Nantucket was a capitalism-driven, capitalist-run society. Its leaders sought to make money to sustain the institutions and the families of that society; their attitude toward work was essentially that of service. Unlike Provincetown, where the vessels (symbolizing the ways to power) would be owned by even such people as Portuguese immigrants, Nantucket kept the ownership in the hands of the mighty, the daring few. And who's to say they didn't serve the cause of civilization well? A solid counter-argument might have been expressed on Front Street; but that voice can no longer be heard here or elsewhere. Macy reports, to be sure, that all people were "comparatively wealthy" and that the town was a social paradise. But not along the now-vanished waterfront, I'll wager. And not out at the "picturesque but profitless" fishermen's community at Siasconset, where a few shacks remained until recently. Certainly not among the imported Negroes, the island Native Americans, and the increasing numbers of extra hands enlisted from the mainland to serve the parochial elite of this town.

Ishmael found not far from the Nantucket wharves a Negro church, a rude lodging place (two a-bed), a dive for a drink or two. One source reports three score grog shops on the waterfront. (It's worth noting that the Quaker proprietors of Nantucket, for all their propriety, didn't care to regulate this slimy business; they would not ever take on the despised role of public authority.) In these wharf-side shadows dwelt and caroused a now-forgotten people, vital to that time's operations.

These were the men who bent their backs at the whaleboat's oars, who slipped and chopped and chopped and slipped as the greasy blubber was prepared for the trypots, who cranked the windless and sweated up the halyards. To coordinate their heavings, these real but apparently forgettable workers sang chanteys like this old faithful:

> *Solo*   Whiskey is the life of man!
> *Chorus*   Whiskey, Johnny!
> *Solo*   Oh, I'll drink whiskey while I can!

Gypped, discriminated against, and subjected to miserable conditions on land and at sea, they cared not a fig for Nantucket's "great simplicity" or for the elite's restrained and tasteful habits.

The city in the sea faded away before the worst of this class exploitation took place; that was left for New Bedford, where exploitation ultimately transcended the parochial and became cosmopolitan. Yet for me, that made the matter all the more painful, for the grandparents whom I mentioned earlier among the whales' teeth had all lived in New Bedford; they had all been Quaker descended. I needed to go there to find out how those pious and severe people, of such lofty, roofwalk principles (favoring Equality of the sexes and of the races, as well as Abolition and Peace) could inflict such conditions on other people.

But perhaps while in Nantucket I could come to understand more about the predilections of these tight-fisted Friends by focusing more closely on their fairest flower, astronomer Maria Mitchell. Perhaps the quality of her life, while not vitiating the meanness of the Quaker elite, would illumine the attitudes which, at this historical remove, I found so puzzling and contradictory. As I turned to reconsider her, I took special note of the sympathetic opinions of that Philadelphia Quaker-spokesman Digby Baltzell. Referring to the perennial social apartness of the Quakers, he wrote: "Members of the upper classes in egalitarian societies that lack a clear hierarchy of values recognized by all classes tend to avoid positions of authority and to protect themselves from the masses behind a high wall of wealth." In other words, public responsibility for what happened across the social range was not the Quaker's concern. Individual contemplations, the family, and business managements, these were what mattered. The rest of the world was to be regarded not at all, neither from the secluded garden nor from the heaven-gazing platform.

Maria Mitchell and her brother (later a famous hydrographer) benefited from the tradition of Quaker education—boys and girls together. So did their cousins—the Coleman brothers who became designers and builders of the town's glorious 1840s mansions. (Here I should probably confess my dislike of mansions—they are generally monolithic and monomaniacal, not of or for the people—but you can certainly read about them, if you desire, in the salivating guide books.) Education wasn't for everyone. Initially Maria had gone to the so-called dame-schools, where well-educated Quakeresses ran the daughters and sons of privileged families through recognized courses of instruction.

But at about this time an educational reformer named Samuel Jenks arrived on the island from Boston. He was outspokenly horrified to find that, as opposed to many of the towns in the Commonwealth, where open schools had been in effect since the earliest times, Nantucket kept to its own practice of Quakers educating only their own. He wrote:

Elegance on Main Street: When photographed in 1905, the showy Starbuck mansions (left) represented a dynamic culture stilled by time. Nantucket Historical Association.

I was astonished and grieved to find that Nantucket with a population of some 10,000 [had no public schools] . . . I sought to arouse the people but met with repeated rebuffs. [The Friends] declared they had schools of their own, and would not mingle their children with those of the world's people.

Jenks was ridiculed on the island as having advanced "a Boston notion." It was quite painful; the Quaker elite was being challenged. Eventually, after his proposition was thrice voted down, and after he had sued the town in the public courts, Jenks gathered enough attention and won the day. By then the town meeting had recognized that there were some three hundred children below the age of fourteen who were simply not being educated. As Quakers grumbled about the perogatives of authority, taxes were levied and public schools were established.

In 1831 there was a solar eclipse which was so astonishing for twelve-year-old Maria that she resolved to be an astronomer henceforth. "I was born of ordinary capacity, but of extraordinary persistency," she said. Later, on the basis of her demonstrated talents, she became librarian of the sacrosanct Nantucket Atheneum. There she tackled Bowditch's *Practical Navigator* and learned Latin, French, and German. But still she kept watching the sky. And finally, like the harpooner his whale, she pegged her great, white comet. Then she went on to become newly formed Vassar College's "most brilliant" teacher. But as a perpetual radical, she scorned the conventional grading system, saying, "You cannot mark a human mind, because there is no intellectual unit." She refused to report student absences.

Sadly, as happened all across her island, she lost her Quaker faith. Or she moved on to another spiritual habitation. First she downright refused to attend Vassar's compulsory chapel service. Then she agreed, taking a place at the rear of the ornate church where she felt free to "think of something pleasant."

Now, I find this pretty refined, as refined and wonderful as the best sperm oil, bright and luminous. And I credit an elite that could produce such a star, even at a social cost. Indeed, for this talent to blaze forth in America at this time—for an insular banker's daughter to become an internationally recognized scientist—called for a special kind of upbringing. First, of course, there had to be that wall of wealth that kept worldly concerns away and allowed for dedication to the selected discipline. Then there must be a society that encouraged education for young women.

Shining talents and university knowledge would be entirely useless here, nay, would be dangerous; it would pervert their plain judgment, it would lead them out of that useful path which is so well adapted to their situation; it would make them more adventurous, more presumptuous, much less cautious, and therefore less successful.

The words are de Crèvecoeur's, written long before.

For all its wealth and privileged upbringings, Nantucket was not producing a Justice Oliver Wendell Holmes or a Harriet Beecher Stowe. Islanders would regard acts like theirs as too showy, too mindful of federal or state authority. The lights that glowed on Nantucket did so privately. Maria Mitchell's prominence was a bit of an embarrassment.

The islanders saw the end coming. Well before the conflagration of 1846, whaling firms in Nantucket knew they faced a combination of negatives, the first of which was geological. The sand bar at the mouth of the Great Harbor was a wild and wandering thing, growing and extending each year. Its presence was felt most intensely at the time when the whaling ships became heavier and deeper. Whereas the whalers of 1800 were of 80 or 90 tons burden, those built in the middle of the century surpassed 300 tons. Even at high tide, for such a ship to cross the bar was a serious risk. Under the leadership of the Nantucket *Inquirer*, a Dutch invention called the camel was mustered into service. This device consisted of two specially shaped half-hulls held together at the bottom by chains. Its first move would be to establish itself beneath and around the whaler at a time when the camel's hulls were deep-laden with water. Then, as the water was pumped out, the next move would be for the whole rig to rise higher and higher, including the whaler. Third move: the tow across the bar.

Despite local misgivings, the system was inaugurated. In 1842 the camel tackled its first incoming customer, the whaler *Peru* of 257 tons. Amazingly, the device worked; 1,340 barrels of sperm oil were unloaded directly at the wharf. But then came the fire. The camel perished along with the rest of the waterfront.

Meanwhile, the Rotches were operating successfully out of New Bedford. Although some twenty-nine whalers sailed out of Nantucket in 1845 (the greatest number ever), and that total fleet numbered eighty-odd vessels, New Bedford then counted more than two hundred ships and schooners as its own. Yes, the tide had turned; fo'c's'le hands found it better to ship out of New Bedford than Nantucket; that island community was closing down. In 1869 the last Nantucket whaler set sail, and didn't return to the island.

Then the summer crowds came. Still standing there by the red Rotch building, I was thinking of how Nantucket must have looked before any of these honeymooners arrived—almost abandoned, shuttered, rotting wharves, but up there in higher streets of the town remained all that treasured purity and grace. It must have been, in its bypassedness, something like a larger Noank. There, too, had been a zest for the sea and its creatures, and people of a stern religious ethic responding to enlightened leadership. That's the New England fishing community at its best, large or small.

Here at Nantucket, even when whaling died and quiet remained, there was a certain superiority. A stepping-up of concept, of daring. Or was I dreaming and letting my love of this place destroy all the facts and figures and industrial pragmatics? No. If not an ethical heritage, then an important and enduring sense of style did survive here.

Finally I remembered that I had seen this island when it was quiet and upon hard times, almost abandoned but still with head up, long ago. Not after the Revolution or the War of 1812, but just after World War II. During that war my father's ketch remained operative because he had used her on various operations for the Coast Guard Auxiliary. So, peace declared and a little gasoline scrounged, we went on our first cruise of the season, sailing through a major storm across to Nantucket. We were the first boat anything like a yacht to have arrived there in years. The waterfront was silent; only at the yacht club, rather to our surprise, did we see a flag at the head of a staff. So we anchored off the club pier, wondering how we might get ashore, or if it would be worth it.

Almost immediately after we'd dropped the anchor, a not-yet-repainted launch pulled out from the pier, boiling across the water in our direction. The fellow at the wheel did not wear a steward's uniform—though he had found a white cap somewhere. Even in the beat up launch and raggedy clothes, he looked pretty good to us.

"Ahoy, *Ruslu!*" he called through cupped hands after idling to a stop nearby. "We aren't open yet. But welcome to Nantucket, anyway. And if you'd like launch service, fly 'Tare' from the starboard spreader." With that, he was off on the foaming waves again.

And I went below to look up which signal flag was "Tare." It's vertical stripes of red and white and blue. What class!

NEW BEDFORD: THE DEAREST PLACE TO LIVE IN ALL NEW ENGLAND

"I AM among the Quakers, thought I, and I am safe." So wrote the escaped slave Frederick Douglass when he arrived in New Bedford in 1838. This captured my attention, for perhaps by following Frederick I could see what it was like for people high and low in this city of my grandparents as it enjoyed its years of greatest flowering. Frederick had arrived north of the Mason-Dixon line with no proper last name, but was soon dubbed "Douglass" (hero of Sir Walter Scott's *Lady of the Lake*) by his black, literarily inclined New Bedford host. He had also arrived in the North with neither his betrothed, Anna, a free woman from Baltimore, nor sufficient funds.

An imposing young man of twenty-one years, his eyes deep-set and flashing, his large and well-proportioned head set on a muscular body, his skin a distinctive "rosy brown," Frederick had been nearly caught, twice, during his escape from Maryland, in the guise of a navy tar. New York, which he reached from Philadelphia, swarmed with agents looking for fugitives to take back into slavery, for a bounty. Frederick was then lucky enough to meet on the darkling street a trustworthy black who not only arranged for Anna to arrive and for the young couple's marriage but also to get them safely off on the boat to Newport. It was this friend out of the dark who explained that New Bedford should be Frederick's objective. There the whalefishery waterfront was booming, with jobs aplenty for men who knew how to wield a caulker's hammer—a skill Frederick had acquired, to his former owner's great profit, in Baltimore.

At last the steamer chuffed into Newport. Yet, the couple must have asked themselves, how to proceed from here? As Frederick later told the tale, when he and Anna stepped off the boat:

the old-fashioned stagecoach with "New Bedford" in large, yellow letters on its side, came down to the wharf. I had not money to pay our fare and stood hesitating to

OPPOSITE. *New Bedford harbor: Small craft cluster about the whale ship* William Hamilton, *moored in the ebbing Acushnet River; scene from a Russell-Purrington panorama (1848). The Whaling Museum, New Bedford.*

know what to do. Fortunately for us, there were two Quaker gentlemen who were just about to take passage on the stage—Friends William C. Taber and Joseph Ricketson—who at once discerned our true situation, and in a peculiarly quiet way, addressing me, Mr. Taber said, "Thee get in." I never obeyed an order with more alacrity, and we were soon on our way to our new home.

That Taber, they tell me, was my father's mother's grandfather.

Frederick went on to write: "I could have landed in no part of the United States where I should have found a more striking and gratifying contrast, not only to life generally in the South, but in the condition of the colored people there, than in New Bedford." Here hundreds of runaway slaves had found a haven (the first of them arriving as early as 1819). More black people lived in New Bedford—6.8 percent of the city's population—than in any other New England city. As pointed out in a thoroughly unromanticized study, *Industrialization and Social Change*, by T. A. McMullin, there was then a notable "lack of an extensive proletariat" in New Bedford; even the blacks fitted into the middle of a striving middle class. Frederick was amazed: "The black man's children attended the same public schools with the white man's children—and apparently without objection in any quarter."

As well as the white Quakers' built-in tolerance of other races, there was something else going for blacks here—namely their recognized abilities and historic success. A heroic figure on the landscape from Revolutionary times was Captain Paul Cuffe, born to a slave father and Wampanoag mother on the nearby island of Cuttyhunk. Freed and moved to the Dartmouth village of Westport, he too married an Indian and led his neighbors and kinfolk to success in the cod and whalefisheries on board successively larger vessels. From the deck of his forty-two-ton schooner *Mary* (crewed by ten black whalemen), he himself harpooned two whales in 1793. Ever a Quaker, he paid for half of Westport's Meeting House from his own pocket; at that site he was buried in 1817.

Nor was the inventiveness of a black blacksmith named Lewis Temple regarded as racially out of place in its own day. Within the same era as Frederick Douglass's stay in New Bedford, Temple fashioned a harpoon head that, once inserted in the whale, turned at right angles to the shaft so it could not be dislodged. These were indeed creative and contributing people.

Frederick had reason to expect that matters would go handsomely for him here. Indeed,

I found that the laboring classes lived in better houses, that their houses were more elegantly furnished and were more abundantly supplied with conveniences and comforts than the houses of many who owned slaves on the Eastern Shore of Maryland. This was true not only of the white people of this city, but it was so of [my host], Mr. Johnson.

In New Bedford the Quaker leaders seemed to be achieving what they had not been able to build on Nantucket Island: an American community free from racial and interclass struggles and repressions (which is not to say that some would be richer than others), a fishing-whaling community strong enough to hold its own among other industrialized cities in the struggle for labor and capital.

From its very beginnings in the 1760s—when Joseph Russell had sold those ten acres of his neatly laid out waterfront to Joseph Rotch—New Bedford had looked to a one-industry, one-way future. Whaling and Quakerism. One family too, an interrelated family to which I belonged, whether volitionally or not: Joseph Russell was my mother's grandfather's grandfather's uncle. And the commanding authority of those original forebears was always in the back of your head, like the shadow of a seahawk. Edmund Taber understated it when he wrote this of the dauntless whaling captains: "I well remember the impression made by their venerable and commanding figures on my youthful mind."

The diarist Samuel Rodman, Jr., was one New Bedfordite who suffered well his surfeit of surrounding relatives. He had sufficient insouciance to risk their disapproval: at his whale oil-lit home in 1823 he threw a *dance*, the first such frivolity in Quaker New Bedford. He also had the wit to understand his cousins and uncles and aunts inwardly, could see through their long, plain coats to the heart of their strivings. Heir to the town's first spermaceti factory, Rodman explained his father's modus operandi in these words:

> Like my grandfather Rotch [William, Sr.], with whom he was long a co-partner, his maxim was never to extend business on credit. They might lose their own property and be poor themselves, but they would not take the risk, which they considered immoral as well as unwise, of making others poor.

In other words, the system was designed to prevent a good worker (such as Frederick hoped to become) from being crushed, should anything happen to the mighty "oil kings." Could that be true, I wondered? Or was this whole picture of a benign, worker-inclusive society merely an agreeable cover story on top of harsher realities? Might not Frederick's comments be but those of a blindly grateful, nonobjective exslave? I had my own memories of the bleak and blackened waterfront, and I had read of the whaling business's darker side in Morison and Goode too deeply to conclude that all here was sweetness and light. What about the fishermen, the seamen before the mast?

Turning to what might be an objective source, a clipping from the *National Magazine* of 1845, I read:

One of the first and most interesting sights which meets the eye of the visitor [to New Bedford], is the great number of neat, modest, and convenient dwellings which are spreading themselves over the beautiful hill upon which the town is situate [sic]. . . . We may be mistaken, but from the observations and inquiries which we have been able to make, we have arrived at the conclusion that there is not a town in New England where so large a proportion of the property is held by what one generally terms the working man, the mechanics and laborers of the place.

No slums? No lousy roominghouses? Remarkable. Another source explained that the reason for this social phenomenon was that New Bedford at that moment (c. 1850) stood forth as the richest city per capita in the world. In a single year during that heady era, the value of whale oil and bone brought into its piers would run up toward $10 million. Municipal expenditures for public buildings and public education were among the highest in the country. Melville called it "the dearest place to live in New England." Apparently, thanks to the beneficent whale and to prudent management, there was enough wealth here for everyone to have a share (and for the have-nots to stay out of sight). Capitalism and democracy and religion and civic pride and natural resources and the goodnesses of God and man were all pulling together.

FORSAKING for a while Frederick Douglass and the unlocatable, impoverished people of the waterfront, I followed my friend of many years, Nancy Crosby, up to County Street to see the preserved glories of what's now called the Rotch-Jones-Duff House and Garden Museum. Anticipating the visit to this huge, gorgeously simple frame house, I had read the prescribed accounts of the years when New Bedford magnates went in for constructing palaces on the Hill. One related that "stately mansions of granite in the neo-classical style, and elaborate Gothic cottages, arose on the high ground overlooking the harbor, amid ample lawns and luxuriant gardens. New Bedford society combined the grace of Newburyport and the power of Federalist Salem." Another (a report in *Ballou's* magazine) marveled at how "the people of New Bedford are [so] remarkable for their tree-loving propensities."

But Nancy explained to me that the elephantine house we were now approaching was built long before those post-Civil War extravagances. It was built in 1833, when the Quaker ethos still demanded restraint of design, if not modesty of size. And it was built by William Rotch, Jr., grandson of Joseph, at a time in his life when he felt free to move upward from the waterfront area. His first house, sited around the corner from Front Street on Water Street, was subsequently moved to Johnny Cake Hill to serve as the mariners' home.

Nancy is a board member of the Rotch House preservation effort, helping arrange sensible yet entertaining and informative activities that relate New Bedford's once private history to the open world of today. First she showed me the basement, in which exists the old kitchen and various work and wash rooms, places for maids to do invisible things. Above that extends the main floor, mostly consisting of four huge, tree-high rooms, opening off a central hall wide enough to drive a carriage through. Not quite knowing what to say about this barnlike vastness, I remarked that the hall chandelier was certainly appropriate; but Nancy confessed that it had been borrowed from a neighboring mansion that had fallen upon hard times. Upstairs, I was not surprised to find that the last family to occupy the house had refused to take the Quaker simplicity seriously: their

Quaker design: Built in 1833, the plain, massive, cupola-topped Rotch house had gained grandeur and a gardener when photographed in 1870. Rotch-Jones-Duff House; photo Thomas E. M. White.

bathrooms were equipped with those lubricious, multilevel shower jets that can be ordered from Midwestern catalogues.

But what captivated me most was the view from the cupola, which we reached by means of a narrow staircase from the third floor. Here I could see, as did William Rotch, Jr., the entire sweep of the harbor, wharves, fishing vessels, hurricane barrier, and all. Far above everything here, I too commanded the view, even as far southwest as Round Hill, the very corner of the bay, around which would have appeared (finally!) those long-watched-for whalers. I stood on tiptoe to see them, excited with the imagining. And I felt I also had a good view into how it must have been to have possessed all this. No wonder that Samuel Rodman had written his diary in a cupola! Here everything was under a powerful man's gaze: the houses, the family gardens, the churches, the ships and sea and sky. Heaven and earth were right there, capable of being monitored. From here, most of all, the oft-told story of New Bedford's perfect society seemed perfectly credible. I climbed down the narrow stairs more than a little shaken by the authoritative vision of "simple grandeur."

Thanking Nancy for the tour, I went back down the hill to the Whaling Museum in order to see if New Bedford's cover story held up there, too. Perhaps the museum's famous paintings of the old city by William A. Wall might reveal something about the whereabouts of those exploited sailors mentioned by Morison. Of course when I saw the paintings, they revealed nothing along those lines at all, they glorified the delusion of perfection, but they had some surprises for me anyway.

The first of Wall's landscapes is called "Birth of the Whaling Industry" (how Soviet-sounding!) and was executed in 1853. It's a sentimental look-back to that time of Arcadian idyllism (1763) when simple blacks, Indians, coopers, blacksmiths, mechanics, and oil-handlers all worked happily together to get this new enterprise off the ground. Oh yes, way in the background, on board the beached whaling sloop one may see a few diminutive figures who might be seamen. But it is the Quaker gentleman Joseph Russell in the left foreground who catches your attention, conversing soberly with an attentive black coachman; or you might notice the beguiling grin on the face of the whale oil-measurer (who looks as if he's come right out of American Genre Painting 101). The seamen in pious William A. Wall's view hovered on the margins of the city's industrial life.

Nor do they appear at all in Wall's better-known, second painting, "New Bedford Fifty Years Ago." Now the date of the imagined scene is 1807; it's the festive New Bedford occasion "Engine Day," and therefore the flag is flown high from the staff of the big commercial building in the foreground, at the corner of Union and Water streets. Everyone's here: men crowd around the fire engine

*Imaginings of the past:
LEFT, "The Birth of the
Whaling Industry" and
BELOW, "New Bedford Fifty
Years Ago," both by native
artist William A. Wall (1853
and 1858). New Bedford
Free Public Library; The
Whaling Museum, New
Bedford.*

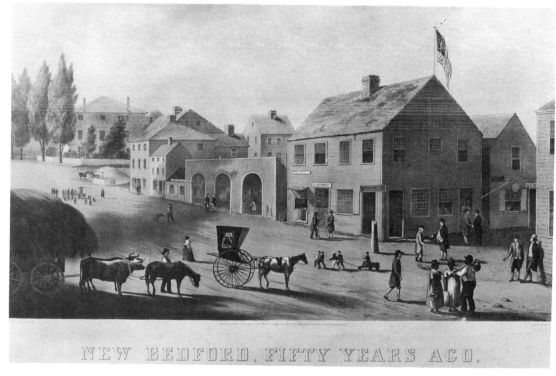

NEW BEDFORD, FIFTY YEARS AGO.

RIGHT AND BELOW. Charles
W. Morgan: *On board the
famous whaling bark (notice
the lack of square sails on
the mizzen, photo and plan);*
BELOW AND OPPOSITE, *the
skipper's son plays skipper.
All, Mystic Seaport
Museum.*

up the hill; our friend William Rotch, Jr., chats with little, infirm Abraham Russell; William Rotch, Sr., stares out at you from his chaise; Barnabas Taber strides across toward the artist's father; the artist himself is the little boy being pulled in a cart by four playmates. But where are the sailors, the whalemen, the fishermen? Nowhere to be seen. Surely they could not all have been off at sea! Interestingly, in the right foreground of this scene (painted "from the artist's memory" in 1855), there are three blacks, two women and a man. None of them look as if they've ever been to sea either; farmers or carriers all.

By now I was getting a bit desperate to find someone other than well-to-do whale oil merchants or upwardly mobile blacksmiths. And, being in the museum that has the superb half-model of a whaler (the *Lagoda*), I thought I might peer through her miniscule portholes and spy traces of the men whose existence was becoming such a mystery. Going into the Whaling Museum's central hall, I saw for the first time in perhaps fifty years the miniaturized but still lofty ship waiting patiently at anchor in her wooden harbor. This was the scene of much excitement for my brother and me as children; here we raced up and down the decks, here we steered the majestic vessel around the Horn and back, here we heard the cry, "Thar she blows!" and went a-whaling.

Down below, all is ideally child-sized. From stern to bow: the captain's and the mates' cabins, the 'tween decks area where specialists like the carpenter and the harpooners bunked, the fo'c's'le where the men sat on chests at the foot of their double-tiered bunks swapping tales and carving scrimshaw. We were with them on many a voyage.

But today I could find not a trace of a real whaleman. Now the whole display seemed strangely sterile, still juvenile, and telling but a small part of the story. I thought then of the later visits my wife and I had made to Mystic Seaport with our children to see that wonderful old survivor, the *Charles W. Morgan*. Though I had first encountered this relic of a whaler in her days on the beach at the Round Hill estate of Colonel Edward H. R. Green, where she spent the insecure years of the 1930s, I was delighted to see her again fully safe and sound at Mystic. Built in 1841, she had been in the business of deep-sea whaling until 1921—what a remarkable span of life. And what a money factory, bringing in nearly $1.5 million in whale oil and bone. In the heyday years before 1880, she but rarely brought back cargoes (whether to New Bedford or to San Francisco) worth less than what she'd originally cost her owners, $52,000.

Now, with the bowsprit jutting out over the Mystic embankment, her jibs and squaresails flying, her masts topped by the distinctive double-hooped look-out perches of whalers, she thrilled the heart . . . and occasioned many questions from our children. Unfortunately, I could only supply imagined answers, knowing next to nothing about the subject; these kids seemed to have become expert whalemen instantly upon birth.

Our older son asked, "Where are the cannibals, Dad?" He had read in *Moby Dick* that wonderfully bloodcurdling passage about a real whaling waterfront:

> in New Bedford, actual cannibals stand chatting at street corners; savages outright; many of whom yet carry on their bones unholy flesh. It makes a stranger stare. But, besides the Feejeeans, Tongataboars, Erromangoans, Pannangians, and Brighgians . . . you will see other sights still more curious, certainly more comical. There weekly arrive in this town scores of green Vermonters and New Hampshiremen, all athirst for gain and glory in the fishery.

For, just as I was to find neither slop chest nor weevil-filled biscuit on the *Lagoda*, so our son found here no clues of "wildmen"—neither in the *Charles W. Morgan*'s spick-and-span fo'c's'le nor on the sun-splashed Mystic waterfront. I explained that Mystic was not exactly in the cannibal business.

Pondering the same question at this later time in the New Bedford Whaling Museum—the question of the whaling community's true waterfront character, despite all retrospective paintings and maritime reconstructions and clean-up tactics—I again sought out the shade of Frederick Douglass. After he'd gotten over his initial enthusiasm and gratitude for New Bedford's open doors, how had things gone for him? His *Narration* (published in 1845) supplied the answer. He'd discovered that "the place was not entirely free from race and color prejudice. The good influence of the Roaches [sic], Rodmans, Arnolds, Grinnells, and Robesons did not pervade all classes of its people."

What he could not forget or forgive was an incident that occurred not long after his arrival. Having just heard to his joy that a Quaker merchant named Rodney French had found a job for him as a caulker on a whaleship under construction, he hurried down to the bustling waterfront. But when he located the right, half-built ship at its float-stage and walked along the hull through the laborers, he heard some all-too-familiar murmurs. They reminded him of a row forced upon him not long before by a gang of white workmen in Baltimore. Now he felt the same stares, the same closing of ranks against the black man holding a caulker's hammer. "I was told that every white man would leave the ship in her unfinished condition if I struck a blow at my trade upon her."

Forced to abandon the caulker's trade (at which he would have made twenty dollars a month), Frederick struggled as a day laborer on the wharves, earning ten dollars a month when he was lucky. He unloaded the whaleships *Java* and *Golconda* for owner George Howland, he toiled in the brass foundry of A. D. Richmond, and he heaved barrels in the whale oil warehouse of Joseph Ricketson. He returned exhausted but not broken to his little house on a back street. Here the winter day began and ended with trips through the snowdrifts to break the ice on a distant well. And here, before the passage of a year, a son was born to the Douglasses. So there was the joy of that, there were the occasional copies of William Lloyd Garrison's Abolitionist paper, the *Liberator*, and there was the comfort of the Christian religion.

Frederick tells the story of his eagerness to join the newly established Methodist Church in New Bedford. Surely in that church he would find a social consciousness, or a holy sacrament that would include the black worker. He described what happened when it came time for communion:

> There were only about half a dozen colored members attached to the Elm Street Church, at this time. . . . These descended from the gallery and took a seat against the wall most distant from the altar. Brother Bonney was very animated, and sang very sweetly, "Salvation, 'tis a joyful sound," and soon began to administer the sacrament. I was anxious to observe the bearing of the colored members, and the result was most humiliating. During the whole ceremony, they looked like sheep without a shepherd. The white members went forward to the altar by the bench full; and when it was evident that all whites had been served with the bread and wine, Brother Bonney—pious Brother Bonney—after a long pause, as if inquiring whether all the white members had been served, and fully assuring himself on that important point, then raised his voice to an unnatural pitch, and looked to the corner where his black sheep seemed penned, beckoning with his hand, exclaiming, "Come forward, colored friends!—come forward!"

One can almost hear the voice of Frederick Douglass, he who would soon be perceived as one of this nation's greatest orators, imitating that sanctimonious minister. He parodied Bonney's burblings:

"You, too, have an interest in the blood of Christ. God is no respecter of persons. Come forward, and take this holy sacrament to your comfort." The colored members— poor, slavish souls—went forward, as invited. I went *out*, and have never been in that church since, although I honestly went there with the view of joining that body.

Within but a few years of this incident, Frederick's outstanding declamatory strengths were discovered at an Abolitionists' meeting in Nantucket (1841), and he became an internationally recognized personage. He moved away from the waterfront, to Boston, to England, to Washington. Thus I could no longer ask him to be my guide to the true character of working New Bedford. But he had helped me turn an important corner of that journey—to understand that there were base attitudes along with high-level tolerance, there were laborers restricted to the bottom of the heap (if not exactly a proletariat)—and for that corrective understanding, I doffed my hat to him, even while thinking less of New Bedford.

SHOCKED back to reality from the heights of Nirvana, I vowed to probe further beneath the surface by means of more detailed people histories and more quantitative accounts. In such infrequently quoted sources I learned that even back at the beginning of the nineteeth century, when the population of New Bedford was a mere 1,800 (at its height in whaling days the population swelled to 20,000), there had been "a great deal of drunkenness among the sailors and some cases of pauperism and crime." The fitfully employed black laborers, who lived in a section of town branded New Guinea, were "given to drunkenness and improvidence." Yet most commentators chose to ignore these social illnesses because they simply did not conform to the city's image of itself.

Slowly but with increasing impact these unfortunate conditions spread, centered on the squalid areas that provided certain services to seamen during their short stays in port. These were places like "The Marsh" down near Front Street and "Hard Dig" and "Cepocket" up in the sparsely settled West End. Within them were the boarding houses, saloons, dance halls, brothels, and taverns for the seamen. Throughout them was thievery and unreported murder; or, if reported, unpunished. For, by common consent, these places did not exist, and thus no constable or reform-minded snoop entered there.

Attempting to interpret this see-no-evil mind-set, Austin McMullin explained in his *Industrialization and Social Change*,

The relationship between the majority of New Bedford residents and the proprietors and customers of these establishments was tenuous. Only the tacit agreement of the townspeople and the residents of the seamen's districts not to bother each other kept the peace. Toward this end the town constables did not enter these districts. Yet on several occasions violent conflicts arose. In 1826, a mob forced the closing and abandonment of a brothel known as the "Ark." Two years later another "Ark" opened in the hull of a ship, and this time a large group of New Bedfordites tore down the brothel and burned the remains. Twice again in 1840 and 1856 mobs burned down buildings in the "low life" districts.

Thus did outrage occasionally break through the sham that New Bedford was purely "a village of wealth and caste and culture." It was also a hypocritical town of vice and depravity. Furthermore, the reason one had such difficulty finding the slums on shore—as I finally came to realize—was that they were at sea. They were the fo'c's'les. "No free American ever worked and lived in such miserable conditions as the ordinary seamen on a whaler," wrote one of our most distinguished maritime historians, Alexander Laing. Other researchers of the waterfront gave me hard evidence as to why it merely appeared that all the housing in New Bedford was so pleasant: the seamen, black, red, or white, were perennially kept in debt; they had no choice but to ship out again. With no chance to establish a foothold on shore, they sailed off again in their slums at sea.

Although the answer to the enigma of the missing men was now unknotted, I felt no victory in the mystery's solution. That is, no passion to prosecute. For was this not simply a situation that had evolved, unintentionally? Surely there was nothing here which, per se, invalidated the brotherly love of the Quakers or put their integrity at issue.

When I discussed this ambiguous pattern with Dick Kugler, director of the Whaling Museum, he pointed out that a modern scholar named Elmo P. Hohman, a protégé of Morison, had drawn a good-versus-bad line at the period 1825–1830. Before that, all was harmony and homogeneity (Yankee whalemen cooperating with Gay Head Indians and local blacks); after that, all was heterogeneity and hatefulness, with the representatives of many races coming under the lash of increasingly brutal masters. And though it wasn't much to take pride in, there *was* an area where the Portuguese (plus Norwegian and other foreign seamen) had been able to establish a living base. It was called Fayal after the Azorean island Faial, where sailors were often pressed into service aboard American whalers.

Dick also showed me (with but a small sense of partisanship) a collection of clippings from local writers who had sought to refute what Morison had so bitingly said in his *Maritime History of Massachusetts* and what Hohman had reiterated. One of their charges, leveled at the basic honesty of Quaker whaleship owners, was that, on the ship's return to home port, the merchants would jigger the actual price of oil (against which the seamen's lays were figured) so that the men

Chores for the hands: Before the chase, the crew searched sea and sky from the crow's nest; ABOVE *and* RIGHT, *after the chase, they cut blubber alongside and* OPPOSITE, *boiled it in try-works on deck. All, Mystic Seaport Museum, Lantern Collection.*

would get less than deserved. In an indignant newspaper article, New Bedford historian Z. W. Pease responded to the contrary:

> If an officer or member of the crew was dissatisfied with the settlement on the basis of the going price for oil, he could have his share of the oil delivered to him and sell it for what he pleased. A captain sometimes took his oil. The sailor less often, because he did not care to bother with the storage and sale. But it was his privilege to take the oil. There were always enough sea lawyers available to enable the crew to secure a fair settlement.

I was not persuaded. The idea of a know-nothing sailor trying to peddle his wheelbarrow of oil casks up and down the city streets and through the system of commerce lacked a certain feasibility.

Another much-argued subject was the embarrassing issue of desertion. Whereas Morison stated that three thousand men deserted whaleships annually in the Pacific, Mr. Pease believed the number to be far less. He admitted, however, that "there were allurements" in the South Sea islands. There now came to mind that curious string of Extracts at the end of *Moby Dick*; one of them seemed particularly pertinent. Melville quoted a source as reporting, "It is generally well known that out of the crew of American whaling vessels, few ever return in the ships on board of which they departed." And of course that act of desertion (whether on the seamen's own impulse or forced upon them by calculating masters) completely dealt them out of the lay-system contract which they'd signed before sailing. Whether it was the allurements of the South Sea islands or the dazzling promises of the 1848 Gold Rush (which many say spelled the end of whaling's easy-to-get labor force) the men found something better to do than stay before the mast on a four-year voyage commanded by a martinet.

In a long letter to the New Bedford *Morning Mercury*, Morison seized the opportunity to refute some of the local writers' refutations. He focused particularly on the fact (?) that, with so many desertions and refusals to sign on for a second voyage, fo'c's'les generally had to be filled with "green hands."

> I have seldom sat in on a conversation between veteran whalemen without hearing them tell, with much gusto, of cruelties practiced by masters and mates of their acquaintance. It must be admitted that our merchant seamen of that era were no mollycoddles, and the fact that they shunned whaling vessels as they would the plague, shows that something was wrong. . . . A New Bedford native, as I understand it [was often given preference. He] generally started as a cabin boy instead of green hand; or else he was promoted to able seaman or boat-steerer in the course of his first voyage. How did the Portuguese first come to New Bedford? Why were agents paid large premiums for gathering in green country boys from the interior?

On this point, I was also reminded of a sea chantey that a friend had brought to my attention. The applicable lines go:

> *Lead:*   Now Ranzo was no sailor.
> *Chorus:* Ranzo, boys! Ranzo!
> *Lead:*   So he shipped aboard a whaler.
> *Chorus:* Ranzo, boys! Ranzo!

My concept of the fisheries, including whaling, as salubrious and life-enforcing workplaces was now good for nothing but throwing overboard, it appeared. This demeaning business—particularly in its post-1850 form—deserved loyalty from neither the seamen of the day nor from me. Dick Kugler sympathized. And he agreed that the Quaker skippers had definitely not seen themselves as running preparatory schools on shipboard. But he thought that Morison had gone a bit far when he wrote,

Three and four-year voyages, touching at no civilized port, brought out the worst traits in human nature. Whalers' forecastles were more efficient schools of vice than reformatories. Brutality from officers to men was the rule. Many whaling skippers who on shore passed as pious friends or church members were cold-blooded, heartless fiends on the quarterdeck. Men were hazed until they deserted, became cringing beasts, or mutinied. The ingenuity of whaling skippers in devising punishments surpasses belief.

It really wasn't that bad, Dick opined. Furthermore, the Quaker ethos had not run dry; there were leaders such as George Howland (mayor of the city in the 1870s) who sincerely sought to build a healthy city. They did, to be sure, favor the lowest possible taxes and restricted sufferage. And superior education for children seemed to be advanced as a passionate cause only when it came to Friends' children. The number of public institutions was not impressive. But what else could you expect of a New England city of this period?

I expected a great deal of this "dearest place."

Dick suggested, then, that I should not get discouraged until I had a more intimate sense of who these people were and what was the particular relationship between them and their sea creatures—I was looking at it now too much from the outside. And I should also get a line on what kept the city driving ahead toward the future. Perhaps whaling had been a corruptive and dead end, with the owners imprisoned in their counting houses just as the men were imprisoned in their fo'c's'les, but something strong and resilient had nonetheless been bred here. For finally, in recent times, the sea as a strength and a resource had been discovered once again in New Bedford. The salty, life-giving breeze was once again sweeping through the city streets.

FOLLOWING Dick Kugler's advice to eschew "social issues," and to dig into those things that were both more whale-related and more technological, I came upon a most peculiar piece of paper. It was a dream-filled page from the diary of Abigail H. Smith, young cousin of the shipowning Howlands. This Quaker maiden's story, penned in the 1830s (that is, exactly at the time of the good-bad line run through New Bedford's history by Professor Hohman), ran as follows:

I dreamed 7th day night that Brother Cornelius was about setting out on A whaling voyage & it seemed as though he was to start from our house & accordingly he was soon ready & all hands on board & set sail the ship standing exactly before Grandmothers East Window, but instead of sailing on Water she arose gradually in the air & after getting nearly out of sight & leaving his son G & me stood watching them he threw A rope by some means or other (but not intentionally) so that G & me caught hold of it & while we hold of it A sudden jerk arrested our attention & we looked and beheld Brother C. & Cousin D. Smith & both looking verry natural with their hats on & well dressed. Brother C. had on a Snuff coloured coat striped vest & Blue pants & white Cravat. Brother spoke to us repeatedly, sometimes would ask if we could now reach the rope. Our answers were in the affirmative—I told Mother I should send them some fried cakes called donuts by tying them to that rope. I first took two then four. I had an exceeding hard time tying them fast & nearly ready to give up and I looked again and there appeared to be A hook at the end to confine them to & I soon succeeded in my undertakings with Georges assistance. In my dream it seemed their ship went with the right course to meet with success—I awoke verry much fatigued so much so that I could scarcely breath.

Ah yes, at this time the pure spirit of adventure, with the whole family participating in the outfiting and the victualing, was still dominant on the land. It had been passed on undiminished from the generation previously when Cousin Cornelius Howland (as Abigail Smith would have called him) teamed up with my great-something-or-other Gilbert Russell to build the long-distance whaler *Rebecca*. Of 175 tons burden, she was considered an "object of wonder" for her size and capacity. She was one of the first two American ships to return from around the Horn with a cargo of whale oil back in those struggling years immediately after the destructive Revolution.

Whaling then was tremendous sport, as even Morison admits. The voyage of the *Rebecca* was made all the more enticing by the action of one Cornelius Grinnell. [Cornelius seems to have been a favored name in the Federalist years; it went well with eagles and Napoleonic haircuts.] Shipped on as first mate, he had to take charge when the skipper became mortally ill. The young man rose to the challenge and succeeded in navigating the ship home after passing through the Cape's storms and iceberg-haunted currents. For this, the hero of the hour was welcomed into the highest levels of New Bedford's society and invited to participate in *ownership*.

Perhaps Cornelius Grinnell sailed under such a lucky star because of an event that occurred at the time of his ship's launching (1785), an event which casts another light on the tensions that animated this then young city. The irreverent shipyard workers, not caring a hoot for the restrained mood of their Quaker bosses, had put a busty female figurehead on the *Rebecca*'s bow. Commanded by the owners to cut off that figurehead, that deplorable vanity, the workmen had no choice but to do so—into the mud. Yet, as the chastened ship sailed out of the harbor, the workmen saluted her with a mock funeral on behalf of their beloved, rejected figurehead. So one wonders which spirits blessed this lucky ship, the holy or the profane? Whichever, she earned her invested funds back many times over, finally was lost at sea when returning from Liverpool in the winter of 1803–04.

The historian who might be called poet laureate of the New Bedford Quakers, Daniel Ricketson, would cap that by telling the following, pertinent and personal story:

> The late Capt. Joseph Wheldon of North Falmouth was a boatsteerer in the *Rebecca*. . . . On a visit to him a short time previous to his death, he stated to the writer that he had received two hundred dollars in silver from the late Gilbert Russell in the settlement of his voyage, and that he never felt richer in his life than at this time.

These stories, these oft-told dreams and encounters reassure me that there was much good here, a continuing theme of reward for the worthy, and adventures for those who worked on land or at sea. For all the horror of what became grotesque, I began to feel and appreciate the original spirit, the spirit strong enough to endure even with its corruptions.

Then, still attempting to get to the heart of the matter, I undertook a task which I had successfully avoided all the years of my life: to go through the painfully intimate stuff of history in my own bureau drawers. To open up those silk ribbons and look into those musty folders, taking apart the crinkly brown papers and puzzling out the self-conscious penmanship of misplaced ancestors had always struck me as spooky and invasive.

But it was in one of those bottom-drawer collections that I found a particularly revealing letter. On the outside of a large sheet of browned paper (15½″ × 12½″) was the address, "Barnabas Taber (he who had been seen striding across the painting, "New Bedford Fifty Years Ago") . . . New Bedford, State of Massachusetts." The letter begins under the date February 17, 1818.

> Dear Parents. I sit down to let you know we are about 8 degrees north of the equator. I have got no whale and the only excercises of that kind we have had was capturing one black fish. We have had a pleasant passage so far and I am pretty well suited with this mode of life as it respects to victuals and the society is not very disagreeable for if any one has a thing the other has not he is welcome to it. I hope I shall be able some time or other to show you how grateful I am for the care you took in fitting me out as you cant conceive how much good the small things did me. I have no time to write anything more
>
> but subscribe myself
yours affectionately
Charles Taber.

No spoiled kid he. Nor an aristocrat unaware of the virtues of the seamen's society in which he found himself. This was, to be sure, on the "good" side of Professor Hohman's line, during the time when whaling was a homogeneous and communal activity. But now I understood what those words meant in terms of one young man's life.

The importance of each man to the other and the ever-present feeling of family closeness even at sea were, similarly, brought home to me by a second bottom-drawer letter, this one dated November 15, 1819.

Honoured Parents, Brothers and Sisters:
This may inform you of our health which is good and has bin since I saw you we are Ten Days from the Coast of Patigonia where we have found Elephant Seals and a number of Ships after them. We obtained about 700 bbls of Elephant oil and have taken Whales since and one sperm [?] Whale on the passage, 75 bbls. We now have on board about one thousand bbls. And whales are plenty but Very Wild so no More but my love and good wishes to My Daughter in a speshal manner Thee must be a good Girl and keep to thy Skool and Close to Styddy and mind thy Grand Parents and ants and what thee stands in need of thy ants wil supply thee with. Dont look for thy par to soon for he has about One third filled his ship So he cant set [forth]. No time [meaning nonetheless?] he has a tite ship and a Good Crew and is in Good Spirits for a Voyage.

Capt Paul Howland.

P.S. I had the misfortin to loos my Carpenter on my outward bound passage by sickness.

Tough and devoted and working like crazy. And those "thees" still make music up and down my backbone.

Yet the styles and the mood were changing. For it was at about this time, 1820, when New Bedford surpassed Nantucket as the chief whaling port, with vast economic consequences. It was also then that a critical split developed in the town's Quaker meeting: the elders cast out those brash adventurers who declined to play by the old rules. As religious scholars now interpret that action, it was not a matter of the new generation tiring of the old strictures but of the proud and antique religion growing increasingly in on itself and being too inflexible to allow variation.

Many who left the meeting became Unitarians—such liberal Unitarians that a twenty-year-long breach sprang up between the New Bedford church and the denomination's base in Boston. In 1854, Abraham Hathaway Howland, still a Friend, advised his brother-in-law *not* to take up residence on the Hill (to which William Rotch, Jr., and others had already moved) because his "inborn Quakerism might be contaminated by those wicked Unitarians." Two years later, Abraham himself moved into a house on the Hill.

There was, indeed, a new spirit in New Bedford as the town became a city (1846). Perhaps that spirit was less devoted to the old principles than in the early years of the century; perhaps it was more venal. But still it was fresh and laced with a passion for the sea (as well as for any other parts of the earth where money could be made). Its pulse beat all the faster after the opening of the Arctic whale fishery just prior to 1850. Dick Kugler directed my attention to one typical striver within this new era, a rather formidable collateral relative named Jonathan Bourne, Jr. who became the greatest owner of whaleship wealth in New Bedford history—and whose fortune originally endowed the Whaling Museum. Dick had been poking into this Bourne's "Letter Book" and had found a treasury of insights.

In those letters Dick tracked the foaming wake of a handsome and successful whaler named the *Hunter* which Bourne had built in 1850, near the peak of this city's whale fishery. In that same year, seventeen brand-new whalers were under construction in the New Bedford area—though of course there was nothing *new* about them at all; they conformed in every respect to time-honored standards. Perhaps because the shipyards were so backed up, but more probably because Bourne wanted to find a way to save money, the thirty-nine-year-old whaleship owner journeyed Down East, to Gardiner, Maine, on the Kennebec, to see about the construction of his projected 453-ton whaler. There both the timber and the labor should be cheaper, he trusted.

But as he agonized over the listed costs, detailing in his letters all that the Maine builders must do to live up to the contract (for example, how the beams should be "bored and pickled"), he knew in his heart of hearts that things were not going right. Finally he paid $14,750 for the completed hull, sparred and masted but not copper-sheathed. Yet more than $20,000 in addition to that was required for the rigging and other gear! Bourne groaned in his last letter to Gardiner that the whole deal had "cost more by $3,000 than I expected"—a total of $47,087. In dismay

Northern Light: *Typical of late nineteenth-century whaling ships, Jonathan Bourne Jr.'s pride and joy was sold from New Bedford to San Francisco about 1880. The Whaling Museum, New Bedford.*

he looked at a comparable whaler that Cornelius Howland had built in New Bedford at the same time, for $46,000.

The *Hunter* proved to be a beauty, however, bringing in $42,294 on her first northern voyage and $48,128 on her second. Furthermore, she was swift. Her master was so confident in her that, addressing his fellow skippers based in Hawaii, he

offered to bet $1,000 that I could beat any whaleship from Oahu around Molokai and back, and would give any man $25 to find me a customer. . . . I make the assertion the *Hunter* can beat any ship out of the river, one hundred miles to windward and back, for $1,025 against $1,000.

As for Bourne himself, he rapidly recovered from that case of investor's agony. By 1852 he was writing the boat builders in Maine again:

Through the winter and spring, I have thus far endeavoured to control my feelings in relation to ship building, and thus far have accomplished it. But I am nearly inclined to do something by way of a contract to have a ship ready the first of May, 1853. . . . My mind runs upon shipbuilding as usual.

Just one month more he resisted; then he confirmed his order for that other ship.

Those relatives of mine, they had this disease of whaling terribly, congenitally, whichever side of that abstract time line they stood on. But why could they not see the inhumanities of it? Perhaps because of whaling's gigantic size and grand fortunes, its built-in flaws could not be seen at the time. By the outbreak of the Civil War, half of the U.S. whaling fleet hailed from New Bedford (300 vessels); 12,000 men were employed in the fishery onshore and off, and the annual revenues were in excess of $8 million. So perhaps a degree of blindness might be forgiven.

Well, actually, some of the whale merchants did get out of the business at this time. Or they hedged their bets, investing in railroads, in Michigan timberlands, or in Pennsylvania ironworks, and keeping their eyes on the thriving cotton mills in nearby Fall River. Abraham Howland, he who so precipitately had moved to the Hill, turned from the waterfront to promote the New Bedford Oil Company, an early attempt to refine petroleum. Jonathan Bourne, Jr. shortly became president of the Bourne Mills in Fall River. Others followed their lead, turning away from the sea, as if in horror at what had been done there—the near wiping-out of certain whale species, the brutalization and death of so many nameless seamen, an average of 1.7 whalers lost each year with all hands.

It may seem ridiculous for me to consider that one of the reasons for this shift of mind and money, this tergivisation of the spirit, might have had roots in social

OPPOSITE. *On the sunny side of the pier: Girls and oldsters pose amid wagons and oil barrels while the bark* Massachusetts *spreads her sails for drying in the background. The Whaling Museum, New Bedford.*

concern. (Dick Kugler would chuckle at the speculation.) But, again, family records tell me that the theory's not totally implausible. The poetic son-in-law of Joseph Grinnell (the initial and patriarchal investor in New Bedford's first successful textile operation, Wamsutta Mills) expressed the family's hope that the new industry should give the common man a better break. That poet, named Nathaniel Parker Willis, wrote expectantly that textiles might be an endeavor "of which the families of sailors and mechanics could avail themselves, independent of the precarious yield from following the sea."

AT THE same time as some whaleship owners were bowing out, the great Arctic whale chase went on—for two and three more frantic decades. And there were many in New Bedford who believed that this continuation of the old game was perfectly sane, many for whom, in the words of New Bedford writer Everett Allen, "the whaling business stimulated the accumulation of money so rapidly as to lead [them] into ways beyond bearing with perspective." So it went on. And, in Morison's view, this distant, difficult Northern business was a special joy to those Quaker skippers whose only pleasure was to work the life out of the their men: "A summer's cruise in the Arctic Ocean gave the keenest delight to owners and skippers, as the midnight sun enabled them to work their crews 24 hours a day." Yes, so it went on, despite the increasing desertion rate, the decreasing profits, and (most important negative of all) the absolutely static technology—that is, the blind reliance on those "simple tools" from the old iron age.

It's not quite true to say that *nothing* had changed on the whalers since those great, slow, chunky vessels began to slide down the ways after the Revolution and the War of 1812. One evolutionary advancement was the distinctive white davits (devices for carrying the whaleboats above and clear of the sides of the vessel). Only American whalers had these ingenious, supple, handcrafted hangers that gave the fragile whaleboats such a secure and springy ride as the ship lurched through the heavy seas. New England carpenters made them by beginning with a solid, squared oak post; next they cut through that post with two parallel incisions, all the way from the bottom to near the top of the post. The result was that the three strips of wood on either side of the incisions could flex independently of each other. Then, after the topmost part of the post had been bent to the desired curve, with each strip taking its own share of that arc, the carpenters drilled holes and drove in trunnels (wooden pegs) to hold the strips at that precise curve.

Another improvement was the shift of rig from ship to bark, a step that many of the whalers took as the century matured. In 1875, when New Bedford's whalefishery was declining from its post-Civil War renascence, forty-nine vessels set sail from the port, of which forty-six were bark rigged and only three were ship rigged. What this step involved was more than just the substitution of fore-and-aft-rigged sails for the squaresails on the mizzen mast; it was a matter of working the vessel and the men differently. Now the whaler became more of a participant in the hunt, driven hard by masters who wanted to outsail their competitors, even while their crews diminished in quality and quantity.

Even so, innovation was hardly the name of the game. The name was status quo, both in rig or design and in shipboard protocol. Such old standbys as the lay system for seamen (with tinier and tinier fractions) and the unquestioned rule of the captain were not to be changed. They were as immutable as the very look of the whalers—black hulls with white stripes or ports, and the square sterns— you could spot them easily in a crowd of other ships. Following the lead of the merchant marine, flogging of seamen on whalers was outlawed (supposedly) in 1850. But in 1857, skipper's wife Helen Jernegan, on board the *Eliza F. Mason* (which established the speed record from Honolulu to New Bedford that year, with a run of ninety-five days), had to watch in shame as her husband's officers lashed the truth out of three crewmen. Eventually they confessed that they had started a shipboard fire so that, amid the confusion, they might escape to freedom in the Gilbert Islands. One needs to think not very hard to conclude why they wanted to escape.

By this time, we are definitely dealing with the "bad" side of Professor Hohman's timeline, the time when the percentage of Yankees in the fo'c's'le was changing from about 50:50 (the others being blacks or Indians or natives of the Azores) to perhaps 10:90. Along with the Irish and the Nova Scotians, the Portuguese played a leading role forward of the mast toward the end of the century (though their numbers did not increase dramatically in New Bedford itself until the time of millhand immigration, around 1900). At first, on shipboard, the Portuguese were regarded as "bestial," with their swarthiness and different personal habits; then it was observed how hard they worked, how fanatical about washing their clothes, how restrained on shore. As a joke, the logkeeper of the *Charles W. Morgan* noted that one Manuel Claudino, while ashore in Durban, had been "arrested for being sober!" These were the people who would help New Bedford find her new life after whaling died.

As early as 1850, less than half of those forward of the mast could read or write English. But what appalled Professor Hohman most was that so many of these wretched seamen came from "the bottom-most parts of society; the dregs of New Bedford's shore life." Degenerates, they were called. It was for this reason that usually charitable George B. Goode, when summarizing the rise and

Baleen and tar: Beneath the arched fronds of baleen ripped from whales' mouths, an aged tar smiles toothlessly. The Whaling Museum, New Bedford.

fall of whaling in his classic study, wrote that the "character of the men engaged" was a major cause of the industry's decline.

Ironically, just as the quality of the whalemen declined toward zero, a whale asserted itself that deserves mention as one of this earth's most magnificent mammals. This was the bowhead whale, also called the Greenland right whale (*Balaenidae mysticetus*), which the New Bedford whaling fleet discovered existing in large numbers among the ice floes north of Alaska's Bering Straits. With the tapping of the petroleum fields in Pennsylvania in 1859, whalemen shifted their emphasis from oil to bone. What was desired most of all was a creature which could supply vast quantities of baleen, that marvelously flexible stuff for which there was an almost boundless market in the days before plastic. Garment stays, umbrella spokes, buggy whips—everything that was light and pliant called for baleen. It went for a dollar a pound.

The bowhead supplied it most prodigiously. One third of this whale's sixty-foot-long body was head, the mouth measuring ten feet wide and fifteen feet high, the height of a two-story house. The gargantuan mouth-cavern was totally hung with feathery strips of baleen, through which the whale sluiced seawater in order to snare krill and other crustaceans. By rule of thumb, a bowhead was said to provide ten pounds of salable whalebone for each barrel of oil; the entire, product-rich creature often weighed over 100 tons.

The bowhead was also attractive for its passivity—though it did have an annoying tendency to head for the shelter of the ice when pursued. But no less courage or skillfulness were called for in the Arctic Ocean whale hunt than in the southerly voyagings for sperm whales. The whalemen's risks were described vividly by T. K. Starbuck, author of the still-definitive history, *The American Whale Fishery*:

With the opening of navigation in high latitudes . . . came increased perils. Not sufficient were the dangers from their gigantic prey, or furious gales, or the losing sight of the ships; to these must be added the risk of being ground between two mighty icebergs, of being caught in some field of ice and forced ashore, of having the stout timbers of their vessel pierced by the glittering spear of some stray iceberg as it was driven by the force of polar currents. [Yet] the season in [the] northern sea lasts but two or three months, and the temptation to incur more risks is too great to be withstood.

From the perspective of the whaler captains, the business became quite routine: where around the Hawaiian Islands to pick up a crew (preferably of the bold Kanakas, not just beach bums), when to sail north, and how to keep in touch with but do better than the other skippers. To make their lives more pleasant, some of the captains invited their wives to join them; these vessels became known as "hen frigates," a not necessarily derogatory term. For, to some extent, the presence of a woman on board modified the rope's-end cruelty that was the daily lot of so many seamen. Owner Charles W. Morgan noted, when one of his skippers advised that he was taking his wife along, that the custom "is becoming quite common and no disadvantages have been noticed, though there are some, but the advantages overpower them. There is more decency when a woman is on board."

It was neither a comfortable nor an edifying life for these whalemen's wives. But as the wives' journals indicate, raising children on board made for moments of family closeness and shared adventure. There were also mini-New Bedfords that were established in San Francisco and Hawaii, and these offered opportunities for civilized discourse. Furthermore, when on board, there was the companionable drive, the husband-and-wife push to get the most possible bone and oil, and the best price. Mary Chapman Lawrence, whose four years on the whaler *Addison* were chronicled in a journal published as *The Captain's Best Mate*, described her reaction to a piece of good commercial news (the great popularity of whalebone-stayed hoopskirts), as communicated by a new arrival:

Captain Curry told us of the still further use of whalebone, which is a matter of great rejoicing for us. An unheard-of event in the annals of history for whalebone to be $1.50 per pound. The ladies are to be thanked for that, and I presume all interested in right whaling are truly thankful for this skirt movement. May the fashion long continue.

But on returning to New Bedford in 1860, she discovered that hoop skirts were on the way out. She discarded hers summarily.

Yet the market for whalebone remained strong. Such doughty, old-fashioned whalers as the *Charles W. Morgan* continued to bring in cargoes valued at $50,000 in the era when the depleted New Bedford fleet was attempting to recover from depredations by Confederate raiders during the Civil War. It's significant, however, that the original owners and builders of this long-lived vessel (now rerigged as a bark) had sold her to new investors, the Wing family. For as noted, the Morgans, the Howlands, and others were increasingly pulling out of the whaling business. It's also significant that at this time when every dollar in and out was being squeezed with special care, the captain of the *Morgan* was no longer invited to invest additionally in the vessel; Captain Thomas C. Landers forever told the tale that he had been "cheated" by the parsimonious Wings. Certainly the time of broad participation by a closely allied community was past.

Then came the terrible ice crunch of September 1871, in which thirty-three whalers (twenty-five of them from New Bedford) had to be abandoned in the Arctic Sea. An unexpectedly early winter had closed in with ever thicker ice floes; what had been but another summer-month operation for the captains became a desperate struggle to save themselves and their wives and their men (some 1,200 in total) before the timbers snapped under the floes' pressure and the ships dropped from sight. By judicious teamwork and good seamanship, all hands escaped in specially coppered and strengthened whaleboats. Nonetheless, ships and cargoes valued at $1.5 million were lost. With that blow, and a major fraction of New Bedford's fleet gone forever, whaling was conceded by all but a few grim loyalists to be on its death bed. A death that had already been too long in the dying.

Incredibly, some struggled on despite the all-too-obvious embarrassments of whaling post-1880. By then the *Charles W. Morgan* was sailing regularly out of San Francisco, for the whaling grounds of the North Pacific were not completely exhausted. A great impediment to the business was the staggering expense of fitting out—to obtain those antique tools and to sign on the men—complicated by the pesky demands of the "crimps" (called sharks in New Bedford days of old). These questionable characters ruled the whaling waterfront on both coasts and worked hand-in-glove with the boardinghouse masters and mistresses; once a sailor was ashore, he was in their untender hands. It was with them that a skipper had to negotiate when seeking a crew. The *Morgan*'s new captain, James A. M. Earle, who sailed with wife Honor and son Jamie on board, complained bitterly about the $1,200 "blood money" he had to pay the crimps on his last sail out of San Francisco in 1904. Thereafter this never-say-die vessel continued her operations in the Atlantic, her last voyage eking out $25,533.90 in revenues.

YEARS before, the New Bedford waterfront had taken on a new character. Into the harbor in the fall of 1848 had sailed a rather strange cargo vessel. She stood in past Palmer's Island and continued upriver, past all the wharves where whale oil and bone merchants were conducting their ages-old business and where the chandleries and ropewalks were still humming with prosperous industry. Beyond the Fairhaven bridge she sailed, finally warping in to a new pier at property under development by the owners of the high-risk Wamsutta Mills. What made the ship so unusual was the massive cargo of raw cotton that she'd brought from the South. Towering bales instead of oil casks unloaded on a New Bedford wharf gave a joltingly different image of the future.

Ever lengthier stone and brick mills extended their bulks along the waterfront while unrigged whalers lay inertly tethered at rotting piers. Recognizing New Bedford's accessibility by water and rail and its favorable climate, more than two dozen textile mills crowded together along the shore. Suddenly the city's population, which had hovered around 20,000 for decades, exploded: 40,733 by 1890; 125,000 by 1925.

So finally the slums became visible on land. The working class, abandoning the fo'c's'les and finding jobs in the new mills, spread into fast-growing neighborhoods in the city's north and south ends. To those tenements came additional immigrants from Europe and Canada. And whereas before New Bedford had been a city of whaleship owners and shipfitting specialists, now (by 1910) it was a city of

Merrill's Wharf: A panorama of contemporary fishing vessels—from catboats and coasters to bankers and whalers (about 1900). Mystic Seaport Museum, W. H. Tripp Collection.

millhands, with more than 75 percent of its population first or second-generation immigrants. To this bustling city of Model Ts and ward politics, World War I brought a wave of prosperity that almost rivaled the grand days of whaling. Yet New Bedford retained much of its gentle charm; the lofty cupolas continued to look down upon flowering chestnut trees and slow-paced strollers.

Just as the very success of the black-and-white whalers had tended to discourage anyone from presuming to improve the equipment or the design or the system, so did this instant industrial boom discourage venturesome deviations. After a damaging strike in 1928, and while the mill owners faced the grim prospect of the Depression, they saw at their backs that the new cotton mills of the South had surpassed them with modern machinery and innovative processes. One by one New Bedford's mills closed, the property seized for taxes by the city. By the 1930s, the most recurrent noise on the waterfront was of boards being nailed across the windows and doors of another doomed mill. New Bedford agonized through a second death.

But at the same time, another kind of noise was heard, singly at first, then in greater numbers: the noise of gasoline and diesel-powered fishing schooners. For at the time of the city's deepest despair in the third and fourth decades of the twentieth century, certain New Bedfordites had turned again to the sea, trusting to find their livelihoods there, in not quite the time-honored ways of their forefathers.

This "Rebirth of the Ancient Business of Fishing" will probably never be portrayed by a painter in the manner of William Wall, for it seems to lack the glamour of whaling. But it's just as worthy; the painting should show how a salty seaman named Dan Mullin went about it by guile and invention. Though born in Ireland, Dan (whose humor-filled voice I've heard on tapes at the Whaling Museum) came to the United States as a toddler. He grew up before the mast, serving time on square riggers and on the seven-masted Maine coaster *Thomas W. Lawson*; then, as the century turned, he was ready to settle down at a business for himself. That meant fishing—which Dan had first attempted from a catboat off Nomansland, then as a mackereler in Provincetown.

By 1907 he was ready to try his luck out of New Bedford. And, having acquired a thirty-six-foot sloop, the *Eda J. Morse*, he rigged her for fishing in the new manner, as a beam trawler. He'd seen how this European invention worked when in Provincetown and Hyannis: you arranged a net so that its mouth was held open by a twenty-five-foot beam; you lowered this over the side and, under double reef with the wind abeam, dragged across the bottom with the tide. To those other fishermen in New Bedford at the time—mostly aboard small, hand-lining schooners—Dan's rig must have seemed suspiciously innovative and backbreakingly laborious. The entire outfit had to be pulled aboard with only the aid of a muscle-powered winch.

Sail was soon supplemented by a two-cycle, single-cylinder, twelve-horse-power engine. Dan called the engine, labeled "T&W" after its builders, his "tired and weary"; it helped him enormously. But, itching to bring back more fish with greater efficiency, Dan looked for better ways.

Scouting down to Montauk, he spotted a number of "Scandanavians draggin' with trawl doors. They were secretive about 'em, put 'em away out of sight at night." Intrigued, Dan went over and got talking. "We went below; somebody had a bottle—best diplomatic tool." And so he learned the secret, that is, how to construct and position the heavy "doors" on either side of the net's mouth. Returning home, he banged the heavy wood and metal pieces together with the aid of a few friends. And thus did New Bedford acquire its first otter-board trawler.

The results were spectacularly successful. Dan then took the course of most other fishermen blessed with good fortune: he set about building larger vessels; and he equipped them with ever more modern devices. The bankers of New Bedford, on the other hand, were not at all convinced that a waterfront renascence had begun or that this daring fisherman represented a good investment. "They thought I was absolutely crazy," Dan recalled.

But his favorite boat builder, Wilbur Morse in Thomaston, Maine, thought otherwise. "Sweetest man that ever lived," according to Dan. When he sailed away from the Morse yard in his new, fifty-seven-foot *Anna* in 1913, Dan Mullin still owed Mr. Morse $8,000 of the $22,000 cost. But it was a loan gladly extended, a loan soon paid back from the boat's earnings. The handsome schooner was equipped with a forty-horsepower engine, reliable enough to let Dan fish confidently out on Nantucket shoals. With this vessel, and with successors powered by diesels, Dan found that he could catch the same number of fish in a week that conventional craft had needed a month to net.

His usual pattern was to fish in about twenty feet of water on grounds where he "knew the bottom" and could expect a fair haul, often of "yellow tails" (flounders). The act of bringing in those heavy nets was eased by another Mullin innovation: Dan contracted with the Hathaway Machinery Company of Fairhaven to build a power winch that could be run off the shaft of his diesel engine. Now the otter trawl fishery became a fully mechanized and efficient, modern enterprise.

Dan's favorite story of a good voyage in those early days ends with a fast run to New York's Fulton Fish Market at the time of a local strike. Thus no other fishermen were there to compete. Dan determined to get what he thought the highest price possible—"one shillin' (meaning twelve and a half cents) for each one o' my yellowtails; and I had twenty bushels (32,000 fish) on board. Well, I got my price, after I'd found the right man, and I felt pretty good. But as I walked away, one of the wiseguys told me I probably coulda got fifteen cents!"

Others followed Dan Mullin's lead. In the words of Portuguese-descended Captain Robert Britto, "For various reasons we all did it . . . we went back to the sea, where we belonged." And by 1938 there were at least a hundred documented fishing vessels sailing out of New Bedford. The banks and other investors had also taken heart and had built refrigerator plants that stimulated the business all the more. In the year 1939 alone, some 1,714,000 pounds of ground fish and 283,000 pounds of mackerel along with 38,500 gallons of scallops were harvested. New Bedford was emerging as one of the East Coast's most dynamic fishing centers, with the Portuguese, the Norwegians (who had suffered a herring wipeout that year in their homeland), and other immigrants applying their talents to the new industry in a town once considered doubly dead.

This was surely not fishing as it used to be practiced in historic New England. In the first place, this was otter-board trawling, the vessel pushed along by 200-horsepower diesels. In the second place, men were paid not as of old, the lay system having become an exploitative farce in whaling times. One boat's account books from the 1930s show how the new system worked, with both salary and profit-sharing:

> The captain earned a salary of $105 a month, plus 2% of the catch ("gross stock") up to $3,000; beyond that target, he got 3% of the gross stock.
> The mate and chief engineer earned salaries of $90, plus 1% of gross stock up to $3,000, thereafter 1¼%.
> The 2nd engineer earned $75 plus ¾% of gross stock up to $3,000; thereafter 1¼%.
> The fireman and cook earned $75; the crew $51.

Thus by technology and human engineering improvements were made over the old pattern: the men would be paid for their work even when the fish declined to cooperate (or when the skipper encountered a run of bad luck). Many of the boats were owned by their own masters. Among the Portuguese families, who mostly left the highly profitable business of deep-sea scalloping to their Norwegian friends across the harbor in Fairhaven, an oft-repeated pattern was for the man to begin as a hand hired by a relative, then progress to part owner, ultimately to own a couple of vessels (or to leave the business entirely).

World War II having been survived along with a couple of hurricanes, the industry has gone on to blossom even more fully in recent years. New Bedford now ranks number one in the United States in terms of its annual catch—$100 million a year, ten times the wealth produced by whaling. Some three hundred

Gasoline breeze: Power-driven hulls facilitated larger catches for New Bedford fishermen; ABOVE, *and gill-netters;* OVERLEAF. *Both, The Whaling Museum, New Bedford.*

fishing vessels operate out of New Bedford, a third of them scallopers. As the harbor's fleets grow, New Bedford—seen by some casual observers as but another Massachusetts location benefiting from the centrifugal effects of Boston's high-tech prosperity—recognizes with a special pride that upward of 30 percent of its revenues come from fishing.

NONETHELESS, the fishermen of New Bedford face a fight for their waterfront. In the name of Development, various operatives have claimed they'll build a nationally franchised hotel and convention center on State Pier, and of course a clutch of condominiums nearby. The argument behind all of these activities (which would eat up highly valued space on an already crowded waterfront) is that New Bedford needs tourism in order to grow and in order to keep marginal businesses in the commercial and restored areas from fading. Promoters say that to bring in the tourists, something more attractive must be put on the waterfront than rusted, net-hung fishing boats and snorting refrigerator trucks. "We've got to build *on the waterfront*," demands one of the eager hotel-investors.

But the city's mayor, John Bullard (who served for several years as head of WHALE, the city's preservation agency), believes strongly in guaranteeing adequate space for the fishing fleet. "What is special about New Bedford and makes it strong," he says, "is that we take pride in and protect our working waterfront and its historic district." Behind him stand the fishing vessel owners and skippers. The supportive voice of organized labor is lacking, however, as a bitter strike and union confrontation in the year 1985–86 decimated union ranks.

To my eye, the opposed forces of avid developers and hold-fast fishermen need not find each other incompatible in New Bedford. Can't tourists and fishermen rub shoulders? Provincetown, in its own way, has made the combination work—why not in other historic locations?

Oddly, in this old city, this city that has realized its destiny in large part because of its rediscovery of the sea, one roams the waterfront in vain search for a certain, lustrous item. Nowhere could I find fish to buy, from one of those treasure chest-like stands that used to spill over with all the silvery varieties. Is this city perhaps ashamed of that humble product—just as it used to feel that whalers' seamen should be kept out of the picture? I could only trust that in Gloucester, long viewed as at the heart of New England fishing, I could actually find some . . . fish.

GLOUCESTER: WHEN THINGS GET CHOPPY, CHANGE YOUR TACK

IN THE middle of Gloucester there's a big hole called Urban Renewal, Phase I. It's a parking lot, actually, in front of a supermarket and in back of the new city offices, with as much flavor of New England as a shopping center in Dubuque. Nonetheless, once you've learned that history is what's destroyed as well as what's preserved, this may be seen as an historic spot. Here exceptionally raucous seagulls turn in the air, here men in fishing boots clamber out of pickup trucks to pick up six packs, and here mighty refrigeration trucks, bearing fish for Boston, muscle down the boulevard around the renewal area. Nothing strange.

Yet at the heart of this city that once epitomized New England fishing I had found a typical turning point, the old abandoned for the new. As expressed in terms of one of those grand Knockabout schooners that used to grace the Gloucester waterfront, this was like the point where the crew had switched the "fisherman's staysail" over to the other side and brought the schooner about on the other tack. (Though more than one hundred feet long, Knockabouts tacked in the stunningly swift time of twenty-two seconds!) And she'd left the rest of the fishing fleet bobbing in the whorl of her wake. Here, in this rain-drenched parking lot, I perceived that Gloucester herself was a vessel which had recently and repeatedly obeyed the local seamen's injunction to "tack when things get choppy."

On an enormous, illuminated sign that becomes visible as you splash east from the parking lot, the famous blue fisherman of the Gorton-Pew fish packing company strains against his ship's wheel. The sign looms over a low-lying glass-and-concrete building which, along with other business structures in this part of town, represents Phase II of Gloucester's urban renewal—the new direction. New but not universally admired: on a previous visit, I'd paid a call at the Fishermen's Institute, which is now housed within the Senior Citizen's Center; there the protests are long and loud. "The environment's all changed. They tore down our Fishermen's Home," the lined-faced men told me, squeezing styrofoam coffee

OPPOSITE. *Tall ships, tall steeples: An 1876 view of Gloucester from Rocky Neck gives a rather empty view of a harbor once crowded with 400–500 schooners. Mystic Seaport Museum.*

cups in huge hands. "There used to be a Fishermen's Corner where we'd sit out on the steps of the Post Office at night and listen to the Salvation Army band play." Worse than that, the whole world of the waterfront is now controlled, they whispered loudly, not by the traditional forces but by tourism and "big money."

Inside the spick-and-span, air-conditioned Gorton-Pew offices (an enterprise which, at $200 million annual sales, represents "big money" quite effectively), the past is remembered with distant fondness but as no guide to tomorrow. Here the most important date is not 1849, when the company was founded, but that splendid day in the late 1960s when the company was bailed out, bought by General Mills, the food-marketing giant. "They put in two really competent managers who turned the place around," Julian Hatch told me. He's director of public relations for Gorton-Pew, sails a lovely, old-timey yacht, and believes strongly that the company would not be where it is today (biggest in the business) if this entirely new way had not been taken.

"Oh yes, we're *in* Gloucester and that's where our roots have always been, but we're not *of* Gloucester," Julian explained. "We buy our fish from suppliers all over the world—Norway, Denmark, Japan—that's the only way we can get sufficient volume to deliver in consistent quantities across the nation, and that's

Working Gloucester: About 1900, New England's new fishing capital was a one-industry city of storage sheds, fish piers, and roominghouses. Mystic Seaport Museum; photo H. D. Fisher.

our commitment. We give hundreds of workers here steady employment with all the modern benefits; that's what counts. But we get a very small portion of our fish from here. That's long gone."

He showed me some photographs of Gloucester a hundred years before. "Rogers Street was just one more bar or brothel after another then. They called Main Street Front Street in those days; it was the same thing, a disgrace. When the fleet was in, they closed the shutters of this city of 25,000 as thousands of brawling Canadians and off-the-boat immigrants roamed the streets. If that's your 'golden heyday,' you can have it."

Walking on around the curve of the harbor, my feet ever wetter, I found a block-large, newly fabricated steel shed which (along with other waterfront constructions of the mid-1980s) represents the third phase of Gloucester's urban renewal. It might be a dairy or a bottling plant, it looks that clean; but in fact the shed is shared by two fresh-fish shippers. At one of them, the John B. Wright Fisheries, I expressed surprise that the building bore no relationship to the odoriferous fish sheds I'd known of old. "Inspectors come here every other week to snoop in the cracks. But we stay ahead of 'em," Bryan Wright, grandson of the founder, told me as hoses sluiced and brushes swept residue down the drains.

Bryan's brother punched out answers to some of my other questions on his calculator: "This is a well-planned investment for the City of Gloucester that has worked out. There used to be nothing but run-down shacks along here, plus rotting piers with rusted gas pumps at the end. And the fishermen were looking at less and less fish each year. For example, they used to bring in something like 120,000 pounds a day to this wharf; now it's 50,000 pounds. But today everyone's makin' money. That happened because of better facilities, and smarter handling."

He clicked out more evidence: "It's not just that the price of fish is up—haddock went for something like seventy-five cents a hundred-weight in the old days, now it's three bucks a piece. We get something to sell from even the worst fish of that half-a-million pounds the boats bring in here each week: the dogfish goes to Europe; the groundfish, which have always been the most popular, goes to Boston for auction; the whiting and so forth go to New York on consignment. You can look at the figures, it's all there; we're selling fewer fish in a better way to a more specialized market. We know what we're doing." He gave me the confident wink of a twenty-nine-year-old professional who likes his bottom line.

Then I spent some time trying to look at this through the fish's eye. For, as the Wright brothers' workers hoisted the boxes of the still-flopping product up off the boats, it was mostly fish eyes I was aware of. Perhaps that was because much of the catch were flounder—those Picasso-style bottomfish that have two eyes on one side, all the better to look up with. And the very biggest of the catch were halibut, called the "giant of the flounders." Seeing a particularly large halibut saved in a corner, a special prize to be carried home, I asked about the dime-sized cut in its tail and was told that only that incision was needed to drain the blood out; thereafter the fish was perfectly prepared for the pan.

Hunter-sleek cod also lolled wide-eyed in boxes, fallen (and gutted) heroes. Then there were some valiant hake, their tough, silver scales comparable to anything a medieval armorer might have forged. But some of the cod did look a bit over the hill. David Wright explained that these questionable fish had been caught with a gill net, a buoyed and weighted net that hangs at a certain selected spot, close to the bottom, all through the night; some of the fish whose gills are caught by the net's mesh hang there drowned for an excessive number of hours before being gathered up.

I also asked about a really ugly fish, a sorry creature that looked as if she had worn her older, bigger sister's dress to the ball and furthermore had delayed too long her visit to the orthodontist. This was an "ocean catfish," it turned out; maybe ugly, but blessed with the ability to crunch shellfish all day long. As a result, the catfish tastes something like a Cape Cod clambake, absolutely delicious, as my wife and I later discovered.

Just before leaving the pier, while watching the skillful young men flip this fish here, that fish there, into their respective shipping boxes, I found myself engaged in conversation with someone who spoke a different waterfront language. A nice-looking, elderly man of smiles and graces, he was mellifluously continuing my course of fish-world instruction (David Wright having disappeared) in English-Italian.

Then came a question, straight from the shoulder: "So you're a reporter?"

"No, I'm writing a book. About the history of fishing in New England."

"Ah, a book!" He smiled at me fondly and finally; his wonderful clothes, his beautifully groomed white hair. Then he turned to one of the men forking the fish—a son or nephew, I guessed. *"Sta minga?"* he asked rhetorically, and went away. I later learned that his idiomatic question—he being a well-known fish trader who does well enough to travel back and forth to his family in Sicily twice a year—means something like, "What *do* these guys want now?"

THOUGH history may not have much value to the successful men of Gloucester's waterfront, it's of intense concern in three buildings up on the ridge that overlooks the harbor. The most prominent of these is the bulky red City Hall, whose clock tower rises an impressive 194 feet above harbor-water level.

City Hall was designed in 1871, when Gloucester, suddenly fish-prosperous (with a population increase of nearly 50 percent between 1860 and 1870), considered itself important enough to have a civic building that "recalled" Philadelphia's Independence Hall. Well, that was the designers' idea, but the Belle Epoque had its own lumpy, anticlassical way of looking at mass and detail. Nonetheless, this is one imposing place for a fishing community of 15,000 souls (1870); it bespeaks power. Yet in the New England manner, for scores of years after the building's completion the power and the glory expressed here seemed to be exclusively those of the Yankee aristocracy, the vessel owners, not of the men who had brought home the silvery wealth in barrels. And many there were of them who had gone down to the sea and never returned, an estimated 10,000 lost since the founding of Gloucester in 1623.

In 1978, however, John A. "Gus" Foote, a retired fisherman, got a hand on the helm and the ship of state took another tack. As a city councilman, Gus Foote proposed that a memorial to the fishermen be constructed, right in City Hall; this became a spectacularly poignant work of art. Within the architectural context of the Hall's main staircase are inscribed the names of those lost from 1874 to 1975—year by year, as in the subsequent Vietnam Memorial. Yet here the artists, Erma Wheeler and Norma Cuneo, endowed each of the 4,000 names with a luminous individuality. They drafted the letters in variously colored pencil, sealed with polymer varnish, on panels of what looks like taut-stretched sail cloth; thus each name shimmers differently, polychromatically, in the dim light, as if seen under rippling waters. It is as unlugubrious as it is memorable. And because names denote races, an astonishing ethnic diversity shimmers forth as you stand in the mahogany gloom of City Hall.

The other two ridge-top buildings where Gloucester's history still lives are the Sawyer Free Library, which stands at one end of the short street that runs past City Hall's front steps, and the Cape Ann Historical Society at the other end. Within the library one can investigate how any one of the memorialized fishermen actually lost his life. For example, on the library's file card for John Phalan (an Irishman?) I read: "Lost September, 1876 on Grand Bank, schooner *Walter M. Falt*. Source, 'Fishermen's Own Book,' page 71 . . . wreck seen dismasted and waterlogged . . . crew never heard from."

Other logs, record books, and maritime exhibits are preserved or handsomely displayed at the Cape Ann Historical Society, which is partly housed in a handsome merchant's mansion. This Federalist house, survivor of the ruinous fires of 1830 and 1844, helped establish the mood of the "Upland" along Pleasant and Prospect Street, where the merchants reigned. The remaining houses from that pre- and post-Revolutionary era remind one vaguely of Marblehead, with their small-paned windows and gambrel roofs. Largest public buildings from the period are the old town hall, a square and heavily quoined white structure which now serves as American Legion headquarters, the beautifully spare home of the Universalist Church, and the still-hospitable Blackburn's Tavern, in whose windows you can almost see oil lamps flickering.

Though famed for its archives, the Cape Ann Historical Society is more popularly known for its collections of seascapes, portraits, and ship paintings—particularly those of luminist Fitz-Hugh Lane. Yet unlike many another art museum elsewhere, the historical society has chosen not to ignore the nonaristocrats in the city's lineage. When it became clear that age and weather were destroying the venerable, fruitwood statue of Our Lady of Good Voyage atop the Portuguese community's church of the same name, the historical society saw to her reproduction in fiberglass, with total accuracy (including the fishing schooner which she holds cradled in her arms). And then they had an all-embracing, all-congratulating reception.

Curious to see the Our Lady of Good Voyage Church, I was also interested to learn about the Portuguese community in Gloucester, expecially after my researchings in New Bedford. What was the connection, and how had the Portuguese fared here? So, after making a few inquiries and being informed of the way to "Portagee Hill," my wife and I headed eastward along Main Street. Then, having spotted on our left the "tower house" that we'd been told about—six stories tall, yellow with orange trim, a real sign that one is entering the differently colored world of the Portuguese—we bore left up the slope. Near the top, on our right, we soon spotted the exotic, smoky purple church, with Our Lady riding the crest of the pediment between two lesser pillars. On either side of the arched main door are corkscrew pilasters that may be traditional in Mediterranean lands but here seem as rare and wonderful as unicorn horns. On the other side of the street stands the Portuguese-American Club, with crossed national flags and a welcome to all.

Inquiries revealed that the first of this salty ethnic group to come to Gloucester arrived in 1847—a refugee from New Bedford's whalers. His name was Francis Bernard. Apparently he had been one of those Azorean whalemen who, picked up on the outward voyage, came to the critical decision: Never again. Within two years, Francis had married, a Nova Scotia girl; a decade later, some twenty-five other Portuguese-speaking fishermen and their families had joined him as residents of Gloucester. One generation later, such names as *Rose Cabral* and *Ida M. Silva* began to appear on the sterns of certain Gloucester vessels. This was the most positive assertion of the Portuguese success: ownership.

But now, I was told, very few Portuguese-descended men walk the decks of

Gloucester's new fishing fleet; they're off on their own new tack. Furthermore, the fishing industry here is shrinking spatially while specializing; its waterfront turf has been reduced to about a quarter of what it once was. As we walked back down the hill, I pondered the negatives I was beginning to hear from all sides: with the prevalent uncertainty about the continuing health of the local fishing business (of which the withdrawal of the Portuguese was but one indicator), investors were inclined to favor not working facilities on the piers but other kinds of construction in the city. There were rumors of ever-threatening condominiums and a splendiferous mall, to be called Gloucester Landing.

Gloucester might soon be sailing off on a tack far away from fishing. The compelling message of history—that the past is prologue (witness New Bedford's return to the sea)—might remain quietly locked up in the institutions on the ridge. The Portuguese would not hear it, being otherwise engaged. And no one but the old salts at the Fishermen's Institute seemed interested in speaking out loudly and rudely for the preservation of essential working space on the piers for future generations. One of the retired fishermen had yelled at me: "The goddam mall's going to make us into another Newport!" I wondered how many other voices might finally be added to his when democracy made its ultimate determination here. Did I expect them to speak forth from cracks in Cape Ann's sea-lashed granite?

WHEN founded in 1623, Gloucester (unlike independent Marblehead) seemed a law-abiding, well-mannered parish within the Puritan Commonwealth's settlement plan. And although the first fishermen and farmers to move there found the place too rocky and exposed to remain, others soon took up the challenge. By Revolutionary times, they had established a thoroughly orthodox town, devoted to ship building (particularly in the nearby Essex County village of Chebacco), to fishing, and to trading. The successful merchants of the latter eighteenth century are particularly remembered for their habit of "Surinaming"—that is, bringing back a sticky cargo of molasses to Central Wharf from the West Indies island of Surinam in exchange for their barrels of salt cod. At pier head the molasses would be made into rum, craved by all New England. A crusty group of Yankee merchants, they hewed to the tenets of the Congregational church, they built their pilastered mansions, and they dominated the town. There was not much need to worry about the lot of the itinerant fisherman.

For anyone trying to discern what happened next—how Gloucester became New England's chief fishing port and cradle of ethnic diversity—it's fortunate that a number of old-timers with long memories were interviewed by local newspapers before their recollections were swept to the four winds. One of these voices from the past pointed out that

> it was not until far into the 19th century that [fishing] yielded much more than a bare substance for the fearless and hard-working men who pursued it, or made the owners more than fairly comfortable. There were no rich fishermen, and no owners grew rich from any of the byproducts.

The slim and rugged times to which he was referring saw men going out to sea in the light and undecked "pinkies" that were the special creation of Chebacco's yards. At the stern, these distinctive double-ended schooners rose to a point that looked not unlike the cross-winged hind end of a kittywake gull, bobbing on the waters. Fisherman Henry Saunders, one of the interviewed old-timers, recalled with more precision than fondness his days long ago on those "red stem boats"—so-called because their black hulls were capped at the bow by brightly painted stem pieces. Of the two masts, one was far forward; on both were raised gaff-headed sails of hemp. That loosely woven cloth held the zephyrs so poorly that, in order to get a more retentive surface, water had to be splashed up on the sails by means of a bucket known as a "scoot horn."

Young Saunders and his master and two other hands would make three trips a year (spring, midsummer, and fall) in their little *Fox*. She carried no real bowsprit, just a pole nailed to the foredeck. From it, a modest piece of cloth known as a Santo jib was flown, helping them maneuver along the coast. The inshore cod fishery was then making the transition from the era when the product was brought back "in the round" (meaning split and cured on shore) to the era when it was salted down on board. Doing his share and more, Saunders worked through the successive stages of ownership; by the age of twenty, he was captain of a boat he owned in partnership.

Fishing in those days had little to do with money as such; Captain Saunders remembered dealing with peddlars from Vermont and Canada, his fish exchanged for their beef and butter. Yes, it was a quaint, preindustrial scene. As sketched by another recollector, this was the action down at Dr. Coffin's wharf:

> It was a small wharf and a noted resort, where Town Meeting orators, waxing warm with each other in the discussion of local affairs, would adjourn to and fight it out. It was the scene of many a hotly contested fight over questions which agitated the minds of those who were interested in town affairs—and perhaps had imbibed too much of the famous New England rum of the period.

Open-air democracy and a communal exchange of goods for services . . . these were ever the essential ingredients of the New England waterfront. Captain Sylvanus Smith, whose colorful memoirs have much to say of these days in the 1830s before fishing became big business, also wrote of the general absence of cash. From Gloucester the manager of a vessel would cart the unculled catch into the market center (usually Boston) and would bring back a selection of goods to compensate each man for the fish he'd caught. The manager would haul home "such articles as flour, corn, beans, as well as wearing apparel. It was seldom that the fisherman had any [money] coming; their families, if any, lived from the

The ancient Mary: *Gliding across Gloucester harbor, a classic pinky shows a salt-bearing bark how to sail with almost no wind. Mystic Seaport Museum.*

[company] store, taking such supplies as were needed from time to time." The barrels in which the much-desired flour was brought were cut in half and taken home to serve as washtubs.

But Captain Smith recalled with more anger than kindness his relationships with the "quarterdeck admirals" who, having made their money in the old days of square-rigged merchantmen, were not about to underwrite the scruffy new generation of fishermen.

> I was going to Newfoundland, and I wanted to place $1,500 insurance . . . on my vessel. I can almost see now those old graduates of the quarterdeck as they sat about the round table in the offices of the company. After asking me all sorts of questions in regard to my vessel, and how she was fitted, they concluded to take the insurance. After leaving their office, I heard someone calling me, and going back to the rooms, they told me that they had neglected to ask if the ballast was stanchioned down. After so many, almost nonsensical questions, this was too much, and I told them they might go to . . . (that hot place), for as I was going in the vessel myself, I certainly would take precautions to safeguard my life. . . . This was a fair sample of their methods.

At that early point in Cape Ann's total development, fishing was carried on from many of the little coves that cut into the rocky peninsula; Gloucester itself, known as the Harbor, was completely in the hands of the old-line merchants whose houses rode the ridge above the harbor (the Upland, "where they speak a different language," as Captain Smith would have us believe). It was only with the decline of the merchant marine and the gradual flourishing of such small-time fishermen as Henry Saunders that the "harbor Boys" saw reason to invest in this most ancient, most forgettable of businesses. Within a few decades, fishing took charge of Gloucester; in the words of Captain Smith, "like the [biblical] stone the builders rejected, it has become the headstone of the corner."

There were at least three factors in this turnaround. One was strictly zoological: for nature's own reasons, the sea all at once was teeming with a variety of attractive fish, apparently eager to be caught. Captain Smith gives us a report of that sudden burgeoning:

> In August of the year 1848, vessels lying about 10 miles off Cape Ann, becalmed, saw what they supposed to be a southerly breeze coming along the water. As it came near, it proved to be an immense body of mackerel, miles in extent. They passed by the vessels with heads almost out of the water, and it was seen that they were very large fish; no such fish as these had been seen before on this coast. They took no notice of hook or bait. Vessels made catches from this immense school, following them as they went South until they passed Chatham.

Mackerel were still caught in those days by jigging with a hand line, the purse seine not coming into common practice for another generation. But even with that crude equipment, the hunt for the tempting new creatures was now avidly pursued. Up to the north where the fish seemed even more numerous, up to the Bay of St. Lawrence sailed Gloucester's eager new mackerelers. They were on the forefront of the renascence in this no longer quiet town.

Relaxed harborside: At another of Cape Ann's communities, Lanesville, fishermen occupy the tiny harbor they once shared with stonecutters. Cape Ann Historical Association; photo E. G. Rollins.

Though the mackerel initially stimulated the fishermen of Gloucester (as it had the fishermen of Provincetown), this was not truly the fish that made the difference here. That pivotal role was played by the momentous halibut. Once regarded as junk fish in comparison with its seaground companion the cod, the halibut came more and more into favor as the nation developed a stronger and stronger appetite for fresh fish. In addition to the firm and tasty meat of the halibut (member of the genus *Hippoglossus*, largest of the flatfish), one has to marvel at the fish's bizarre sexual differentiation: while the females occasionally weigh 500 pounds or more, the males rarely exceed 50 pounds.

At first the halibut seemed even more numerous and inexhaustible than the mackerel. "They were like sand on the beach," remarked Gloucester's Captain W. H. Oakes; "the more you catched, the more there was." And although the halibut dwelled at great depths—100 fathoms and more—the fishermen thought nothing of pulling them up and up and up by hand, over the sides of their little schooners. Then the massive, struggling fish would be done in by a blow to the head from the "gop stick" and heaved forward to the "checkerboards" (pens to hold the fish on deck, made of crossed beams) for freighting home. Working farther and farther out into Massachusetts Bay, the fishermen would haul in 12,000–15,000 pounds of the monstrous halibut a day.

Not long after the opening up of George's Bank to halibuters (1830–1840), the railroad came to Gloucester. And with it came the realization that the fleet could now deliver fresh fish to any market in the Northeast. In this highly competitive market-fish business, ice made all the difference; schooners that had been off shore for as long as three weeks could land bright-eyed fish, preserved in mounds of winter-harvested ice. (A French wit noted that *Le sel a cédé la place à la glace*.) So the zoological blessing was enhanced by ice and the railroad. But something else was still necessary—quantities of men.

Men of many sorts and many races and minimal expectations were required to do this labor-intensive work. Marblehead had not willingly welcomed such men to its narrow streets and tilted houses—swarthy strangers like that Portuguese exwhaleman, Francis Bernard. Gloucester, by contrast, opened its doors happily (or is the word *hungrily?*) to newcomers from Canada, the Azores, and Europe. And here, as in Noank, the immigrants had a particular Christian denomination to thank for the relatively open minds behind those open doors.

The scene shifts back to London in the mid-eighteenth century, when John Wesley and George Whitefield were shaking up the ecclesiastical establishment with their unorthodox interpretations which came to be called Methodism. Working within that same, lively religious tumult, a preacher named James Relly took the rather extraordinary theological step of extending Christ's salvation to the entire human race, not just to the elite as endorsed by the Calvin-inspired churches of the day. Young John Murray (1741–1815) listened hard at Relly's knee, then put his mentor's saving words into action.

Excommunicated (and thus removed from any pulpit in England), Murray came to North America in 1770 and preached his way through several colonies before coming to Gloucester, where a few other Relly-influenced Christians were to be found. Under Murray's leadership, this small band established itself as the American Universalist Church in 1779. It gave Gloucester a unique spiritual slant—a notably different view of humankind.

For not only did the Universalists believe in the "supreme worth of *every* human personality" (italics mine), they also shied away from that Brahmin intellectualism which is so much the hallmark of New England Protestantism. In the words of Sydney F. Ahlstrom, author of the *Religious History of the American People* (one of the few historical works from modern pens to come to grips with religion as a generative part of U.S. society), Universalism in Gloucester and elsewhere "began as a revolt from the standing order by humble, unlettered people rather than by the intellectual and social leaders." Here was a native religion that could offer to the fisherman welcome and salvation on his own terms (as opposed to Frederick Douglass's experience with Methodism). Or, at the very least, here was a religion that urged upon the fixed minds of the Yankee property owners the idea that these foreigners might have some claim on earth, too, as well as their abstract claim on heaven. Despite the manifold storms and fires that have swept through old Gloucester over the decades, the securely founded, proudly plain Universalist church building (1805) still raises its prominent steeple and its Paul Revere bell high above the city.

Many of the people who came through Gloucester's wide-open door brought their own religions with them, of course. First were the Irish, who, along with the fishing technique known as beam trawling, brought the Roman Catholic faith to Cape Ann. They established St. Ann's parish in 1849; today their handsome and massive granite church, around the corner from the Sawyer Free Library, stands as the city's most capacious religious structure.

Elsewhere around Cape Ann sprang up Methodist and other churches for the Nova Scotians and additional Canadians. Of particular charm were the wooden and brick Lutheran churches crafted by Finns and other Scandanavians—some of whom preferred stone quarrying to fishing. By denominational leaps and bounds, the population grew from 6,350 in 1840 to 16,754 in 1875 (as the property valuation rose from $1 million to more than $9 million). For anyone who cared to count, it was clear that those foreigners, whatever their religion, were producing fish richly; their catch in 1875 alone was worth $4 million.

Nonetheless, a journalist of the time described the town like this:

Of the courage and tenacity of the Anglo-Saxon blood in keeping its grip on this rocky Cape, a walk through the streets of Gloucester furnishes hourly evidence. . . . For years the increase in the population of Gloucester was a natural increase, barely affected by the coming of new people. It was this which preserved [the city's native] characteristics; the marriages among the original families produced a sturdy race physically and morally—a race of patriots.

To a certain extent, the journalist was correct: the Yankees continued to run the show; and, as we've seen in other seaport communities, a shift of complexion among the laborers was but slowly reflected at the top. When looked at by one nineteenth-century writer, it added up this way:

The native-born citizen makes but a small element in the catalogue of the fisheries [meaning the roster of deckhands]. The men who sailed with the fleet a quarter of a century ago are largely included in the ranks of the fitters and buyers today. Their early experience proves their best capital in conducting their business, and gives them success where others may fail.

Thus, even as the numbers increased, there was no real confusion about whose town it was—a situation that lasted for all of the nineteenth century and beyond. "The owners provided the purposeful delusion that this was still a Yankee town," joked a later commentator.

Yet aboard Gloucester schooners, at sea, that delusion was battered by the storms of reality. The captains ate at the same table as all the polyglot men; unlike the whalers, the schooners had no mates. Off Cape Ann, democracy ruled the waves, though there was steady and unquestioned guidance from the man at the helm.

AS IF GOLD had been discovered on the Grand Banks, just as it had been in the Sierra Nevada Mountains of California (1848), fishing boomed in the years immediately preceding the Civil War. And fishermen flocked not west but east to make of the underwater grounds what they could. The Banks fleet out of Gloucester swelled to enormous proportions: counting only the larger schooners, 301 vessels sailed forth from the harbor, engaging the services of 3,568 men and boys. And the complexity of business multiplied, both on land and on board ship. There were now a dozen professional fishermen on board (four times as many as in Henry Saunders' day), each of whom carried out a specific set of functions.

The men on the powerful halibut schooners were considered staunchest of all. Dr. Goode wrote of them, "There is no branch of the fisheries which demands . . . more skill, endurance, and courage."

On the swift-flying mackerelers, a landed fish was first cut open by a "splitting keeler" then disembowled by a "gib keeler." On a codfishing schooner, the snagged fish was met by three processors: the "throater," the "gutter" who took out and saved the oil-rich liver, and the "splitter" who removed the bone. Yet the majority of the men were engaged in the prime business of catching—first from the deck, then (post-1850) from dories that tended trawl lines, or seine boats (post-1870).

The processes of catching and cleaning and icing-down went on all day, all night, and in all weathers as the hunt became more and more intense within the different fisheries. Now the fishermen had not two lines in each hand, for a total of four hooks, but four or five hundred hooks stretched out along the one-mile length of the trawl line. And the numbers of fish, iced or salted, rose geometrically as the on-shore capability to market them also expanded. The numbers for that pre-Civil War year of 1859 were: 60,000 barrels of mackerel, followed closely by 11.4 million pounds of codfish and 4.6 million pounds of halibut, plus other millions of pounds of haddock, hake, and other seasonal fish, not to speak of the shellfish or of by-products such as cod liver oil, glue, and isinglass.

Before the lamp is lit: As dories surge astern, a Gloucester fisherman baits his yards and yards of line above the schooner's transom. Mystic Seaport Museum.

With the competition so fierce and the need for packing in more ice and salt so urgent, builders were called upon to provide larger and swifter vessels. The original schooner design—the foresail smaller than the main, with the idea that when out on the fishing grounds the main could be stowed and the vessel pushed slowly along by the foresail alone—was a Gloucester creation, way back in 1713. Now designers sought to catch up for two generations of no progress. New sails of canvas and even of lighter, more tightly woven cotton came to the fore; jibs were set out on longer and longer bow sprits (called widow makers, with complete justification), and topsails were raised above the gaffs on higher and higher top-masts. "Fishermen's staysails" were devised, vast and overlapping sails that spanned the gap between the maintopsail and the foretopsail.

Yet one critical item changed not at all: the ballast, which had always been of stone, loaded into bins not much below the water line, continued to work as a negative force when the schooner was knocked down. By this common practice, the self-righting capabilities of the vessel "were reduced to a minimum," in the words of Raymond McFarland.

And, as might be expected, the loss of life under these combined conditions was scandalously high. In the twenty-five years from 1866 to 1890, according to Joseph E. Garland, 382 schooners set sail from Gloucester and never returned, with a total of 2,454 men drowned at sea. *Century* magazine, in a tone more sentimental than activist, reported that in the ten years preceding 1886, "over a thousand Gloucester fishermen have laid down their bones on the drifting sands of the fishing banks."

It would be pleasant to say that this appalling loss of life (and recognition of the old schooners' imperfections) sparked the reform in schooner design that occurred in the last two decades of the nineteenth century. But that's not the case, according to the late, great authority on American fishing vessels, Howard I. Chapelle of the Smithsonian Institution. In looking at the slow and conservative advancements from the "heeltappers" and "dogboddies" and "pinkies" to the splendid schooners that characterized Gloucester at the end of this period, he says that the need for larger ice compartments and greater fish storage capacity had far more to do with it than human safety. His final verdict, "the brutal facts [are] that the men lost cost the ship owner nothing, and insurance could take care of the loss of vessel property." Hence the leisurely pace of reform.

Yet advancement did occur (as it did *not* in the whalefishery), initially for the sake of speed-to-market alone. First came the "sharpshooters," most of them built at the highly productive yard of Andrew Story in Essex. The *Romp* (1847) was a typical example of this design, according to Chapelle, measuring 65' 3" × 19' 9" × 7' 1". She was said to have looked something like a Boston pilot boat of the period, yet seamen were reported to have been fearful of shipping on her because she was so "sharp" (severely angled at the bilges). Built simultaneously with these tall-rigged schooners were the famous "clippers," of handsome profile and shallow draft. Both types might have been even longer (and more dangerous) were it not for the limitations of Gloucester's wharves, where the slips were rarely more than seventy-five feet in length and ten feet in depth.

Increased rather than diminished by the success of these unstable, overrigged vessels, the death toll finally began to cause concern. The editor of the *Cape Ann Weekly Advertiser* and Captain Joseph W. Collins at the U.S. Commission of

Fish and Fisheries were but two responsible voices demanding that the industry take steps to modify the situation. With no response forthcoming, Captain Collins attempted to show the way out of the old, lethal pattern by designing a research vessel named the *Grampus* (also credited to builder D. J. Lawlor), launched in 1885. Deep and plumb-bowed, she had a shorter foremast than most fishing schooners of her size (eighty-eight feet in overall length), a double-head rig (forestaysail and jib rather than one, backbreaking jib on a jumbo boom), and iron-wire rigging—innovations that made her both safer and more seaworthy. These improvements were not lost on other designers . . . though the *Grampus*, a smack, was plagued by rigging and balance problems. Then, two years later, the notable schooner *Carrie E. Phillips* was launched from the Story yard, a creation of the distinguished yacht designer Edward Burgess of Boston. Like the *Grampus*, she had double headsails and wire rigging and lots of fish storage room below. But unlike the *Grampus*, she was well balanced, handy to sail, and successful as a fishing vessel. She became the prototype for many others in subsequent decades.

Most famous of these later schooners was the so-called *Fredonia* class, named after a beauty that Burgess designed in 1889. Extraordinarily yachty, with a double-curved bow decorated at the bowsprit with a complementary scroll, she became a model for many future New England pleasure and fishing boats, including the Friendship sloops. She herself, sadly, met an untimely end. Having served as a yacht for J. Malcolm Forbes, she was struck by a monster wave in December of 1896. As her twenty-three-man crew watched in horror, the sea raised the schooner's "great beam" two inches off the main deck. The water poured in and she rapidly filled, sinking swiftly, with two men lost; the others were picked up by a passing steamer.

And so the search for a commodious and swift yet humane schooner went on. Ultimately the problem was tackled by a designer named Thomas F. McManus, who, Chapelle relates, had grown up on the fish piers, talking with sailors about precisely how and why so many of those accidents at sea occurred. From them he learned that the all-too-frequent causes were the bowsprit, from which a man might easily be swept off, or the poorly maintained rigging, a vital line having broken under a man's weight. McManus became the enemy of bowsprits and other nautical equipment that threatened the fishermen, many of whom were scarcely spit-'n-polish sailors. His radical schooner *Helen B. Thomas* (1902) strove to cure some of those threats to life by both the unusual design of her hull and the careful detailing of her rigging.

She was nicknamed a knockabout because, as with the bowsprit-less racing sloops of that class, her hull was carried forward to receive the jibstay. At first

Glory of Gloucester: The Gertrude L. Thebaud, *built in 1930 with both fishing and racing in mind, takes aboard a foaming sea to leeward. Mystic Seaport Museum.*

the fishing community scoffed at this schooner without a bowsprit; then they saw how agile and swift-tacking she was, despite her 105-foot length. Although many builders continued to turn out bowsprit-wielding fishing vessels, the Knockabout was a design much flattered by emulation. Several of the grand racing schooners (that sportsmen helped evolve from the fishing vessels and that dominated the waters between Canada and the United States after 1900) like the *Gertrude L. Thebaud,* were either bowsprit-less or extremely modest in that department. Good design and seaman safety had teamed up, and Gloucester had been the scene.

Beauty at wharfside: *Known for her good looks,* Laverna *(a "knockabout" with a rounded bow) brought in a record catch worth $6,396 in 1918. Cape Ann Historical Association; Gordon W. Thomas Collection.*

Ready for launching: Grace L. Fears was a typical Gloucester halibutter with a heavy clipper bow; lost crewman Howard Blackburn won fame by his survival. Cape Ann Historical Association; Gordon W. Thomas Collection.

BY THE 1880s there were more than 350 schooners sailing out of Gloucester. The town hummed so loudly that someone coined the phrase, "Who *wouldn't* sell his farm and go fishing?" And the shipyards—including the big ten in Essex— were employing teams of specialists to construct schooners in a way that might possibly be called mass production. But it should be remembered that all of these large and carefully wrought vessels were made by hand, with simple tools, every inch of the way. The highly skilled borers, for example, earned a penny for each hole bored, for an average of five dollars a day—that's 500 holes. Into each hole,

to mate the beams, not bolts or rivets were driven in but hand-whittled, locust trunnels. There was not even a steam-powered band saw at Essex until 1884. Yet Garland recounts that in 1874 the Essex yards employed 150 men who succeeded in turning out twenty-two schooners of (slightly) varying designs plus a number of larger vessels.

It should not be imagined that these yards were elaborate affairs. As seen at the Burnham & Story operation, there were only two or three ways, a little shop in a single shed, plus an ox for hauling. The owner family's investment in the place was assessed at $4,000—less than the cost of one of the schooners. Few made much money: the men of lesser skills than the borers were paid two dollars a day for a ten-hour day, six days a week. In 1910 the men struck for an eight-hour day and got it. Pressed by such demands on his fragile economy, nearby shipyard owner Aaron Burnham went broke.

At about the same time, the average Gloucester fisherman was earning something like $175 a year. But Dr. Goode's researchings indicated that, if the fisherman went back out to sea in the winter (usually after haddock), he might earn twice that. It was still essentially the same method that had always obtained: 50 percent of the vessel's gross fare for her owners, 50 percent for the crew. But in Gloucester (which Morison considered less "democratic," meaning fair, than Provincetown) the following, lengthy list of charges was deducted from the crew's portion: so much for fresh water and firewood; so much for medicine; so much for certain "safety rigging"; and .05 percent for the Gloucester Fisherman's and Seaman's Widows and Orphans Aid Society Fund. Nobody begrudged that .05 percent.

That was the fisherman's life in terms of wages (though, in fact, some owner-agencies paid a combination of salaries and "lays"). But what of his living condition on board? At the Gloucester Fishermen's Museum—an institution that seems to be troubled by lack of continuing support from its big business funders—I saw a rather stark collection of clothes and gear. The means employed by the fishermen to protect themselves from spray and weather were quite the opposite of high tech: wool mittens were boiled and beaten, beaten and boiled until they were tougher than felt; then they were worn among the muck and oil of fishing until they were virtually impermeable. Similarly, long wool stockings (to be pulled up over the hips) were deliberately subjected to grime and oiling until they could warm the lower extremities like a wet suit. Jackets and hats were of oiled canvas (the "Cape Ann hats" being more like flat derbies than sou'westers). But with all this heavy duty protection, wrists and necks were still exposed and chafed, subject to the particularly painful boils that were the fishermen's own stigmata.

Yet no description of the seaman's rigorous life on a Gloucester schooner would be complete without mention of the saga of Howard Blackburn. Lost in the foggy emptiness of the ocean, Blackburn and his dory partner, Thomas Welsh, looked in vain for signs of their schooner, the *Grace L. Fears*. Night came on, a night of freezing rain, and by morning both men were, literally, freezing to death. They determined not to continue the hopeless wait for their mother ship but to pull for the coast of Newfoundland, though it was five rowing days away. Welsh soon succumbed, frozen at his thwart, and Blackburn deposited his body in the bottom of the dory. Recognizing that his own fingers and hands would also freeze, Blackburn deliberately positioned them around the oars; so, as they froze, they would remain locked in position for him to continue rowing. He made it to the coast and survived. But the heroic tale is made bitter by its ending. The *Grace L. Fears'* owners, figuring precisely how long Blackburn had and had not been with the vessel, minus several other charges, gave him $86 for his trouble. More happily, Blackburn lived to a ripe old age, profiting as a tavern owner from his fame, and sailed twice across the Atlantic in boats less than thirty feet in length. Without hands.

In those high-rolling days, when fortunes and reputations were made and lost at sea as if in a gambling saloon, the fishermen had no kind of labor organization, any more than the whalemen did. But on land, some workers sought to organize themselves. The Gloucester sailmakers undertook a three-week strike in 1899 and won three dollars a day from their bosses for a nine-hour day. But no one listened to the crazy rantings of Cape Ann's Finnish quarry workers who, according to Helen Carliss Babson's *History of the Fishing Industry in Gloucester*, were "pouring their splendid ideas of democracy into the forming of socialistic [American] societies." In 1915 they organized the Essex County Socialistic Convention in the New Hall of the Finnish Workingmen's Association. Gloucestermen labeled their meeting place "Red Hall" and stayed away.

Although the peak of those grand fishing times had been reached and passed about 1880, no one truly knew it. The fish were obviously declining—first the ever-spooky mackerel went, then the halibut became smaller and smaller to the point of near disappearance, and fishermen concentrated again on the faithful cod. Also new technological developments had revolutionized the business: the building of freezer plants, the advent of gasoline and diesel engines to power the schooners, and the arrival of draggers for the deep furrowing of the fishing grounds. To many observers it appeared merely that, with all these changes, Gloucester was merrily sailing off on a new, more efficient tack. But to others, who rued the passing of the magnificent sailing vessels and feared the effects of mechanization on both man and fish, it appeared that no skipper who knew what he was doing now stood at the helm.

LEFT. *Tarps on the flakes: Before the start of a working day, cloths still cover fish-drying racks at Gorton-Pew's Reed & Gamage wharves, East Gloucester. Cape Ann Historical Association; Eben Parsons Collection.*

BELOW. *Splitting and salting: Workers process the catch from the* Evelyn M. Thompson; *at left, a fisherman unloads another basket of cod for the waiting pitchfork. Cape Ann Historical Association; Eben Parsons Collection.*

THE face of the town began to change. But still schoolboys were hired to put the codfish out on the flakes and to arrange the shading tarpaulins over them. A genius named George Smith invented a way of skinning and boning the cod; Gorton-Pew packed the salted, boneless fish in attractive wooden boxes and merchandized them successfully through advertisements across the country (one pound for fifteen cents). People still wanted to believe that, despite the packaging, this was real fish, not just processed stuff. So Gorton's assured them that it was truly cod as in days of yore, "Indeed some of the directors [of our company] have actually served aboard fishing vessels in earlier days." Well into the 1920s the company continued to own and operate a fleet of schooners; but by the 1930s all but the *Thomas Gorton* had been sold off. Why stay in?

Annabelle Firth, in her reminiscences entitled *Rewinding the Skein*, let us know what it was like then for a young Gloucester girl on a summer's day:

> Going up to the Square to get some groceries, a newspaper or a spool of thread from my house, I would pass Fletcher Wonson's Fish Plant. . . . Walking by Reed and Gamage's we saw spread out on flakes, row after row of them, cod and pollock being salted and dried. . . . It was interesting to watch Mr. Elwell tarring the seines and nets at his loft next to the Reed plant. The smell of tar was so good, and often we reached up to the top of the building and got a piece to chew. I don't suppose this was very sanitary but we didn't think a whole lot about germs then. It was the same with the ice truck. We would run after that and take some of the small pieces that had been chipped from the block. To suck these chips on a hot Sunday was so refreshing.

There was a slight odor of decadence in the air (which made the tar taste all the sweeter, perhaps)—those powerful, Old Gloucester names painted on the sides of the buildings Annabelle passed had been there forever. Yankee power, epitomized by the "Big Four" (the major seafood companies and suppliers), controlled politics and trade equally. Whenever you went to the store, they'd always let you trade," one old-timer remembered. "You'd hand the man your slip of paper and it would be honored because they knew your father did good work."

That was only slightly less true if you happened to be Portuguese. By then the Yankees regarded their sometime shipmates with tolerance verging on re-spect. One said: "Rarely is a Portuguese seen in police court. . . . They are law-abiding people. None will strive harder to better their condition." They paid their taxes. But the same respect was not accorded to the Italians. Whereas the names of Portuguese schooners and skippers were to be found up and down the news-papers' lists of arrivals, only way down at the bottom of the listing would there be mention of this or that "Italian boat," without skipper's name.

In the terminology of the townspeople, they were simply "Guinea boats." Astonishingly early each morning, the thirty-foot, gas engine-powered, brightly painted craft went out; back they came with fresh fish for sale at day's end (with no clues having been given to their skippers by Yankees or Portuguese about the fishes' favorite schooling places). Why give 'em a break? Furthermore, these ghetto-inclined people had opted to move into the "Fort," the tenements down at the hook of the harbor built years before by the George Tarr Company for the Irish (who had long since moved up and out). Inquiries revealed that these new immigrant fisher families were from two quite different, even opposed, ports on the island of Sicily. Never mind: they were all "Italian."

The women of Gloucester perceived the ethnic situation in much the same light as the men. Whereas Helen Carliss Babson had written of the Portuguese people's "love of adventure, fearlessness in danger, propensity to take a chance, and their keen ability as bargainers," among the Italians she saw indolence. And whereas the Portuguese had "attractive, small houses, tidy yards," and households that were "well kept, simple, and unpretentious, she found squalor at the Fort.

> Untidy women sit on the doorstep or lean out of the windows, while a brood of nearly naked, dirty children play in the streets. . . . No attempt [is made] to become part of the larger community. [The men are known for] clubbing together to purchase small, clumsy sloops generally equipped with gas engines.

On the other hand, Mrs. Babson did spot a certain pertinacity.

> The whole family turn to, to prepare the boat and tackle for the next day's trip. The women, their babies in their laps, untangle the trawl lines, the small children coil them in the tubs with the hooks in careful order around the edge, while the men scrub down the boat and make the necessary repairs on sail or gear.

It seems gratuitous to remark, today, that both the Portuguese and the Italians had creative strengths and virtues; that both made contributions to Gloucester's economy and society as the tacks were changed. But the difference in those contributions is important to understand, not only for the sake of history but for today and tomorrow. The Portuguese gave Gloucester some of its finest moments both in the closed era of sail and as men and women took up new opportunities in the broader society of this century. The Italians, wedded to the family and to the sea, chose to stay and fight for their life on the waterfront.

Perhaps it helped the Portuguese in the public eye that they produced a recognizable local hero: Joseph P. Mesquita, fondly called Smoky Joe. Working his way up through the Yankee fleet along with his fellows, he acquired a share here and a share there. Finally, in the 1880s, at the height of Gloucester's fishing days, he was able to purchase his own schooner, the *Mary P. Mesquita*. But one grim night on George's she was cut through by the New York-bound liner *Saxonia*—death by liner being a dread but not uncommon fate on the Banks. Rescued, Joe Mesquita went on to build another schooner which became one of the fleet's "highliners" before World War I.

Later, fishing on the Banks in 1917, he was hailed by a British trawler. She came closer and only then revealed herself as under the command of Germans who had captured her from an Atlantic-roving U-boat. Despite all pleas, the Germans sank Joe Mesquita's schooner as an act of war.

Frances P. Mesquita:
Queen of Gloucester's
Portuguese fleet, this swift
schooner (shown racing, with
full sail) was sunk by a U-
boat in 1918. Mystic Seaport
Museum.

But, for all such adventures, Captain Mesquita is best remembered in Gloucester for his fulfillment of a vow made when the sharp bows of that liner destroyed
his wooden hull and dropped him into the sea. Near drowning, he vowed that, if
saved, he would demonstrate his allegiance to God by renewing a devout custom
of his ancestors. He would "see to it that no fisherman or his family [would ever]
go hungry." Thus commenced one of the city's grand ceremonies: each year a
man from among the membership of the Portuguese-American Divino Espirito
Santo Club is selected by lot as the *"imperator,"* to symbolize the generous
benefactor.

Brass-banded through the streets and up the Hill in a procession of Silvas and

*Disasters at sea: The
schooner* Arthur James
*(shown dousing its fore
topsail) had a history of
collisions; the ship's cat was
once rescued from crosstrees
in fifty feet of water. Mystic
Seaport Museum.*

Pereiras and Souzas and Costas and attended by maidens in white, the *imperator* advances into the deep-sea-blue sanctuary of Our Lady of Good Voyage. From there, after the priests have placed a crown on his head at the climax of the religious observation, all participants progress to the church hall or to the club across the street for baskets of Portuguese food and wine. Particularly visible and irresistible among the mounded food (*linquinca*, "Holy Ghost soup," and spicy meats) are ring-shaped bread rolls known as *"rosquilhas,"* which hark back to the charitable predilections of a medieval Portuguese queen. Originally all of this (which takes place on the first Sunday of Pentecost) was managed within the Mesquitas' home on Prospect Street. But now it's been taken over by a variety of societies. They also see to the distribution of food to the poor.

This is not to say that the Italians, for their part, lack in public occasions. Far from it. In June, some six weeks after the grand event on "Portagee Hill," all people of Gloucester and many from beyond throng to celebrate the four-day Festival of St. Peter, which terminates in the highly publicized Blessing of the Fleet. On the given Friday night, eight selected fishermen solemnly carry the heavy statue of their patron saint along Main Street from the men-only St. Peter's Club to the fairground near the Fort, where the statue is enshrined amid band music, fireworks, and patriotic American speeches in Italian. On Saturday come the boat races and opportunities to eat, among the bunting and balloons and American and Italian flags, quantities of American junk food, and specially prepared Italian cuisine. Then on Sunday, after a thumping parade of religious floats, of young soldiers equipped for the American Revolution, and of high school baton-spinners, the gorgeously robed bishop appears down on the beach (where stands the ever-watchful, ever-indifferent bronze statue of Gloucester's fisherman). With as much grace as possible, the bishop boards the boat that carries him out and around for the blessing of all the dressed-up vessels with their more or less attentive crews. It's the kind of festival, however ancient and religious, which tends to include everyone today, both the devout and the beery. The distinct categorizations of history are blurred into the happy belief that all national strains can mix, and are brighter in the mixing.

Ethnic harmony, it must be said, has been rather evasive in Gloucester. The Italians' celebrations were ignored for some while, not recognized as something for the whole city to join, until the late 1930s. The Yankees of the Uplands, not above playing off one group against another as jobs became scarce during the Depression, reacted in Protestant shock to newspaper stories of the Italian youths ascending "Portagee Hill" to crash local dances. And to fight over the women. Stories too of how the wild Latin youths had wrecked the homes in which, traditionally, certain fisher families had held open house on St. Joseph's Day (mid-

March). Few attempts were made, and they all failed, to integrate the ethnic groups into a consolidated band of fishermen, strong enough to contend for rights against the owners.

AS GLOUCESTER tacked into the mid-twentieth century, the question was heard again: Whose hand was on the helm? Certainly it was not the Yankee establishment, whose rotting wharves and rusting facilities fell claim to the tides as the number of fishing vessels fell from 400 to little more than 100. Rum-running gave the economy a little shot in the arm (and had a certain influence on speedier marine engines) but could provide nothing constructive or long-lasting.

Not fully recognized, two profoundly affirmative forces were at work in the background. The first was the family system of the Italians. Analyzed by economists only recently, this "kinship" system allowed owner/skippers of the Italian fleet to employ or to lay off family members in a more flexible and protective pattern than anything the capitalists or unions could ever design. In lean times, the working-age males were rotated about the fleet, each having a chance to earn his worth. In richer times, money went into the purchase of more boats and the hiring of cousins at the fringe of the family circle. No one ever starved. Furthermore, all members of the family used their minds and talents to plan for more productive and rewarding lives. As one woman explained, "Always we wanted to buy a house of our own. But my husband says, 'First we get a boat. A boat will buy a house, but a house no buy a boat.'"

The second constructive force came from Michigan (of all places) about 1910. This was gill-netting, the complex but effective practice of arranging a large, floating net so that its lowest part sweeps the bottom and blocks a passageway through the sea where the fish are believed to run. At a time when venture

GILL NETTING

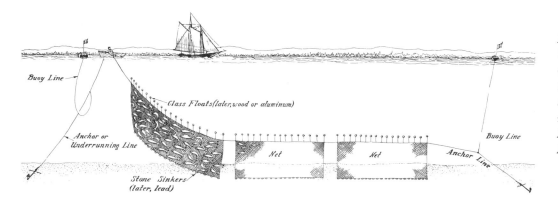

Beneath the surface: Gill-netting arrived on the Gloucester scene early in the twentieth century; current-borne fish are snared in a mesh of net. Mystic Seaport Museum; diagram John F. Leavitt.

capital was wanting and when great fishing vessels were too manpower-hungry and costly to be practical, this new method was in the right scale and the right place. For a few men in a moderate-sized boat, working within known, in-shore waters, it was a smart way to pick up some money directly from the fresh fish marketplace—particularly in the fall when the other fisheries were slack. The technique continues to offer advantages today (though the original Sea Island cotton nets, whose line had to be dried daily to prevent rot, have been replaced by nylon mesh); it offers the best opportunity for the young or the old or the otherwise underemployed to go fishing successfully and to be home the same night.

If any doubt remained about the demise of Yankee power—the mighty firms with their seemingly unalterable names having merged forces in 1906 for mutual protection—that hope was blasted in 1939, when the few fishermen still employed by them went on strike. They attempted to break, finally, the shackles of the fifty-fifty split that had for so long made them losers when catches were lean. One of the spokesmen at the Fishermen's Institute remembered the miserable times that had led up to the strike: "My dad would have been off four or five weeks halibuting and come back and get nothin'. Halibut was supposed to be ten cents a pound, but he never saw any of it; he'd go months and months without settlement. Finally he was forced to stop work entirely."

"But we got 'em finally, didn't we?" another old fisherman joined in. "Took six months, until the middle of August, you see. They finally gave us the sixty-forty lay that we'd been workin' for for so long. And d'you know what? Afterwards one of the owners came up to me—it was midnight when we settled—and he said, 'You woke us up; we've been sleepin' all these years.' " What the owners woke up to, it seems, was the fact that they had been cheating the men (and thus strangling the industry) for decades.

World War II made for a certain easing in ethnic relations; by the 1940s, Italian skippers were mentioned by name in the press. But by the 1950s, with foreign factory ships taking what fish there were by "vacuum cleaner," as New England journalists complained, the big business of fishing from Gloucester was no more. If anyone's hand was at the helm, it was that of the little man—who might have come from a Portuguese or Italian family or who might spend his time gill-netting (like Gus Foote, initiator of the City Hall memorial). It was time for the independent fisherman to take a turn at the helm.

"There's something about fishing that requires an independent skipper with an individual stake in the vessel," Julian Hatch told me, speaking from his big desk at Gorton-Pew. After his firm sold out and abandoned their in-charge approach to the Gloucester waterfront, they altered course in their policy of owning schooners and employing their crews. Henceforth they would own no vessels and engage no fishermen but would help talented individuals with good reputations acquire their own boats. Gorton-Pew would handle the packing and the shipping but would rely on the men to be their own masters. Did this then mean that the industry and the city really belonged to the individual fisherman?

ON A dark Saturday night of a recent September, someone up-ended a barrel of fish, particularly malodorous fish, on the lawn of Gloucester Mayor Dick Silva's house. This was the second such deposit: in June of 1985 an even larger load of gurry had been left on the mayor's front walk. A carefully typed note had come with it, pointing out that the disgusting mess was "an expression of non-appreciation for your attitude toward the fishing industry."

The irony in this was that Portuguese-descended Dick Silva could not be more of a Gloucesterman if he tried. "I was born and brought up here" he told *New England Monthly* magazine. "My family was in fishing." He was well aware of the fact that the fishing community despised the projected Gloucester Landing mall and that his Redevelopment Authority had approved the mall. Nonetheless, he believed that all aspects of this proposal should be considered. "There's no way I would give away waterfront property," he continued. "But look at the plight of the fishing industry—and it looks like it's going to get worse."

At issue here also was that the mayor's health board had closed down an obsolescent fishmeal plant called Gloucester Marine Protein, a rather grandiose moniker for a stinking facility. Its function had been to turn the large, local catch of the oily menhaden ("pogie") fish plus vast amounts of waste fish into pet chow and protein supplements. When the GMP was shut down because of its unconscionable stench (which, it must be said, the residents of East Gloucester had been able to live with for more than twenty-five years), three big pogie fishing boats and about a hundred fishermen were put out of business. And the city's fish-processing plants no longer had a legal and local place to ship their waste.

What connects the GMP to Gloucester Landing is mutual distaste: the need for a new plant, a dehydration plant, obviously runs counter to the real estate developers' desire to build a glitzy mall on the pristine waterfront. The two would hardly get along with each other. So the city braced for a major fight concerning the future of the waterfront—which is the same as saying the viability of the fishing industry.

Whereas the mayor of Gloucester believed that certain $300,000 condominiums and a glamorous, business-stimulating mall might be a safer bet for the waterfront than Gloucester's historic but diminishing fisheries, the Fishermen's Wives Association—to identify one important and vocal group—argued to the contrary. Most of the women in this dynamic and increasingly effective group are from the Italian community. "They tend to be vocal, vigorous, and devout," said the former head of the Association.

I talked with Lena Novello, who emphasized that there's no reason to give up fishing simply because it's termed imperiled. Mrs. Novello, having seen the ups and downs of the business for many years, has concluded, "God gave us fish for food. And he isn't going to take it away now." That's pretty much the way I feel about the world, nuclear-imperiled though it may be.

Mrs. Novello admits that, for a while, the situation looked grim. The diminished fish species and the increasing costs of vessels and on-board equipment were making it difficult for the individual fisherman to bring back a profitable catch and to keep his business afloat. That was the first matter that the fishermen's wives needed to address. They understood that their husbands were working as diligently as they could to make ends meet, with no time or energy left for taking charge of industrial policy-shifting at the local or national level. Therefore Mrs. Novello and the other association members determined to go and lobby in Boston, in Washington, anywhere. Perhaps there was nothing they could do to bring back the cod bounty that had been cut off a hundred years before. [But why not? Farmers, after all, get a subsidy to preserve their land.] And there was surely nothing the association could do to persuade the bottom-line, international corporations to put more muscle behind the fishermen's cause in marginal New England. But the wives could, possibly, strengthen the backbones of legislators who were debating how to turn back the foreign invaders.

The Gloucester women did indeed go to Capitol Hill, armed with indignation, eloquence, and the facts (some of the weapons that had put the Marblehead women into history's black books, but out of peonage, so many years before). The result of their adept lobbying, and that of many others, was the establishment of the 200-mile limit, by which our own waters were, at last, preserved for American fishermen. Surely this was the most important accomplishment on the First Frontier since our initial fisheries treaty engineered by the insistent John Adams after the Revolution. But unfortunately when the negotiators finished their work, the final borderline of 1974 banned New England vessels from the most valuable part of the Georges Bank fishing ground. Outraged (and knowing that a woman's work is never *done*), the fisherwives understood that they would have to assert leadership and common sense again. They had a definite role for the future.

"If we could only get some of those legislators to come out on the boats with us," muses Mrs. Novello. "Then they'd understand that there's a lot more involved—like insurance and apprentice-training—than just picking up off the bottom a product that doesn't cost anything." She's thinking about the eighty-five-foot dragger that she and her family own—will her son who operates it now be able to train his son into the business?

As for Gloucester's real estate wars, Mrs. Novello believes that here too the historic, common-sense position of the fisher families can be asserted successfully. She tried to make that point at a meeting she attended not long ago:

> They were talking about the smell of the [dehydration] plant, and how the waterfront, the new waterfront shouldn't smell. So I told them what it was like to walk along Main Street today: you go past a lumber place and that smells nice from the wood; you go past the gas station and that smells bad from the oil and exhaust; you go past St. Peter's Club and that smells funny from the liquor and cigars. But the point is, there are good and bad odors that are a part of life here. The only thing that doesn't smell is the bank—that's weird. Now, if we were talking about a real stink, that would be something else again.

When I walked back to the Wright brothers' fish pier, other boats had come in. It had been a pretty good day. So I expected David to agree when I asked him about the preservation of the waterfront for the fishermen. A two-year moratorium on new building had been imposed by the city to allow a cooling-off period in the big business grab for waterfront property. And it was contemplated that only commercial fishing enterprises would be allowed to build here in the future, should pending legislation be approved. That would mean no mall.

"That certainly sounds like the way to go," I said, having come to understand that this was an acceptable and feasible decision in some New England ports. "Don't you think so?"

This was David's father's building we were standing in. It would belong one day, presumably, to David and his brother. He looked thoughtful as he computed my question about the restriction of potential sale to just one type of buyer.

"What if the fishing business goes bad?" he asked. I had forgotten that I was dealing with the New England mind.

VIII

MAINE: CHILDREN OF THE SALTWATER FARMS

BETWEEN uninhabited islands and lurking ledges the ferry slalomed, lobster buoys bobbing in the wake. Then, in a rush of green waters, we took a hard turn a-port around Norton Point and faced a very special kind of civilization. The white narrow houses and sweepingly sheered boats swung to look at us as we entered Carver's Harbor, major port of Vinalhaven Island in the middle of Penobscot Bay. Black windows from beneath gables, secretive portholes gave us the eye as we foamed across toward the Steamer Pier.

We watched the leggy wharves and unpainted town (only one church tower) come closer and we counted the lobster boats—nearly fifty. Not a yacht club burgee nor a welcoming wharf-restaurant enlivened the scene with saucy colors. No crowds awaited the boat; this was definitely not Nantucket we'd steered into. Roger Duncan, author of the infallible *Cruising Guide to the New England Coast* writes of Vinalhaven that this is "one of the few places on the [Maine] coast . . . where fishing totally eclipses *tourism*."

Young men unloaded gear from trucks at the dark mouth of the Lobster Co-op, ignoring us as we trudged through dust and exhaust from the landing to the town. Farther along, carpenters banged away at the roof of the old fish factory, either raising it or razing it. The chalkboard at the pizza place had nothing much to offer that would tempt a traveler. Finally a wide-open-doored hardware store and an attractive stationery shop came into view at a bridge: downtown.

Two blocks of confused architectural history stood before us, shades pulled to varying levels. Because convention in Maine towns calls for houses to turn gable-end to the street, you might think the townscape would have looked sharply angled and lean-fronted. But no. Here, as in a Western town, horizontal store-fronts had been superimposed on gable-ends—merchandize advertised in no longer legible letters. Adding to the frontier town look, a couple of large, blockish buildings had shouldered their ways in between the original houses. "BARTON'S"

OPPOSITE. *Airview of Vinalhaven: At the entrance to the island community's busy harbor in 1893, an outbound fishing schooner meets the inbound mailboat. Vinalhaven Historical Society.*

was one of these big, three-storied Victorian citifications, its uppermost floor a fantasy of dormers and carved shingles in the mansard manner. How odd, I puzzled, that Vinalhaven doesn't look like a fishing community.

Farther along, an even bulkier and more elaborate hall dominated the next block, piercing the skyline with wrought iron embellishments. This Odd Fellows Hall, built at the height of what I later learned to be the granite quarry prosperity, is now the residence of artist Robert Indiana, famed for his LOVE poster. Gratifyingly, he emerged from the central portal, leading a chow which wore a large, plastic ruff around its neck—some kind of anti-tick device, I believe. Vinalhaven, Maine?

"Oh! Mr. Bourne?" The supermarket door opened and the friendly wife of the president of the historical society burst out. (The eyes of this small town had indeed seen us, it appeared.) Esther Heisler not only confirmed our plans for the next day at the society but drove us around in her little car, waving at acquaintances at every turn. Her patience with our questions was extraordinary.

Who would not be curious about this unlikely-looking town? A strange plaque in front of the library thanked a certain Martin Pring for discovering the island in 1603. Who in the world was he and why had he been so interested in this offshore location? A big house across the harbor was pointed out to me as the former residence of the man who had taken the fisheries here to tremendous heights simultaneously with the 1890s granite boom. But how could that be? The salt cod business in Maine was supposed to have died a sudden death with the end of the bounty (1866). And speaking of anomolies: right above the waterfront rose a jagged collection of modern townhouses; but these I learned were not the expectable, deplorable condominiums for outsiders, they were moderate-income housing for Vinalhaven's own population. Here we seemed to be looking at a series of contradictions deeper than the central paradox, that this place looked more like a suburb of Lodestone, Colorado, than like a fishing village. There's obviously a need to review the bidding.

Maine had grown up apart from the rest of New England, that I knew—its ragged sea islands and its fog-shrouded spruce headlands appealing to settlers quite different from the Roger Williams Baptists of Rhode Island's waterways or the proper Quakers of Massachusetts' sandspits. Settlers with different ambitions and different tools. Along the glacier-carved coast of Maine, in towns strung upon Route 1, vacationers today gaze at the distinctive and splendid houses built by merchants whose fortunes came from fish-shipping and shipbuilding. Historic restorations at Bath and Searsport confirm that Maine sea captains' wives decorated their parlors with silks from the Orient; their library shelves spoke foreign languages.

Far from being isolated, these Mainers on island and peninsula looked at matters globally. In Sara Orne Jewett's *Country of the Pointed Firs* a seaman remembers that

> in the good old days, a part o' the best men here knew a hundred ports and something of the way folks lived in them. They saw the world for themselves, and like's not their wives and children saw it with them. . . . They were some acquainted with foreign lands an' their laws . . . they got some sense o' proportion.

Maine's distinguished sense of proportion was precisely what I yearned to find as I set out along the coast, attempting to resolve Vinalhaven's contradictions.

But perhaps those fine proportions had been warped down along the line of history. Had periods of economic depression and cultural apartness reduced people in the fishing communities to mere hardscrabble endurance? Lobstering, to take a typical fishery, would not seem to open broader vistas for humankind. A hundred years ago, Dr. Goode reported with little respect on the undercapitalized, solo operations of Maine's proudly independent fishermen:

> They could aspire to no culture or respect. We refer to those men who are engaged in the shore fishery from little boats and who spend their lives in solitude, fishing among the ledges near their homes. These men are seldom brought into contact with the world, and acquire peculiar mental traits, and in the course of dozens of years of solitude develop a bearing and physignomy which mark them unmistakably as men of a peculiar class.

So here was a *sociological* contradiction. I added this one to those other confusions in my head as I laid it down on the pillow at Vinalhaven's Tidewater Motel (a contradiction in itself, since this lodging place seemed utterly disconnected from any highway). Confusions of architecture, of historic interpretation, of economic thrust. . . . I struggled to sort them out. The rushing out of the waters from the tidal pond above the town soothed my thoughts; the answers could surely be found. But still the worry wrankled of how to avoid the fake and clichéd interpretations that seem to booby-trap so many writers in Maine. Attempts to put the region's people down on paper too often end up as unreal as the sheriff with the Down East accent on *Murder, She Wrote*.

The worry was eased somewhat the next morning when my wife and I opened the curtain and looked out upon the harbor. A red-shirted, bearded fellow was sculling out to his red-painted boat. Neither sharp-chinned nor pointy-nosed was he; not one of Dr. Goode's "men of a peculiar class." Methodically he hoisted gear aboard, leisurely he checked the engine's cooling system, casually he dropped the mooring line overboard and powered south out the channel.

The fact that he had sculled—or "oared," as they say in these waters—impressed me. So salty and easygoing (but try it one day). In its own way this forward-facing stance is a symbol of the professional waterman, as opposed to the rest of us who row facing backward. This could also be a clue to how to avoid too-easy answers here.

A year or so earlier, I'd been talking with a neighbor of my daughter's at Gouldsboro on Maine's distant Schoodic Peninsula. Mark, whose grandfather had been a sea captain and whose father a lobsterman, was uncomfortable in responding to my nosy questions about his world. Breaking free, he referred to the matter of how a lobsterman rows (and thus looks at the world). Mark hitched up his pants and spat out: "Hell, I already know where I've been; I just want to know where I'm goin'!"

That's it, the clue. And it coincides with Maine's stately motto: *Dirigo* (translated herewith as, Hey, I'm steering the boat). These people whom I would be meeting along the coast would steer me, straight ahead, to their perception of Maine's unique world.

"WELCOME, Englishmen!" Samoset had called out to the Pilgrims. Astonished at being greeted in their own language, the settlers of 1620 soon learned where the Indian and his companion Squanto had picked up their English (as well as a few good-looking items of clothing): in Maine, among the fishermen.

That revealing bit of information stayed in the hungry Pilgrims' minds as Plymouth suffered through initial years of near-starvation and misery. It jibed with reports that many Englishmen had already established themselves at fishing stations on certain islands off the Maine coast—primarily Monhegan. Finally, when famine threatened the very existence of the Pilgrims' colony in the spring of 1622, Edward Winslow sailed east along the coast, embarked on a begging operation. At Monhegan he found that the rumors had been true: Here was a busy and productive fishing scene, some thirty vessels making ample fares and flaking the fish on shore, in the "dry" or English style. (The salt-poor English used this technique, but the French cured their fish "wet," by salt aboard their vessels.)

Winslow could not persuade the fishermen to sell him any of their food or supplies, but they willingly parted with enough extra fish to aid their Plymouth brethren. And so Maine saved England's first permanent colony in the New World.

Two of the earliest New England explorers—Samuel de Champlain and James Rosier—had noted the magnificent abundance of fish in the Gulf of Maine. They did not know the geobiological reasons for the teeming multitudes and varieties:

the fortunate circumstance that off the Gulf's mouth the Arctic current's waters circulate in a counterclockwise pattern, sweeping such species as the herring into the warmer-water shallows, where the fish spawn and multiply; the happy coincidence that the Gulf Stream introduces there such plankton-eating, warm-water fish as the menhaden to the oceanic ranges of the great Atlantic hunters. But the explorers did perceive that in Maine, even more than along the coasts of Canada, there was a meeting place of big fish that hunted and smaller fish that supplied.

Rosier, after bringing in a particularly encouraging catch of large fish, observed that "a few good fishers" were needed to reap this splendid harvest. The men would "make a more profitable return from hence than from Newfoundland; the fish being so much greater, better fed, and abundant with train [livers, for oil]." Martin Pring, who had spotted tawny "beastes" on Vinalhaven and its neighboring, spruce-topped islets in Penobscot Bay and thus called them the "Fox Islands," reported to his merchant-backers in Bristol, England, that these waters would richly yield what they valued above all: fish. Thus did this rather obscure explorer help determine Vinalhaven's destiny.

The English expected much from Maine (named for a French province owned by Henrietta, bride of the new king, regicide-prone Charles I). But along with the riches that would be pulled from Maine's waters there went a concomitant: this would never be a soft or a princely way of life. Although John Smith had remarked of New England's fish wealth that it would be greater than the gold of Spain's colonies, the usually game explorer was put off by the harshness of the Penobscot territory. "It is a country rather to affright than delight one," he wrote. "And how to describe a more plain spectacle of desolation or more barren, I know not."

The thousands of islands wrapped in varieties of fog, the apartness from the civilization of the "Meyne," as Smith called the mainland—these natural qualities seemed to have an influence on the humans red and white who came here in pursuit of wealth from the sea. In 1610 Champlain noted that fierce Indians had established the pattern long ago of coming down from their mainland encampments to the islands for the summer months to hunt and to fish and to barter with the seventeenth-century Europeans: liquor and metal goods (plus firearms when they were available) were traded for fish and furs. On either side of Monhegan, fish merchants set up rough and ready outposts at Damariscove and Matinicus. These were no Renaissance-style investments in the concept of the New World; they represented business as usual, with rum for persuasion and flintlocks for backup.

As in other frontier communities, the men who chose to come and lead this crude life in Maine were themselves subject to exploitation. Sloops called walking taverns habitually visited these bachelor-populated posts, to the great disruption of business. On Richmond Island, off Portland's Cape Elizabeth, all fishing ceased for a week when the tavern sailed in. The high pay earned by the fishermen (eight or nine pounds a week) was blown away in "drunken revels." The newly arrived Puritans of the mainland watched this offshore debauchery with disgust and nonsurprise. Their courts duly heard the case brought by the owner of Damariscove, Jonathan Parker, who demanded compensation for his business loss in 1645, when a sailing tavern had left his men too drunk to go to sea. At the height of the season!

Gradually the islands took on a moderately civilized character. In 1673, Massachusetts having taken over the governance of Damariscove, a constable and military officer were named to bring Puritanical order to this fishermen's community. But in view of the people's recognized habits, and to keep a good business going, a license was granted for a liquor-dispensing "house of public entertainment."

Along with civilization came palisades against marauders and houses for families. A permanent fleet of seven vessels was formed, a year-round codfishery; word went out that there were good locations on Damariscove, "free for any person to fish," under established terms of island ownership. In those productive summers of the seventeenth century, many dropped anchor here in these relatively secure bases, the first real Mainers. But in 1676 King Philip's War spread along the coast, and soon the islands were ablaze with the continuing struggles against French and Indians. Boston absorbed boatloads of terrified refugees. Not until nearly ninety years later, after the Treaty of 1763, did settlers again seek out the islands and peninsulas of Maine—wondering if it were true that once there had been here a rich kingdom of the sea.

FROM well-populated Massachusetts towns and from ports in southern Maine, hopeful families caught the southwest winds in their sails and turned helms "down" east. They landed at once-again wild islands and harbors all the way from Penobscot Bay to the high-cliffed peninsulas beyond Champlain's Mount Desert. Today you can find a notable similarity between the names of early families in Jonesport, Maine (only a day's sail from the Canadian border), and those in Martha's Vineyard, Massachusetts—Looks, Plummers, and Nortons abound.

Jonesport had been known by a number of Indian-derived names until the next pivotal episode along this troubled coast, the Revolution. Then a local fish merchant named John Coffin Jones (descended from the Nantucket Coffins?) chose the cause of freedom and donated one of his vessels to the war. It sailed as one unit within the New England states' navies that attempted to storm into Penobscot Bay and deliver the key town of Castine (Indian name: Majabigwaduce) from its British captors. But the result of the naval assault was a military fiasco—whether because of incompetence or treason. Nonetheless, after victory at Yorktown, Mr. Jones sought and received compensation for his contributed ship, which had been destroyed: a grant of nearly 50,000 acres was ceded to him (including present-day Machias), and "Jonesport" became a focus for the fisheries at the eastern end of the state.

Recovering from the Revolution and the War of 1812, the immigrating Maine families could pursue the dream of the saltwater farm—a dream quite different from that of the seventeenth-century pioneers. One such farming household was led by William Gilley and his wife Hannah (originally from Newburyport, Massachusetts); their self-sufficient homestead was set up on Little Baker Island, out to sea from Mount Desert. The life story of their son John, as respectfully told by Harvard president Charles W. Eliot, gives an idea of the qualities engendered by this unique mode of existence.

The boy was the tenth and last child born to energetic father and teacher mother. His initial tasks on the island farm were to cultivate the seemingly endless rows of potatoes (yielding 200–300 bushels a season) and to cut and store the nutrient-rich hay for the cattle. But fishing also occupied his youthful years: lobsters could easily be picked up in the dark places between the rocks at low tide; fresh fish could be pulled out of the water by casting a line. The family preferred fresh mackerel to salted-down cod.

Though butter was the most cash-productive product from the Gilleys' farm, smoked herring was a steady source of revenue. (This business peaked on the Maine coast between 1845 and 1865.) John and the other children spent winters nailing together one-bushel boxes for the herring, which were to be processed in the dirt-floor smokehouse. During the summer, when the weather was exactly right, they would take the herring caught in their brush weir and impale each fish on a separate stick along the wall; then the fire of green wood could be lit and the smoking begun. When the fish were finally cured, dry and aromatic, they'd be packed tightly and sealed in the boxes; the children would then climb to the headland to hail one of the coastwise schooners that would take the homemade product to the markets of New York City.

The sea beckoned to John. And by his own industriousness (plus a cash boost from his father), he was able to buy a one-third share in the small schooner *Preference*. Paving stones from island shores for Boston wharves were the schooner's first cargo, but dried fish followed close behind. Two vessels later, John was part owner of a thirty-five-ton fishing vessel, off to the Banks for cod and haddock.

Throughout his life, through two marriages and the building of a farm and a smokehouse on his own island, John Gilley epitomized the fisherman-farmer of the Maine coast.

Evenings, John and his wife would read books aloud to their three daughters (one of whom went on to become a teacher). They planned the work of their abundant days to make maximum use of the materials at their command—there was simply no need to rely on others or to compromise themselves. Once disaster struck: John's greatest asset, his smokehouse, went up in flames and burned to the ground. And once fortune struck: summer people from Mount Desert took a shine to his island and he sold a part of it for a tidy sum. Finally the end came: when rowing back from the mainland one day, he and his partner were overturned by an errant wave; his aged fingers could not cling to the keel long enough. The sea claimed him; nor can it ever be trusted, for all its gifts.

For the formative half-century from about 1820 to 1860, John Gilley's was the preferred way of life along this geographically distinctive coast. Maine flourished not as a tight, organized society but as a series of only occasionally connected points. And to a degree all Mainers remain sons and daughters of those early saltwater farms, cherishing the simplicity and the integrity and of course the independence.

DURING this pre-Civil War era, the small Maine schooners, many of them pinkies, regularly went out to the Banks off Newfoundland at the end of March, just as the land began to show green. The eighteen men of the crew stayed off shore fishing till mid-June, when they returned to plant the season's crops. In the ages-old pattern of hand-liners, the men fished from set positions, those amidships ranked as best. And at the fishing day's end (three-thirty or four o'clock), the dressing and salting of the catch began.

Skipper and crew all fished on shares; only the cook was paid a wage. On Maine boats the system worked "at the fifths": that is, the owners, who had supplied the vessel and a fifth of the salt and the other supplies, took one fifth of the sales price received; the crew, who supplied four-fifths of the provisions, divided their four-fifths income according to who had caught the most fish. The food they ate aboard ship—fish and potatoes, salt pork and Indian cornmeal— was reported to be not bad; a special treat was "scourer," cornmeal mush with pork fat and scraps, topped by daubs of molasses. For those who cared to make a second voyage, leaving the planted crops to the attention of their families, it was a six weeks' passage out to the Banquereau and a stay of six weeks before returning in September with the last harvest of the sea. Fishermen-turned-farmers would then take in the last harvest of the land.

Pinkies closely observed: ABOVE. *The foremast of the smaller pinky is set almost in the eyes of the vessel;* RIGHT, *the wheel is solidly braced before the stern overhang. Maine State Archives, Davis Loring; detail Mystic Seaport Museum.*

The fishermen were professionals, very much so, even though they had their dryland worlds to manage as well. Raymond McFarland in his comments on the U.S. fisheries sought to make a clear distinction between the organized, well-capitalized fishing operations in nineteenth-century Massachusetts and the independent, individualistic activities in Maine. Nonetheless, by 1860, Maine stood in second place among the nation's fishing states—a volume of more than $1 million annually—and it counted along its shores more fishing establishments than any other state. Of these not all were small operations like John Gilley's smoke-house; Portland hosted seventy-five Bankers and Vinalhaven and Southport had fifty or sixty, while Bucksport, Castine, and Lamoine also claimed sizable fleets. That near-primacy among the states was naturally to be expected, given the unquestioned wealth of Maine waters and Maine fishermen's ready access to the Banks. Yet the success speaks well for the zeal and dedication of Maine fishermen, who were called in contemporary accounts: "Baymen, Labradormen, and Bankers." Not to be found among them were those pathetic, ineffective drudges of whom Dr. Goode wrote.

To test this delicate matter with greater accuracy, however, it would surely be well to look at one of the centers where fisheries thrived at that time in a peculiarly Maine way. Not far from Vinalhaven, out at the end of a peninsula that terminates in a headland visible up and down the length of Penobscot Bay, stands Castine, once the citadel of French, then British power in eastern waters. In this midcoast area of Maine, Castine became the dominant town among the fisheries by the middle of the nineteenth century.

It was the wealthiest town per capita in Maine—and, indeed, the second richest, after New Bedford, in New England—combining the quaint charm of an ancient port with the new bustle of an industrial center. That dominance occurred not only because of Castine's magnificent deep-water harbor, capable of holding an infinitude of Bankers, but also because of its control of the one ingredient central to the cured fish business, salt. Dr. Goode's researchings informed him that it was about 1825 when a Castine merchant, recognizing the importance of that commodity, seriously "turned his attention to it, and began the importation of salt from Liverpool and Cadiz."

Thus it was to Castine that the Bankers from all regional ports came to be manned, rigged, fitted out and filled up with salt before their April departures. As portrayed by W. H. Rowe's *Maritime History of Maine*:

Sometimes as many as 500 fishermen assembled in the capacious harbor in the spring waiting to take in salt and other supplies for the four-month voyage to the Grand Banks or the Bay of Chaleur. During the summer would come the salt fleet from

Cadiz or Liverpool, Castine ships with great cargoes of coarse salt, to be stored in the staunch salt houses and sold by the ton to the fishermen coming from all quarters. Of this trade the town had almost a monopoly. In the fall the fishing fleet would return with the harvest of the sea and dispose of their cargoes. Again in January [the fishermen] returned to collect the bounty with which the United States encouraged them in their labors.

As county seat or "shire town," as shipbuilding center (more than a dozen yards), as legal-financial headquarters for the area, and as port of entry for incoming ships from overseas, Castine was obviously more than a humble fishing town. But fishing—smelly and disreputable fishing—was at the heart of Castine, however much denied that may be today by the appearance of its constantly mowed lawns, immaculate houses, and Cinzano-umbrella'd waterfront.

When you drive down the peninsula into the town, with the Penobscot River on one side and the Bagaduce on the other—a route I have followed for almost every summer of the last thirty-five years—a sign greets you with the straight-

Low tide, Castine: A captain's house up among the elm trees (at right) looks down over the community to shacks, a shed, and fishing sloops. Maine State Archives; photo George French.

faced claim that Castine was *established* in 1613. That's only off by a century or so, for the first permanent settlers arrived here about 1760, emigrants from the Puritan Commonwealth in the traditional Maine coastal pattern. But one must admit that the hackmatack trees do hum here with wondrously ancient tunes, that the soil does yield occasional Indian hatchets and European flintlocks, and that the historic signs around town do tell great tales.

Focus of imperialistic struggles between the French, the Dutch, and the Plymouth-based Englishmen, Castine enjoyed a Shangrila-time in the years between 1667 and 1693, when it was the personal fiefdom of "a wanderer from the shores of France," Baron Jean Vincent de St. Castin. Henry Wadsworth Longfellow was one poet unable to resist the romance of the baron's tale. But what poets and publicists for local lodgements continue to leave out of the story is *fish*. It's all very well that the baron's courtship of the reigning Indian chief's daughter was colorful and fruitful, but it's a bit more to the point that the baron was a successful investor in the fisheries at Matinicus and other nearby islands. Castine would not be left out of that business in the first century of settlement or in the next. The product that brought wealth to the English Colonials who followed along after the French was, undeniably and unsurprisingly, salt cod.

John Perkins, who had moved with his family to Castine among these first homesteading Colonials, stands forth in records of the period and in his boardwood portrait as the typical, prosperous farmer/fish-shipper of the late eighteenth century. He built larger and larger vessels for Castine's basic industry, retaining ownership of several. One of these was named the *Eight Sisters*; for as well as son Robert (my wife's great-great grandfather), there were that many daughters who survived infancy. They had a tendency to marry captains of their father's ships, ships which sailed farther and farther to sea in order to trade and capitalize on the products of the Bay and the land. (The oldest daughter, however, married a British officer at the time when strategic Castine was occupied by King George's forces; she was all of sixteen.)

Captain Richard Rider, one of the Castine fishing skippers who served under Robert Perkins' management, wrote a revealing letter to his employer. The letter spent a good deal of its life as one of those wrapped-away items in my mother-in-law's bottom drawer.

> . . . going in Newfun Land. Take this time to inform you of my misfortune on the 2 day of July the wether bein thick . . . the wind bloen a fresh brease . . . at 5 a clok am the chain plat parted & the mast brok. . . . Ebenezer Rider was Nokt overboard by the main bome & ketch by the Rigen we got him in in about 30 minite & then went to work as quick as posebel to get up a gunl mast to save our Lives . . . the

wind howlen to the westerd . . . am very sorry for my Loss . . . the bills are aboute two hundred dollers.

So the first matter of concern to Castiners at sea was the welfare of a man (a relative), and the second was the welfare of the ship—quite different from the order of things in the more heavily capitalized industrial areas to the south. There was nothing soft about Castine life in this era, however; one still lived on the edge of the wilderness and at the whim of the sea. Losses were high, and expected. Bodies of victims not swept away by the wild wave were either consigned to the depths by surviving shipmates or brought home wrapped in tarred sailcloth. One skipper's deceased wife came home in a rum cask.

The shingled or clapboarded buildings that sprang up along Water Street and Front or Fore Street were plain and generally unpainted, heavily timbered and functional, whether residential or commercial. Many of them were sheds of the salt repository. The fisherman climbed a flight of steps along the outside of Castine's "brick block" in order to report his completed voyage to customs house officials. He obtained his load of salt for the new voyage by driving a freight wagon beneath the overhanging, back ell of the storehouse on Sea Street. (The exterior staircase may still be seen, as may the massive, natural timber knees of the overhanging structure—the latter between the allurements of two waterfront bar-restaurants.)

Though hard to imagine now, the concentrated bustle of this forgotten fishing community is well described in Ellenore Doudiet's splendidly illustrated volume, *Majabigwuduce*: "there were in Castine a rope and line factory, sailmakers, pump and block makers, expert riggers, blacksmiths who forged chains, anchors and iron work for hulls and rigging, numerous shipyards, wharves, warehouses and salt storage buildings."

Noah Brooks, the local housepainter who went on to become a journalist and one of Abraham Lincoln's secretaries, was fascinated by another aspect of the town. He referred in many of his *Tales of the Maine Coast* to

> that part of the shore which lies between Jarvis's and Perkins's wharfes, sweeping inward with a flattened curve a scant eighth of a mile. . . . [It] was and is known as Oakum Bay. There were the sailor boarding houses, there the cruising and fishing schooners of the port were beached for repairs.

And there, at Oakum Bay (so-called for the sweet-smelling tar that sealed the hemp caulking between the careened vessels' planks) were the grog shops and rum houses and brothels. They flourished, parasitically, in the oldest part of this ancient town.

As in New Bedford, the Yankee aristocracy began to turn its backs on this lower section, moving up to the quietude of Upper Main Street (nicknamed Quality Avenue), where the merchants and *arrivistes* would build pilastered mansions. But what they left behind, as well as the scruffy sections of Oakum Bay, were a number of remarkable, commodious, and straightforward houses—workaday masterpieces of the shipbuilder's art. Whereas most of Oakum Bay today has been prettified out of reality, with blue shutters and geraniums and Palladium-windowed lofts above two-car garages, the dignity of these ship captains' houses is so profound and the space so complete that they need no enhancement.

Castine is richly blessed (though not alone, of course) in its possession of a number of these "four-square" houses dating back to the time of the early Republic. Whenever along the eastern coast the trade in fish and other goods spawned a certain affluence and an occasion for pride, there you're apt to find two or three of these perfectly symmetrical, hip-roofed houses. Even Monhegan's rugged waterfront is graced with one of them. Architectural critics, flummoxed that anything so up-country could be so grand, often resort to adjectives like *sublime.*

In 1796 Captain Elisha Dyer built such a house for his twenty-one-year-old bride, Sally Perkins (Robert's sister). Restored to glowing good health by recent and present owners, it looks out from its high terrace above Castine's harbor as if with unceasing curiosity. Though such events as golf parties and Maine Maritime Academy football games may take place in other parts of town, for this house there seemes to be nothing so important as which ships in, which out.

If you start your tour in the attic of the Dyer house, you'll get an instant impression of its character. For here you'll notice first two enormous oak shafts, measuring only slightly less than a yard on each squared side, each of which holds up an end of the ridge pole. Slanting in toward the tips of these shafts, the beams from the four corners of the roof come hugely together. It's as if you were standing in the hull of a ship, looking up at the timbers angling out toward the bow and stern—but of course this hull is upside down, with its masts pointed down rather than up. You can readily imagine the shipwrights bending to their work in this nave-shaped space, fitting together the notches and corners of their carefully adzed tree limbs.

The "masts," as I conceive them, do indeed go straight down through the Dyer house, all the way to the foundation stones, and everything ties in to them. But what makes the image of an upside-down vessel all the more vivid is that here, in one of the house's four main-floor rooms (now used as a library), a very unusual picture has been carved into the panel of an interior shutter—a picture of an upside-down schooner. Why would a vessel with keel turned heavenward and all sails drawing at the bottom of the sea have been incised here? Either someone saw the same analogy that I did and scratched it into the wood as an architectural memento, or a British occupant of the house in the War of 1812 sketched the schooner (as legend has it) to suggest the proper position of all American frigates.

Two other structural features of the house are equally remarkable: the brick arches in the basement that hold up the weight of the house's eight fireplaces and the front and back stairways in the space at the center of the house. The two arches stand as lithe and graceful as Roman aqueducts (one of them more massive than the other because of the extra burden of the kitchen hearth) and are built with such finely detailed craftsmanship that one almost forgets they have the single task of bearing loads.

Front and back staircases meet each other, rather courteously, at a landing three-fourths of the way up from the first floor to the second. The climber-up from the front hall is given the opportunity at this landing of either taking a jog and continuing the rest of the way to the bedrooms at the back of the house or of turning around and rising to the bedrooms at the front. It's all as neatly worked out as in a ship's companionway.

Throughout the white pine-sheathed house the cabinet work also reminds you of cabins and staterooms. In the passageways between the corner rooms, cupboards or closets open at a finger's touch. Behind the panel beside the fireplace of the old kitchen, a miniature fireplace holds a copper basin in a special recess, ready for heating. And when the broad, paneled front door is swung open, filling the hall with morning light, one can hear the whole house echoing with sounds of bygone shipyards and fitters' lofts.

Resonance lingers, but the time for sea captains' houses on the waterfront was passing. Not far from the Dyer house, the Georgian-style "Whitney Castle" degenerated into nothing but a house of ill repute; a sailor had been rolled there and his companions had attacked the place in reprisal. Therefore, when Captain Moses Gay, Jr. (nephew of Sally Perkins), was at sea, he wrote to his brother requesting that his house be built far from the combat zone—up on Main Street.

Similarly, Main Street became the site of the newly fashionable, very conservative Trinitarian Church, its members having broken away from the original Congregational church (whose new pastor showed astonishingly liberal tendencies). It must be added that the next denomination on the Castine church scene, the Methodists, had suffered the indignity of seeing their first preacher ridden out of town on a rail. Today the Unitarian-Universalists occupy the original First Congregational Church on the Common, a glorious, towered structure whose nearly cubic interior recalls such Maine community-religious halls as Harpswell's Meeting House of 1757.

Away from Main Street and the Common, the commercial focus of the town remained where it had always been: the waterfront. The enormous hoist that raised hogsheads of salt and other goods to the warehouses' upper stories (which hoist is still visible in the cobwebbed attic above Castine's beauty parlor) continued to grind away against the day when another Banker sailed in needing outfitting; one writer reported that the fishing vessels came in so frequently and so thickly that you "could go from the upper to the lower wharf upon the decks of vessels." The waterfront expanded along all the harbor's shores. In 1830, the astute William H. Witherle, who "owned [many] fishing vessels and used to fit them out for a three-month trip to the Banks," had built an exceptionally large wharf across the harbor on Nautilus Island and had retained Benjamin Coombs to manage the storehouses and fish-drying processes. The Witherle team subsequently succeeded in sending ever greater volumes of salt cod overseas and in energizing the entire town toward the peak of its achievements.

Between 1830 and the Civil War (the "Silver Age" of U.S. fisheries), Castine prospered as both a place to work industriously and a place to live well—hardly the conventional idea of a small-bore, Down East community. Gloucester luminist Fitz-Hugh Lane painted the busy place at this time, his harborscapes accurately showing the sprawling sheds, the houses grand and humble, and the diversity of activities. The view from Front Street, Castine, at this point could not have been much better; one of the songs rendered at the Universalist Meetinghouse on a March evening in 1846 was "The Fisherman's Glee." A photograph possessed by the local Historical Society and entitled "Main Street from Sea Street, ca. 1850" shows the populace looking confidently toward the waterfront, expecting more riches to flow.

For Castiners of all ages and genders there were opportunities; from farmsteads and nearby villages workers came in for jobs in fishing-related industries. As a typical example of an associated industry, the famous Dresser Ropeworks—"mackerel and cod lines known around the world"—employed thirteen men and two women plus numerous boys. (This little factory was still puffing away in later years when the local fishing industry was no more.) Castine historian Dr. George Wheeler recalled of the ropeworks that "it was pleasant to stand just within the door and watch the lithe boys run with their hempen thread the length of the worn floor; a delight to sniff the clean balsamy tar and feel the little flecks of fibre settle with downy touch on the cheek."

It was the loss of the cod bounty in 1866 that pulled the bottom plank out from this many-layered industrial structure. They all collapsed one by one—the shipyards, the chandleries, even the livery stables. Perversely, a salmon weir out at the head of the peninsula began to yield big catches, upwards of 1,600 pounds of Maine's anciently most treasured fish annually; but eventually (1880) the Penobscot joined the list of rivers from which the salmon was banished by either mill dams or paper-making chemicals.

Sadly surveying Castine's empty wharves, and remembering as a historian the passing of two other times of glory in Maine, Dr. Wheeler attempted in 1875 to nail down the reasons for this collapse.

> The loss to navigation caused by the late Civil War—which is said to have taken from the town shipping to the value of one hundred thousand dollars—and the inability of our merchants—for lack of a near market—to compete successfully with the merchants of Cape Ann engaged in the fishing business, in consequence of which the pursuit of that business from this port has been entirely given up, have almost completed the commercial ruin of the place.

Though the lobster canneries and, later the sardine-canning plant would pump some new life into Castine's arteries at the turn of the century, the town was an invalid, a shadow of its former self. Summer people brought it back to a new kind of charming but artificial existence. In the elegiac words of Raymond McFarland: "The fisherman's hut [gave] place to the cottage of the summer visitor."

OTHER species of fish beyond the old cod kept offering opportunities for Maine communities to expand in the direction of the sea. The lowly menhaden—subject of more than thirty demeaning nicknames, of which "pogy" is Maine's favorite—played a brief role as local hero. For one generation in the depressed decades following the Civil War, menhaden seemed to constitute an in-shore fishery that would employ both men and women in the production of a nationally valued product.

This little "pogy" (but what a splendid real name it carries: *Brevoortia tyrannus*!) is basically a warm water fish, thus does not show up in the bays of Maine until June. Then, like summer folk with school kids, it disappears by Labor Day. When it swarms in from the ocean, it comes in schools of hundreds of thousands, compacted into dense disturbances. Looking down into the waters of a cove, you would see the brassy flash of myriads of scaly sides, the semblance of a coiling serpent.

The dollar-worth of the menhaden lies not in its meat but in its oil, and this is an astonishingly oil-productive fish. It is also virtually defenseless, easy fodder for successive waves of mackerel and bluefish.

When mature, the skittery, toothless pogy measures about a foot in length, about a third of that length devoted to the oversized head. When swarming and feeding, the snout of that head can be seen out of water, eagerly ingesting the microscopic plants, diatoms, and tiny crustaceans which are its exclusive food. Like the huge baleen whales to which it is related not at all, the pogy filters its slight food, passing the nutrient-rich waters through comb-structured gill rakers. In summer off the Maine coast, where the pogy finds up-rushing sources of the food it likes best, the fish grows with special vigor; it becomes unusually fat and heavy with oil. Industrial sources confirm that Maine pogies put out nearly twice as much oil as do their kind south of Cape Cod.

Already desirable before the Civil War as a source of fish oil for medicinal and industrial purposes (including curing leather), pogies became particularly esteemed during the war, when the need for oil to tan cavalry saddles became acute. By 1874, the production and sale of pogy oil nearly equaled the fish oil yield from all other sources, including whales, seals, and cod; in 1876 enough pogies were caught off the shores of Maine's Lincoln County alone to yield 2 million gallons for the eager market. The price simultaneously rose from $0.25 a gallon to $1.25. Owners of menhaden fleets and oil factories in Maine acquired fortunes and respectability.

For the average fisherman and his wife (if such exist), the era of the pogies was also heaven-sent. Within Blue Hill Bay—where once, according to fisherman Gooden Grant, "the water was so thick with pogies, it'd be black"—the fishery flourished as weirs and gill-nets corralled great catches. As early as 1850, a Blue Hill woman found an efficient way to press the oil from the fish. At the Blue Hill Historical Society today, a black iron pot greets visitors, typical of the steamers employed by local folk to process the fish; the residue could be sold to farmers for fertilizer. Later, as the industry matured, hydraulic presses were brought into play.

But suddenly it ended, in part because of "big steam vessels from Norfolk, Virginia" which (in the recollections of Gooden Grant) "cleaned out the Bay in three years." Certainly by 1878 menhaden were few north of Cape Cod. Optimists pegged 1889 as a "recovery year"—10 million pounds were taken from the Gulf of Maine. But in these waters the fishery (like how many others before and afterward?) had reached the point of overexploitation from which it would recover only sporadically.

However, if menhaden blessed Maine only briefly, herring have blessed it eternally. As herring elsewhere decline, you might even say that Maine's blessing is so complete as to be monopolistic. Atlantic herring, whose smaller members are most often consumed in the form of "sardines," are a pelagic fish swept upon Arctic currents into shallow Maine coves and estuaries to spawn in great numbers. The slim *Clupea harengus*, like its chubby cousin the menhaden, is a summertime visitor, feeding on plankton. But unlike the menhaden, herring feed slightly below the surface, revealing themselves to watchers on the surface by great, gray, gull-swept swirls at feeding time. Or by a weird and wondrous flare of phospherescence at night. In modern times, airplane spotters have been retained to radio in reports of where these gigantic concentrations are trending up or down a bay. Then it's a matter of swiftly getting the net in place, encircling the fish, and holding them until a herring carrier arrives.

The silvery herring have been a subject of wonder ever since the history of Maine began to be written. In 1670 the chronicler John Josselyn wrote that the

herrin [were] so numerous, they take of them all summer long. . . . They are driven into Black Point Harbor by the other great fish that prey upon them, so near the shore that they threw themselves (it being high water) upon dry land in such infinite numbers that we might have gone half-way-the-leg amongst them for near a quarter of a mile.

Thus did herring, appearing at the fishermen's doorsteps, become Maine's most sustaining and most vigorously pursued fishery—as food for man and as bait for lobster. Yet the mystery of catching herring (which will not take a hook) has always been: how to lure the easily spooked creatures into the net. And one dark night in Passamaquoddy Bay, legend has it, a marvelously illicit answer to that mystery was revealed. A fisherman, as the story goes, was rowing home one night across the bay and bringing with him a skillet of chips and coals to relight his cold stove; during the crossing, the chips took fire and blazed up, with

Postcard from Downeast: Boasting the coast's largest sardine factory in 1900, Eastport still pursues an industry abandoned by many Maine towns. Maine State Archives; postcard Ruth McInnes.

a strange stirring of the waters below. On landing, the fisherman found that a mass of herring had followed his light to the shore's very edge—he could scoop them up with his hands! So torches became the key to the easy collection of herring in great numbers along the frontier coast.

As described by Lorenzo Sabine in his official *Report on the Principal Fisheries of the American Seas* (1853), the sport as practiced at night in Maine's harbors and river mouths was both productive and exciting.

> Far in the offing the torches, no larger to the eye than a candle's flame, move and dance, approach and cross each other, and then vanish away; while nearer, and perhaps within a stone's throw of the position which he occupies, their red flare will reveal every act of the fisherman, as, time after time, the fish are bailed into the boat. On shipboard . . . when entering or leaving Passmaquoddy, these lights, seen in all directions, serve to relieve loneliness, and to excite imaginings.

The harvest was tremendous—indeed, excessive. The Quakers led by Manwarren Beal to settle along Mossabec Reach realized that torching was too much of a good thing. In 1800 these fishing-farming families petitioned to ban the "driving" of herring along the reach by torch; perpetrators were to be fined ten dollars for each barrel taken (half of the income would go to the town of Jonesport, the other half to the complainant). Manwarren Beal's reasoning ran as follows:

a. Mass destruction of the fish by torch-and-"mash" (mesh-net) destroyed the fingerlings as well as the mature fish;
b. if all the generations of herring were destroyed, the all-important codfish would no longer come in after them;
c. tearing off birchbark strips from the trees for torches was so destructive that soon all the islands along the reach would be bare.

His logic was sufficiently powerful to win the case.

Although torching was banned along the coast, the lesson had been learned that nighttime was when the mysterious herring could best be lured into a net. That, evidently, is the time when they gather in a tractable school, dispersing in daytime on their separate feeding quests. Thus it is at dusk that you will see today's herring fishermen setting out, waiting upon the nocturnal whim of their prey. In generations past, however, herring fishermen would set out to sea day or night, whenever the schools were running.

My favorite depiction of these fishermen at work, by the nineteenth-century American artist William E. Norton, is called "Herring Catch '68." Against a backdrop of the Isles of Shoals, three typical small craft are struggling against the seas while tall-masted fishing schooners strike off for the Banks in the distance. All three of these undecked craft, some thirty feet in length, resemble the sturdy, keeled "Hampton Boats"—originally from Hampton, New Hampshire—which were the standard, in-shore vessel for much of the New England coast. But instead of the usual spritsails (fore-and-aft sails raised and stretched out to their peaks by means of a diagonal staff, the sprit), these carry gaff-rigged sails. There were varieties upon varieties: farther east, one might have seen a single-masted version of the Hampton boat known as a Matinicus sloop; in other places (such as Casco Bay), the Hampton boats assumed a form more like a pinky.

In Norton's painting, men in the nearest boat are completing the set of their herring net—you can see the massing fish and the excited gulls. Beyond their boat's stern, two other fishermen strain to pull in a net with its encircled harvest; off their bow, men on the third craft are setting sail to pursue a school sighted in the distance, their net coiled (or "made") neatly abaft the mast. For all of them, it's tricky work in a sea not known for its forgivingess.

When George Burnham, Jr., of Portland upped the ante in the herring fishery by figuring out how to sell four-to-six-inch fish under the label *sardines* (1879),

"Herring Catch": Off the Isles of Shoals, three teams of fishermen wrestle with herring nets and sailing gear amid choppy seas. Peabody Museum of Salem; painting William E. Norton.

Maine communities like Castine were delighted to have new factories replace the failed lobster canneries. Other sardine manufacturers followed Burnham's lead; other uses for the "silver" scales were invented (cosmetics, jewelry). A new line of spoon-bowed, deep-hulled service schooners was built to carry loads of shimmering fish from weirs to factories. Toward the end of the era (1910), there were sixty-eight sardine factories along the Maine coast.

A contemporary account now in the files of the Penobscot Maritime Museum describes the impact of this sudden boom on the populace of a typical port: first the great brass bell was rung, indicating that a shipful of herring had arrived and that shift-workers were needed; then

> from almost every house in the village came women and young girls all dressed in large snowy-white apron and large white cap. All were headed for the plant. . . . As they filed in, [the owner] called them all by name. They took their places at their bins and soon the tiny fish were running in and the ladies began to deal swiftly with the supply. Looking at those who responded to the bell, we saw they were all ages from 16 to 90.

And although the number of sardine-packing plants in Maine has decreased radically (only three now function in the Penobscot Bay area), the piecework labor of the factory women remains very much the same. On invitation, I stopped in at the Stinson cannery in Prospect Harbor on Schoodic Point (Stinson being the largest processor now operating in the state). The summoned workers, wearing red kerchiefs rather than snowy caps, also wore special, fingertip-less gloves, seemingly made of gauze, to protect digits from sharp and fast-flying scissors. As the cans to be filled came remorselessly along the belt, the women snipped the ever-flowing herring into a number of just-right-sized pieces to fit into the can.

I was pulled away from watching the seated, aproned women—particularly from one rather frantic worker who jerked irregularly with her scissors and body, struggling to keep up, ever faster—by the words of president Cal Stinson. "We can keep these people employed quite steadily, not off and on as in the old days," he said. "That's because we're not localized in our supply of herring. When the fish aren't swarming around here, our boats bring in the catch from somewhere else—some years as much as 85 percent from Canadian fishermen."

Cal took me outside to look at the vacuum system that suctions herring up from the one hundred-foot carriers and launches them into the shoots that supply the worker stations. As we gazed down into the deep water, something shimmered, out beyond the seal that was gamboling and feeding at the mouth of the factory's discharge pipe. "What do you think those little shiners are?" I asked.

"Why—they're herring!" Cal answered, as if surprised to have them come knocking at his door. The wondrous bounties of the sea.

AS THE historic fisheries waxed and waned, Maine smallcraft continued to develop for the fulfillment of specific tasks. Dories, common by the late eighteenth century as the craft for in-shore hand-liners, were admired for their ruggedness and ease of building (you could slap one together in a day), if not for their sea kindliness. They were no treat to push through the waves; for that purpose Mainers preferred either peapods, so-called for their just-alike bow and stern, or Moosabec Reach boats, known for the greater stability of their generous bilges and full stern sections. For purely aesthetic reasons, I find the Reach rowing boats, with their heart-shaped transoms and their lap-straked hulls, ideal.

These local craft and their slightly larger, sailing sisters were pressed into service by lobstermen harbored all the way from Kennebunkport to Eastport.

Crowding Biddeford Pool: Above drying sails of coastal fishing craft rise the skyscraping spars of the Bankers. Mystic Seaport Museum.

To many observers those lobstermen, whatever their home port or preferred vessel, epitomize everything that's right and wrong with fishermen along this coast. They or their successors, one suspects, were the incorrigible characters Dr. Goode had in mind when he wrote that Down East fishermen showed a "lack of enterprise." He cluck-clucked that they put off going to sea just as long as possible, sitting out a blast of breeze or a thick o' fog in the comfortable lee of a fish shed, waiting with other laggards on the "liars' bench" until the last tale was ended. And commented on. Goode was distressed that, rather than organizing themselves into profitable industries, they "*subsisted* upon [such] products of the sea" as lobsters and clams plus their wives' garden vegetables.

I prefer to think of the lobstermen as existing on quite a different track from most Americans. They are the living representatives of the traditional fishermen whose sea-booted footprints I had been following through history for these months, following but never really meeting. They are the men of the sea whose cussedness and skill and inventiveness allow them to live independent of others' expectations. One of the few recent writers who has tried to hear the lobstermen speak of their lives in their language and without imposed judgments is Louise Dickinson Rich, who summered for years on the Schoodic Peninsula. Of the lobstermen she knew, she wrote

> [The sea] offers them nothing of warmth and comfort, of repose, of easy gain or future security. It demands everything a man has to give—his time, his thoughts, his whole strength, all his vigilance and skill. In return it promises only hardship, danger, even death, and a bare living; only these things and personal freedom of thought and action and a philosophical tranquility of spirit as undisturbed by the world's alarums as the depths of the sea are undisturbed by surface tempests.

Sometimes their tranquility can be misinterpreted, their mood considered "peculiar" (Dr. Goode's word).

Sometimes their industriousness can be misread, their caution questioned. But what a tremendous, dynamic industry they contributed to for many years, all constraints tossed to the winds! In the year 1880 alone, before the lobster canneries had been put out of business by their own efficiency—as well as by resource-protective legislation and by competition from the fresh-lobster market—9.5 million pounds of lobsters were gathered and processed and sealed into tins. It was then an all-consuming, mass-production business (though not one that might make a poor man rich): in the lobster-canning town of Jonesport, they were paying $1.25 per 100 pounds of lobster delivered; no sex or size differential mattered, just the thousands and thousands of pounds. This was a complete reversal from early times, when lobstering was not a business at all . . . in the

1700s lobsters were a common food for shoredwellers; in John Gilley's day, a family member could gaff 150 a morning if he wanted to, no sweat.

Suddenly lobstering was called upon to become an industrial giant. And it responded magnificently. Castine boomed with five lobster canneries, employing 190 men and women. To these plants, employed lobstermen brought more than *2 million* pounds in that year, 1880. The result of this tremendous output, the work of all those fishermen and tin-stuffers, was an annual take of only $52,000. And this dollar total was supposed to be the rationale for a business which, in fact, was right neither for the lobsters nor for the people who lived in the same sea-universe with them. By nature, it could not be borne; the industry swiftly faded, the buildings were abandoned. Lobstering again became the individual concern of independent fishermen. In Castine, the fifty lobstermen who had declined to work for the canneries, preferring to supply the fresh market, must have chuckled that they'd stayed on the smart side of the business.

For centuries there had been a taste for lobsters but little thought that their catching and selling as fresh produce might become a respectable fishery. There had always been something weird and unpredictable about these claw-wielding, multi-jointed beasts. Enthusiastic accounts by early travelers had pointed out the superiority of *Homarus americanus* to similar European crustaceans; the New World's species sometimes reached four feet in length. Here lobsters were so easy to pick up that (even when the selling of them became a coastwise operation in the 1840s) they were regarded as appropriate prey only for old men and small boys. Then, after the passing of the industrial spasm, lobsters again became a bit of a joke. In the youthful days of Gooden Grant on Isle au Haut (about 1890), the fishermen were wont to swap stories about their largest catches. Of his father's Gooden recalled,

> We was standing on the dock pressing pogies just before dusk. He saw something moving around in the eel grass. He went and garfed [gaffed] that lobster into his dory . . . it was 36 pounds! Tough eatin' . . . we used to cook [the big 'uns] in an old wash boiler . . . still had to break the claws off so they'd fit in the boiler.

Later Gooden told how he solved the matter of his own largest trophy, that weighed in at some twenty-three pounds: "On Congress Street in Portland you can see that lobster today . . . I sold it to [a restaurant owner] and it was stuffed. There's a plaque there sayin' who caught it."

But along with the laughter went serious contemplation of how to turn the somewhat whimsical fresh-lobster game into a regular, year-round business. Attempts to capture the lobsters more efficiently and to market them more effectively spurred the design of sturdier and better-adapted working vessels.

Encouraged by rising sales prices, lobstermen wanted to get out to pots that were placed competitively, in set territorial patterns of ownership, farther and farther off the ledges. Gooden recalled one of the most important changes: "The Friendship sloops were startin' to be built when I was about 15. They were funny lookin' when they first came out. But a lot of fun to sail."

They were indeed wonderful sailers, with broad decks that gave good working platforms for the lobstermen. Light enough to row through morning and evening calms (so the men would be home at night), the Friendships were heavy enough to stand up to the storms that blew as the lobstermen of summer became winter fishermen, out for hake or winter flounder. But in any season, these sloops of varying sizes, ballasted with beach rocks and equipped with cockpits that did not drain, were no playthings for inexperienced skippers. They had evolved, as

Working rig: Trimmed down for pleasure sailing, the Friendship Estrella *still shows the great lines and speed of Maine's classic fishing sloop. Mystic Seaport Museum.*

described in Roger Duncan's lovingly written *Friendship Sloops*, from the earlier and cruder Muscongus Bay sloops, but they remained working vessels.

Nonetheless, for working vessels they were unusually handsome: their clipper bow, hollow entrance, slimness (beam one-third of overall length), and sharply raked sternpost and transom reflected the latest schooner designs (1880). Builders produced the distinctive dark buff color of the decks (which contrasted pleasantly with the generally white hulls) by mixing locally mined ochre with oil from pogy or seal and then stirring in some skim milk. The very beauty of the Friendship sloops seems to have been a factor in their popularity, existing alongside their utility—a happy combination of form and function and hue.

When the fishermen nosed out of harbor in gray winter or early spring two or three generations ago, the Friendships might be glimpsed reaching off the spray-dashed islands beyond the mouths of Muscongus Bay's Medomak and Meduncook rivers, their rig severely shortened and dory or peapod astern. When at sea in Maine's hazily blue summer or sparklingly bright fall lobster season, they might be seen shooting up into the wind alongside a striped buoy, preparatory to hauling it, or roaring home with topsail and flying jib stretched taut by southwest winds.

Wilbur Morse of Friendship was the best-known builder of these adaptable vessels. His yard's output was extraordinary: between 400 and 500 sloops in the twenty years after 1900. The end came only when the one-cycle gasoline engine forced fishermen/lobstermen to become mechanics rather than sailors. Along with Wilbur Morse, a number of other builders had helped their saltwater farm neighbors obtain one of these sloops that everyone loved to sail. Typical of these other builders were members of the McLain family, who had been in the habit of producing a sloop each winter. In the spring (when the cod would have come into Muscongus Bay's waters to spawn) family members would launch the boat and fish with hand lines; then in the late summer and fall they'd go out lobstering and setting trawl lines before selling that boat and planning the next one.

Just as the lobster boat grew up as a response to the fishery's needs and the fisherman's ways—and because of a surging fresh market—so has the trap (called the pot by lobstermen south and west of Vinalhaven) evolved along with the industry. All shifts toward modernization have been taken in the face of the most stubborn conservatism, the first big step being the invention of lath pots with oak-bowed frames in Casco Bay about 1830. Eventually they were recognized as superior to the ancient, Cape Cod model.

The system of luring lobsters by bait into an initial section of a cage, then through woven "heads" into another section from which there's no escape, seems hopelessly low-tech and chancy. But the whole system of pot and warp works,

and it all can be handled by one man in his own boat, so why change it? Even today's rubber-coated metal traps (which *do* rust, my lobstermen friends tell me) follow the convention of a cage placed in a certain spot simply because a lobster once wandered there before.

Similarly, the distribution system has remained about where it was after the first buyer's smack cruised into Casco Bay's Cundy's Harbor in the 1840s, looking for fishermen who might be holding lobsters in reserve for city markets. By 1857, the smacks were including Swans Island and the harbors beyond in their tours, serving as middlemen between the lobstermen and the mainland. Although that general pattern has remained unaltered for more than a century, there have been such significant improvements as the "lobster pounds" (fenced-off coves which can hold a great number of lobsters against a more favorable swing in the mainland market price). And of course the New England states have all agreed on the 3¾₆″ minimum size regulation. Only Maine has, in addition, a maximum size regulation—a legal lobster's carapace cannot measure more than 5³⁄₁₆″—supposedly because these big breeders help repopulate the tribe. But generally the simple and singular tradition continues: one man and one boat, armed with a hundred or more traps, out after a fierce though smallish animal whose habits remain unknown.

Lobstermen believe, for example, that lobsters migrate first in shore then off shore as the year advances. It's a fascinating scenario. In May or June the lobsters swim into warmer, more protected waters to moult (they must shed their old shells in order to grow), as well as to mate and to lay eggs. Somehow a female communicates to a male of the right body size that she's ready to cooperate. Another form of communication exists to prevent all lobsters in a given group from shedding at once. Then, after all this warm-weather sociability—during which the recently shedded, "soft" lobsters cannot legally be caught, if only because their flesh then tends to be soft and untasty—lobstermen believe that the critters start moving off shore again. (They are most active at night.) So during August and September, the men in daytime pursuit will transfer their lines of pots, marked with their distinctively painted and numbered buoys, farther and farther off shore.

Scientists tell a different story. They claim that lobsters do not migrate seasonally, that the only reason for the richer harvests farther off shore later in the season is that the traps have caught all the in-shore lobsters. The scientists also seek to explain communication patterns in terms of hormones and enzymes. The researchers are not able to explain, however, how it happens that in the midst of a battle one of the cannibalistic creatures can "throw off" a claw, being empowered by nature to grow it back from the stump over the years. Nor do they

OPPOSITE. *Lobsterpots unlimited: On the shore of Gouldsboro* ABOVE *and the pier at Bailey Island* BELOW *fishermen have a choice of two standard trap designs, square or bowed. Both, Maine State Archives; photo George French.*

know how water temperature changes affect the productivity and survival of lobsters (an increasingly important issue) or what kind of territoriality exists among them, controlling where a particular animal may hide his own cache of scavanged food. As with the moon before man's great landing, lack of scientific knowledge has led to lots of anthropomorphic interpretation (viz. lobsters keep moving from a trap's first chamber to the second because they like to proceed from the "kitchen" to the "parlor.") and to highly individualistic explanations about why lobsters do what they do.

"Clannish" may be another word along with "independent" that applies to the lobsterman and his view of the world. Certainly the crucial issue of which lobsterman controls what territory around an island or off a point is determined by the traditions of his clan—and the next island better beware that its lobstermen do not intrude on the places preserved for the inhabitants of the first. Isle au Haut is but one special and fiercely protected preserve; its wars against raiding lobstermen from Stonington on Deer Isle are legendary. The lobstermen of Matinicus meet annually to put the dates on a closed season for their ledges and shallows in the name of local conservation; neither then nor at any other time would fishermen from elsewhere dare put down pots in those rich waters.

There's also the question of who is really *in* the island's lobstering clan—who's entitled to "the privilege," as it's called, of "haulin" at a spot along this coast. Lobsterman Mike Brown (who also writes a column for the *National Fisherman*) has discerned that the rights to certain territories and to joining the local clan are passed on strictly from father to son. By high school time, the lad has learned enough from working with his father and has saved enough to start operating on his own with a little outboard on his skiff's stern; his pots are tolerated along with his uncles' and those of his father's friends. Soon he's talking with the bank about a larger boat and more traps—he's in the business.

But anthropologist Jim Acheson from the University of Maine thinks that the "privilege" is not necessarily restricted to the father-son line.

> It's whom you know and trust when you're a teenager, and who goes fishing with you and your dad. Once you've gotten in with the harbor gang, you'll be tolerated even if you aren't related. The guys who will *never* make it drive cars with out-of-state plates, have other incomes because they're part-timers, and start off too big with too many traps.

Probably Jim Acheson is right. But nonrelated lobstermen who have tried to break into island groups have found their pot lines cut one morning; they have found no one to help them hoist the engine out of their boat. Scenes of harassment and worse occurred frequently after World War II, when servicemen were returning to waters dominated by men who had been on the scene for four years, and prospering. One needs to be careful.

Thus along with the individualism of the lobstermen goes a certain clannishness. But that's not getting in very close to these fishermen; they remain essentially beyond scientific-sociological entrapment. As practitioners of one of the few American businesses that has gone through industrialization and out the other side, they may indeed represent not only a traditional kind of *Americanus* but also a species of postindustrial man for others to contemplate as their model. By their closeness to the land and water, their freedom from modern society's artificial stresses, perhaps they have proposed another way of going into the future. I certainly respond to it positively. And that may be why my wife and I understood the family happiness when Esther Heisler in Vinalhaven reported that her daughter, a successful artist, had married a lobsterman.

BUT in Maine they tell you it's impossible to know anything about lobstermen without going to the "twin" communities of Jonesport and Beals Island. This is where lobstering may be observed in its rawest (meaning poorest) and most authentic form. Jonesport-Beals is also the source of the boats accepted by most lobstermen as the best in the business.

Years ago when I sailed Down East in a family yawl, we rounded Petit Manan, poked into Jonesport by passing inside Beals Island, and continued down the Moosabec Reach to Roque Island (the loveliest and most surprising stretch of beach this side of Oahu). It's a breathtakingly beautiful run but full of all the horrors—such as swirling back eddies and uncharted ledges—that every lobsterman learns to live with. It also has an oceanic wildness: you see the long-winged shearwaters cutting across the sky; you see in the chillingly clear waters the great red jellyfish (among whose lethal tentacles Rachel Carson says young cod and haddock find haven in storms); you see a kind of viscous fog that, independent of mainland weather, enwraps headlands and invades villages. This is Down East, a different (you might even say an exaggerated) Maine. One is reminded here of the remark attributed to essayist Elizabeth Hardwick that if in Massachusetts you succeed, it's because you've changed the environment; whereas if you succeed in Maine, you have simply survived along with nature.

The appearance of Jonesport had changed since my sail-through days. A bridge had been stretched over the passageway between Jonesport and Beals Island in such a way that no yawl with tall masts could now sail in from the west. This steel and concrete construction, I was told by our host Cliff Davis, had been hailed with much community enthusiasm when the engineers built it in the 1950s.

But soon relations between the two towns, never good, were made worse by nearness. "They ended up wanting to tear it down," Cliff said, shaking his head at the clannish antagonisms.

By the parsonage door where he greeted us were stacked cartons of food cans and supplies for the community's poor. Cliff is parson of the "Stick-Victorian" Sawyer Congregational Church, down at the end of Jonesport called Sawyer's Cove. There my wife and I found evidences of an 1880s shipbuilding era's prosperity: large houses in browns and yellows looked haughtily out at the harbor from their lofty towers; an American flag strained in the gathering wind at the top of its mast; somewhere nearby a church carrilon electronically played "My Faith Looks up to Thee."

In our walk we met youthful John Sawyer, who explained that from his perspective as a Jonesporter, in-shore lobstering was but a small part of the regional picture, past and future. There had been the shipbuilding in the last century, now there were the processing plants and the off-shore lobstering, and in the future there would be more intensive scalloping, aquaculture, and the raising of mussels

Jonesport. Me.

BELOW AND OPPOSITE. *Turn-of-the-century Jonesport: Three views of Sawyer's Cove show a part of town where fishing, canning, and summering came pleasantly together. Postcards courtesy John V. Sawyer II.*

on leased land. The government was definitely promising a new breakwater to help protect the town's growing fleet of diversified vessels.

This was not really the down and dirty Jonesport I had expected; what we'd just heard was up-and-coming, even visionary. But I was reminded now again of the resilience of these fishing communities, of their perpetual determination to find other ways of making the sea yield unto them. And I remembered the report of one Maine fisherman: "When I was a boy and a young man, no fisherman could make a livin' from just one kind o' fishin'." That's the way it would be forever on the waterfront; and the statements that we'd heard John Sawyer make were evidence that Jonesport, too, declined to be locked into one fishery.

Elsewhere in town, I got a good look into the past. Again, it was not the lean, crude Jonesport that I'd expected. Lawrence Norton, ninety-one, is descended through all four of his grandparents from original settler Manwarren Beal. He talked of fishing and showed me his garden. On the fishing front, there were tales of the bountiful yields of the old saltwater farms, with the fish in their season and the great numbers of migrating birds that could be shot and pickled. Maine's abundant way of life was there for the taking—if that was the husbandman's total way of life, him on the land and him on the sea. That point was gently and repeatedly made as Mr. Norton led me around his, or actually his late mother's, garden. The need for the man to stay with the land.

Poking a clump of sequestered pansies with his cane, Mr. Norton asked, "See these? They wintered over. Can you imagine?" The wind had by now turned to the kind of wind-rain you must lean against to stay a-foot. I was impressed with the pansies.

Mr. Norton pushed aside some of the surging wildflowers, the lupine and the English buttercups, and showed the young woman who worked with him where he wanted the dahlia bulbs and nasturtiums planted. "That's right, dear; along here in a curve like this." Then he showed me the forest of green at the corner of the barn that had been his mother's delphinium bed. "Last year I had some nine-footers. Can you imagine?"

Though Mr. Norton might be called an aristocrat by some, certainly by me, and though he has dwelled in and made contributions to History in southern parts of New England, there is still something of northeastern Maine in his speech. This comes forth as a classless gentleness, an empathy with nature and God's creatures that includes, of all things, you yourself. Now, as a shaft of sunlight briefly replaced the rain, I heard those sentiments in Mr. Norton's garden talk. Not long before I had been reading of such cadences in a haunting book by Castine's Katherine Butler Hathaway called *The Little Locksmith*. Listen as she hears her Maine neighbors speaking:

Their voices kept going up and down, up and down, indulgent, humorous, and persuasive, no matter what the subject of the conversation might be. The effect of this inflection is that even in the most casual remark the inhabitants of [the village] always seem to be insisting gently and homorously that they want to comfort you for everything and want to excuse you for all your faults.

By my conversation with Mr. Norton, I felt so excused. In scruffy Jonesport.

Later, pastor Cliff Davis granted us the kindness of a ride over to Beal's Island. On the way, he spoke most sympathetically of the plight of younger lobstermen today, the high school lads just starting out. " 'They'll never make it,' the oldsters say. 'There's all kinds tryin' to be fishermen, but they'll never make it.' The old guard's wrong, of course: somehow the youngsters sacrifice enough and work hard enough to come up with the $50,000–100,000 you need to get going. But it's incredibly tough, since you can't build your own boat any more, and you need all that new electronic equipment.

"Oh . . . see these five houses here? We've got a real problem: deaths from cancer in each house; radon gas from all the granite, I think. But the state won't investigate for some reason. That nice, new house over there? That was built by a fella's done well with gill-netting."

We were still on the Jonesport side of the bridge, and Cliff attempted to explain the difference between the two communities. "There are lobstermen on both sides, and lobster-buyers too. The co-op's over here, and that's the biggest of the three shippers. They do lots of quahoggin' and clammin' over there at Beals too; I guess you could say that's more of a fishing community. But of course they do the boat-building over there too." He scratched his head and smiled apologetically, then turned over the bridge. "The only thing I can really tell you is that they're separate."

Beals Island turned out to be a craggy, treeless world of mobile homes and fisher-made shacks. In rock-and-weed front yards we saw, as we had seen in other Maine communities, brightly painted wooden figures of donkey-with-cart, fat-Fanny-gardening, whirligigs and spotted butterflies. Flannel nightshirts and pantyhose streamed in the wind from the wash lines. The bay window of one little place right on the road and been knocked out so many times by the snow plow that they'd simply given up the battle and boarded it over. Another home-maker had found that a barge on the beach gave him a quite adequate shelter, particularly when fitted out with stove pipe and mail-order front door.

At nearly every corner there was a church of another denomination, many of them Adventist or Pentacostal by persuasion. Cliff explained that each one of Jonesport's five Protestant churches was duplicated here at Beals Island, plus several more that the Beals churchgoers claimed individually. As we drove up to the grade school, he pointed out a white trailer: "That's another, an Adventist breakaway. We all try to get together at Thanksgiving and Easter, a total of something like three hundred Christians; but not everyone will come—they consider some of the churches to be just sects."

Such a proliferation of denominations was beyond my understanding. Again, not what I'd expected on this no-nonsense coast. The diversity of religious outlook must, I speculated, have something to do with the individuality of the fishermen and with their seamen's sense of the imminent end of things. "That's a pretty good guess," Cliff nodded. "One of the lobstermen in my congregation told me that every time he goes out . . . he knows he may not come back in."

In subsequent reading, I found a lobsterman who had his own way of explaining how religion had hit him. Charlie York of Bailey Island had fished up and down the coast of Maine for some seventy-five years before his reminiscences were collected by Harold Clifford. In those memoirs, Charlie told of how the urge to repent struck him in his twenty-fourth year:

> As the service went on, it seemed as if every word was pointed straight at me. . . . I was convicted of my sins. When the altar call came, I went forrard and two of my friends done the same. I gave my heart to the Lord. When I returned and told Millie the good news, it was the most joyful homecomin' I've ever experienced. The next summer I was immersed at Garrison Cove Beach and joined the church.

Yet one cynical commentator noted that Christianity seems not far removed from alcoholism, child abuse, and even incest in some of Maine's impacted communities. He went on to remark that "liquor should be blamed for 85 percent of Maine's religious conversions." On the other side of that argument, an historian of the Adventist movement points out that these passionate outbursts of the religious spirit have much to do with reformers trying to "impose moral direction on social turmoil." A slightly apologetic spokesman for the Congregational church (New England's largest Protestant denomination) admits that breakaway groups indicate areas of service that the church is not fulfilling. "Cults are the unpaid bills of the church," he confesses.

This is important stuff on Maine's islands and peninsulas, and has been for generations. An 1872 article in *Harper's*, rather than finding that the fishermen of Mount Desert were roistering carousers (as in the seventeenth century) or devil-may-care dreamers (a view of fisherfolk held by many romanticists), reported,

The islanders were, in fact, of a decided seriousness. . . . The concerns of the meeting-houses, Seventh-Day Baptist, Close-Common Baptist, Communion Baptist, and Adventist, by preference, were among their strongest preoccupations. . . . Men on barrels in the store [could be seen] discussing the conditions of grace and the higher life, with the same animation as if it had been politics or the scandalous chronicles of a neighborhood.

Superstition also plays a role, to be sure. As we drove back toward the bridge with Cliff Davis, we spotted a small boatyard in which men were working on a typically racy Beals lobsterboat. Cliff regarded her as a good example of what he was talking about. To my eyes she seemed a magnificent exercise in close-spaced frames, producing sternward curves of grace and power; a working boat you might drive so fast as to *plane* in; an investment to be treated with more professional care than superstition.

"You'd think they'd trail her over to Sawyer's Cove where there's a good launching place, wouldn't you?" Cliff asked. "Well, they probably won't; they'll manhandle that hull right across the road here and bump her down over the rocks to the water. Damnedest thing: Bang, bang, bang! But their superstition is that when they've banged a boat around like that, and if she's still OK, then she'll leak less. They swear by it."

My last conversation on these shores, back in Jonesport, was with Larson Alley, a retired fisherman who gave me a pretty good idea of whether this life was worth the struggle. He personified that tranquility of which Louise Dickinson Rich had written. The house that Larson and his wife share was floated to its present location on a barge from a failed fishing community down the line. It now sits perched on a rock base, fresh-painted yellow, with sprightly artificial flowers in the windowboxes. Charles Pratt wrote of this local mode of decoration in *Here on the Island*.

Often there were little bouquets of plastic flowers amid the real grass, real leaves, and real flowers. This bothered me at first, but after a time spent among the pretty spectacular natural wonders of the Island, I began to think of these colorful little bits of fakery as evidence of *human* memory and concern, manmade outposts of resistance to the leveling of natural decay and to the impersonal strength of the sea, which is never far off.

Larson's father began life with not much more than a homemade, family boat kept on the beach; he'd go out with his three brothers and their father. The women in the family would contribute what they could by stripping herring for the smokehouse (herring being "the people's greatest food fish") or, later, working as sardine packers. Despite the lowness of the wage, Larson said, the women would never go out on strike. "There warn't much reason to strike, o' course; they'd just bring in some other body, see."

Soon Larson and his brothers started helping their father, finding a boat for themselves. "One year, after a whole year, my brother and I counted up what we'd got and, you know, 'twas only $18 between us. But we got by; we got by."

He did have his times of terror and misery at sea. "Once the sea was so high the owner of the bo't came down where I was below and jammed himself in forrard just as far as he could get in the bo't's eyes; that's the only way he wouldn't be thrown right out. You couldn't hold on, see."

"But Larson loved the water, you know," his wife told me. "His leg bothers him now, but he misses it out there."

"Bothers me awful to see the bo'ts go out sometimes," Larson admitted. What he said wasn't sad only; a kind of triumph could be felt.

LIKE Larson Alley's house in Jonesport, the Vinalhaven Historical Society's museum once voyaged across the waters. Back in 1838, the structure started life in Rockland as a simple little Greek revival Protestant church. Then in 1875, a time of social change when Vinalhaven went through one of its few religious disruptions, a breakaway faction from the Union church moved this transported structure to its present location, upon a hill on the other side of town. Within it Roy Heisler of the historical society showed me old photographs and well-displayed artifacts that told the story of this island town at the time of its greatest wealth.

If I had not been prepared by my recent Maine peregrinations, I might have been fooled by what was here displayed; I might have thought this was just like any other Victorian boomtown on the mainland—or in Colorado. I might not have recognized, beneath the mining town façades, the continuing reality of the fishing community.

It was a proud and yeasty community of some 3,000 families in the 1870s, boasting a 350-foot granite wharf and 50,000 square feet of processing plants for the fisheries. Since Edwin Lane and Thomas G. Libby had come on the scene, the salt cod industry had been turned around from its pre-Civil War days, when lack of salt had demanded dependence on Castine and lack of capital had negated competition with major mainland ports—and then the cutoff of the salt bounty had killed the whole thing. But Lane and Libby seemed to have made such solid connections with Gloucester and Boston that capital and commodities now flowed freely: huge, iron salt barks sailed in from Sicily; more than 20 million pounds of fish were shipped out each year in some form or other (including fish oil and hake sounds for isinglass).

But the even more spectacularly successful business was granite quarrying. Stones for a confident nation's new Romanesque halls and monuments were pickaxed out of the island's granite heart. During these splendid "Government Times," when Uncle Sam delighted in building such piles as the State, War, and Navy Department building next to the White House, immigrants' hammers rang to fulfill federal orders. Quarry owner R. R. Bodwell got himself elected governor.

The rich folks, of which there were enough to give the island tone, expressed their satisfaction by putting up filigreed castles and setting the bandstand out on the green for the people and planting the trees that kept down the noonday dust. The ladies joined such organizations as the Ocean Bound Rebekah Lodge; society swains and their long-dressed lasses looked forward to the next "Grand Soiree Musicale"; the gentlemen got together and marked out a sporty racetrack.

Yet apparently this was also a democrat's delight and a worker's paradise. Workmen flocked to the island. Whereas there had been only a thousand men a generation earlier, three quarters of whom were fishermen, now there were thrice that many, with less than half fishing. In the words of a local rhymster:

> The island blossomed like a rose.
> A kingdom out of the sea arose,
> Two thousand hammers daily rang,
> And shools and churches upward sprang.
> No snob sat on her social throne,
> Each man's success was all his own.
> And in our country's diadem,
> This isle was then the Granite Gem.

But of course it was not that way at all. The Lane and Libby fish operations were living on borrowed time and capital, borrowed from such operatives as Slade Gorton of Gloucester. As the century wound down, the Gloucester and Boston corporations, with their freezing facilities and command of the newly popular fresh-fish business and superior transportation to the rest of the country, merely tolerated their suppliers up and down the coast. And at the quarries, the primitivism of the technology—oxen and cart being only gradually replaced by steam and rail—saw to it that the industry would slide out of favor in the Age of Progress. Architects began to choose facile concrete over stubborn granite; the business degenerated to supplying granite paving blocks.

The quarry workers, under the lash to produce higher quality carved stone for a diminishing market, at less money and for longer hours, could only go on strike. In 1890 they won a ten-hour day, an eight-hour day in 1900 (when "Government Times" were long past); in 1892 there was a grim and successful lockout. Throughout all these years, the workers themselves had been "owned by the quarries"; most of their compensation came in the form of goods from the company-owned store. When the company chose not to (or could not) pay, the workers had no recourse.

The fishermen, no longer able to find berths on Bankers as Lane and Libby declined, returned to their own smaller vessels, pursuing inter alia the lobsters (which had become Maine's most income-productive fishery for the individual fisherman). As they returned to their in-shore fishing lives, they watched the destiny of the quarrymen work itself out—and were glad to be free of all that. And the exquarrymen looked seaward, noting that each fisherman worked as his own boss, or was paid for his share of the catch. Many of the quarrymen, particularly the Italians, got the idea and sought places for themselves in the fishing fleet. Workmen from Vinalhaven's other failing industries also decided to try their luck with hook and line. The big-deal industries having blown away, the town and its work became easier to see for what they were. In the words of Vinalhaven historian Sidney Winslow:

> Other enterprises have come and gone, and even the fishing industry has had its ups and downs. There have been intervals when the pursuit of this occupation has been a rather poor means of gaining a living, and the fisherfolk oft have been obliged to seek employment on shore during these dull times, but their hearts and hopes were elsewhere and they inevitably returned to their true love, the sea.

So the "Kingdom out of the Sea," the bustling industrial port, was revealed as unreal as silver-mine stock certificates. As the new century began, after the excitement of the canneries had passed, the most fun people seemed to have along the decaying waterfront was "rat shooting day," when the business of cleaning out the vermin from the old plants caught everyone's attention. But mostly the fishermen had learned that their real call was to seaward; shore-side entertainments came and went.

AS STATED a while back, I'm inclined to view the Maine lobsterman as on a different track from most Americans. Perhaps I'd even say that this individual, the representative survivor of the centuries-old New England fisherman, is more sophisticated than most of us, more solidly and pragmatically based on an agricultural system that will not let him down. And that will let him live in his own way (so long as he stays out of the collection agencies' hands). He will become a part of the consumer society but will not be consumed by it. His communities and his waterfront—when he, with the help of his wife—succeeds in controlling them, will not tart themselves up for the benefit of tourists; the yards will prosper with plastic flowers. In his heart he is the wise son of the saltwater farmer, self-sufficient and solitary.

He's learned not only to work with the seasons and to work in step with technological changes but also to keep himself, his mind and his body, flexible. One Maine lobsterman, quoted by Margaret Dewar in *Industry in Trouble*, explained his routine:

Lobsterboats waiting: At Cape Porpoise, the flat-bottomed skiffs in the foreground seem to urge owners to row out to boats at anchor, then to sea. Maine State Archives; photo George French.

You quit shrimping because the shrimp disappear, usually around the tenth of April. And then you've got your choice: you can either go dragging for fish, or you can go spring lobstering, which is a short season. Now, I could keep dragging all summer if I wanted to, but I prefer to go lobstering then, because there's more money in it, and besides after you've been dragging all winter, you kind of welcome a change.

Furthermore, the lobsterman is not just surviving but is laying new plans to stay on top of his business for the upcoming generations. Since the plague of overfishing was overcome in the 1970s by the application of measurement and other conservation principles, there's little doubt that the lobster, unlike the menhaden and other fish, will be here to stay: Maine landings remain at a fairly constant 22 million pounds annually. (This is speaking only of in-shore lobstering; the off-shore fishery in far larger boats operates under completely different limits and possibilities.) And, with some exceptions, the lobsterman is succeeding in retaining an increasing share of this traditionally middleman-heavy business. Greatest example of how that's working is the lobster cooperative. Like the one at Vinalhaven.

"To call the business their own" was the objective of the men who organized the Vinalhaven co-op back in 1974," I was told by Gerry Dowdy, the present manager. "It wasn't easy," he remembered. "There were guys who thought that only the buying companies could handle things . . . everything. But we made it work."

And in the Northeast Folklore Archives at Orono, I found a spokesman who recalled those days even more vividly—Vinalhaven's Edward Holmes:

In village after village [around Penobscot Bay] the fishermen were afraid to organize cooperatives because they were so deeply in debt to the lobster buyer. . . . [But] the lobster buyer is not necessarily a villain and thief. If you had access to his books, you'd find that he was deeply in debt to the jobber or wholesaler . . . the thing was a chain of command. The lobstermen at Vinalhaven were *not* afraid, however. They— it kind of tickled them to screw the buyers, I think.

The system now is that about fifty lobstermen belong to the co-op; they're all skippers of their own boats. Their best and easiest harvest come at the end of July and early August; then they move their pots farther out (sometimes four or five hours away from Vinalhaven harbor). The working year ends October 1, at which point the co-op's books are reviewed for the division of profits among members in January. Those profits come both from the co-op's herring-bait business (bushels are bought from local herring fishermen at seven dollars and sold to the lobsterman at nine dollars) and from the sale of members' catch to a variety of mainland buyers. "The more pounds you catch, the more dividends you get," Gerry explained.

I watched as herring fishermen unloaded the night's catch from their boat. Each week they and other harbor vessels bring in to the co-op's pier about 500 bushels ("Those are *Vinalhaven* bushels, packed to the top," one of the young men pointed out). Their entire catch is turned over to the purposes of the lobstermen.

Last year revenues at the co-op topped $1 million, on the rise from the year before. Looking at the need for expansion and more efficient operations, Gerry and the co-op board are getting ready to talk with contractors. The co-op backers and associated commercial fishing interests are the power on the waterfront.

Watching the success of the young men, Esther Heisler pondered what to do about the fact that at the other end of the harbor the old canning factory was being looked at as a possible site for a condominium. Did this mean that the waterfront, which for so many years had simply deteriorated, was now slated for upgrading? And that, as in so many other New England communities, the nature of that improvement would be determined not by the fishing community itself but by outside investors? But this time, rather than turning the waterfront and the town into an 1890s mining scene, they'd build it up as a 1990s rich folks' summer preserve. With the time-sharing provisions, you as owner, could swap your place in Vinalhaven for another owner's equally beautiful place in Hilton Head or in Miami.

That would not be the kind of community Roy and Esther Heisler had chosen to move to. Their choice had been to come here and open up a restaurant, "The Haven," that would serve the lobstermen and would help build up the waterfront on its own terms. They put out the restaurant's OPEN sign every morning at five o'clock, they serve the kind of muffins that flow over the sides of the pan. Robert Indiana admires what they've done enough to have designed a bright poster of circles and stars called "The Four Faces of Esther." The Heislers hung it on a wall, but liked even more what lobstermen have had to say about the quality of their coffee.

"No. I'm not going to let that happen," Esther decided, thinking of the canning factory being turned into a condominium. "This isn't any investor's waterfront; it's the lobsterman's." Then she put herself at risk to demonstrate her beliefs: she bought the old canning plant. It's now called, fondly, by her husband, "Esther's Folly."

So it looked as if the real Vinalhaven, the one that I'd struggled to see through the storefront façades and beyond the turn-of-the-century pictures, might become the Vinalhaven of the future. Here's a fishermen's community that has remembered its past—and has been saved by the memory.

Tattle Court, Nantucket: Along narrow paths between backyard gardens, the ancient "city in the sea" retains its charm for new generations. Nantucket Historical Association.

ACKNOWLEDGMENTS

This book, the author proudly confesses, is the creation of historical societies up and down the New England coast. Their devoted work in collecting the artifacts and recording the not-always-stirring tales of fisher life on sea and land has preserved the authentic qualities of this phase of American social history. The recognition of specific societies and personnel that follow, chapter by chapter, is hardly adequate expression of the author's indebtedness and gratitude.

I am furthermore indebted to the authors of certain seminal and basic resource volumes within this rather neglected field of maritime history. Among the works that I must acknowledge as having played significant roles as guides and data bases are the following:

Albion, Robert G., Baker, William A., and Labaree, Benjamin W. *New England and the Sea*. Mystic, Conn.: Mystic Seaport Museum, 1972.

Bigelow, Henry B., and Schroeder, William C. *Fishes of the Gulf of Maine*. Washington, D.C.: Government Printing Office, 1953.

Boorstin, Daniel J. *The National Experience*. New York: Vintage Books, 1965.

Chapelle, Howard I. *The American Fishing Schooners*. New York: Norton, 1973.

Goode, George Brown. *The Fisheries and Fishery Industries of the U.S.* 5 vols. Washington, D.C.: Government Printing Office, 1887.

Laing, Alexander. *Seafaring America*. New York: American Heritage, 1971.

McFarland, Raymond. *A History of the New England Fisheries*. New York: Appleton, 1911.

Miller, Perry. *The New England Mind, from Colony to Province*. Boston: Beacon Press, 1961.

Morison, Samuel Eliot. *The Oxford History of the American People*. New York: Oxford University Press, 1965.

———. *The Maritime History of Massachusetts*. Boston: Houghton-Mifflin, 1921.

O'Sullivan, Judith, and Gallick, Rosemary. *Workers and Allies*. Washington, D.C.: Smithsonian Institution Press, 1975.

Vickers, Daniel Frederick. *Maritime Labor in Colonial Massachusetts*. Ann Arbor: University Microfilms International, 1984.

Ziff, Larzer. *Puritanism in America*. New York: Viking, 1973.

CHAPTER ONE

Within the several fishing communities encompassed by this chapter, I would like to extend my thanks particularly to the following historical societies: Norwalk, New London, and Stonington, Connecticut; Little Compton, Rhode Island; Rockport, Massachusetts; Stonington and Deer Isle, Maine. John Hightower, director of the yet-a-building Maritime Center in South Norwalk, and his staff and board members were of special assistance in helping me understand how fishing (in this case oystering) can make a continuing contribution to the well-being of a reconstructed, historical waterfront.

Chase, Mary Ellen. *The Fishing Fleets of New England.* Boston: Houghton-Mifflin, 1961.

Huntington, Gale, ed. *Tom Tilton, Coaster and Fisherman.* Old Town, Me.: Northeast Folklore Society, 1984.

Jenness, John S. *The Isles of Shoals.* New York: 1875.

Johnston, Paul Forsythe. *New England Fisheries, a Treasure Greater than Gold.* Salem, Mass.: Peabody Museum, 1984.

Keating, Bern. *The Grand Banks.* Chicago: Rand McNally, 1968.

Kochiss, John M. *Oystering from New York to Boston.* Middletown, Conn.: Wesleyan (Mystic Seaport), 1974.

Netboy, Anthony. *The Atlantic Salmon.* Boston: Houghton-Mifflin, 1968.

Robinson, William F. *Coastal New England.* Boston: New York Graphic Society, 1983.

Swann, Marshall W. *Town on Sandy Bay, a History of Rockport, Mass.* Canaan, N.H.: Phoenix, 1980.

CHAPTER TWO

The men and women of the Noank Historical Society were unfailingly generous of their time and information. I am particularly grateful to the following individuals for their guidance: Louise Anderson, Mary Andersen, John Beach, Aldo Bacciocchi, Adrian Lane, Mary Virginia Goodman, and Bulkley Smith, Jr.

Ansel, Willits D. *Restoration of the Smack Emma C. Berry.* Mystic, Conn.: Marine Historical Society, 1973.

Chester, Claude M. *Papers.* Essex, Conn.: Noank Historical Society, 1970.

Dreiser, Theodore. *The Twelve Men.* New York: Boni & Liveright, 1919.

Dewar, Margaret E. *Industry in Trouble: The Federal Government and the New England Fisheries.* Philadelphia: Temple University Press, 1983.

Oppel, Frank. *Tales of the New England Coast.* Secaucus, N.J.: Castle, 1985.

Sabine, Lorenzo. *Report on the Principal Fisheries of the American Seas.* Washington, D.C.: Armstrong, 1853.

CHAPTER THREE

My guides in Marblehead were the ever-generous Russell W. Knight and Paul Forsythe Johnson of nearby Salem's Peabody Museum. The Marblehead Historical Society, under the leadership of Bowden G. Osborne, was also of stalwart assistance. I am personally grateful for the help and hospitality of my cousins, Judy and Andy Skinner, of Barnegat.

Barnard, John. *Autobiography of John Barnard.* Boston: 1836.

Bowden, William Hammond. *The Commerce of Marblehead.* Essex, Conn.: 1932.

Breen, T. H. *Puritans and Adventurers.* New York: Oxford University Press, 1980.

Bridenbaugh, Carl. *Mitre and Sceptre.* New York: Oxford University Press, 1962.

Heyrman, Christine Leigh. *Commerce and Culture: The Maritime Communities of Colonial Massachusetts.* New York: Norton, 1984.

Roads, Samuel, Jr. *The History and Traditions of Marblehead.* Boston: 1881.

CHAPTER FOUR

As is clear from the chapter on Provincetown, the Heritage Museum and the Provincetown Historical Society are rich with both information and interpretation. Without the friendship and guidance of Josephine Del Deo and George Bryant, I would have understood neither Provincetown's historical evolutions nor its present-day potentials. The many articles and booklets created by both Mrs. Del Deo and Mr. Bryant are examples to all of how accurate recordkeeping and vivid storytelling can bring a waterfront community to life.

Dwight, Timothy. *Travels in New England and New York.* Cambridge: Harvard University Press, 1969.

Fiore, Jordan D., ed. *Mourt's Relation.* Plymouth, Mass.: Plymouth Rock Foundation, 1985.

Jennings, Herman A. *Provincetown.* Boston: Peaked Hill Press, 1975.

Raynard, Elizabeth. *Tall Tales from the Narrow Land.* Boston: Houghton-Mifflin, 1934.
Thoreau, Henry David. *Cape Cod.* New York: Norton, 1951.
"Walking Tours" of the Provincetown Historical Society. Provincetown.

CHAPTER FIVE

At the Nantucket Historical Society, Bruce Courson set my feet on the right pathways; his colleague Victoria Hawkins was most gracious in introducing me to pertinent documents; and Peter S. MacGlashan was particularly creative in locating photographs.

Baltzell, E. Digby. *Puritan Boston and Quaker Philadelphia.* New York: Macmillan, 1979.
de Crèvecoeur, Hector St. John. *Letters from an American Farmer.* New York: Duffield, 1904.
Giambara, Paul. *Whales, Whaling, and Whalecraft.* Centerville, Mass.: Scrimshaw Press, 1967.
Hohman, Elmo P. *The American Whaleman.* Clifton, N.J.: Augustus Kelley, 1972.
Kugler, Richard C. "The Whale Oil Trade, 1750–1775."
Laing, Alexander. *American Ships.* New York: American Heritage Press, 1971.
Macy, Obed. *The History of Nantucket.* Boston: 1835.
McDevitt, Joseph L. "The House of Rotch."
Melville, Herman. *Moby Dick.* New York: Random House, 1950.
Nordhoff, Charles. *Whaling and Fishing.* Cincinnati, Ohio: 1856.
Shapiro, Irwin. *The Story of Yankee Whaling.* New York: American Heritage, 1965.
Stackpole, Edouard A. *Rambling Through the Streets and Lanes of Nantucket.* New Bedford, Mass.: Reynolds-DeWalt, 1981.
Starbuck, Alexander. *The History of Nantucket.* Rutland, Vt.: 1969.
Starbuck, Mary E. *My House and I.* Boston: Riverside Press, 1929.
Stevens, William Oliver. *Nantucket, the Far-Away Island.* New York: Dodd-Mead, 1936.
Trueblood, Elton D. *The People Called Quakers.* New York: Harpers, 1966.

CHAPTER SIX

Richard C. Kugler, director of the New Bedford Whaling museum, was both a resource and a conscience during the times spent in New Bedford. Virginia Adams and Judy Lund of his staff and Philip F. Purrington, creator of the Museum's whaling and fishing archives, were also unfailingly helpful. Mayor John Bullard, Nancy Crosby, and David Riley of the Rotch-Jones-Duff House, and Thérèse Kelly of the Waterfront Historic Area League (WHALE) all gave me fresh insights to the city's fishing past and its urban future. So did Captain Dan Moreland of the restored schooner *Ernestina* (on which you should try to get a sail). In the area of New Bedford's recent ethnic and economic development, trustworthy guides were my friend David Ransome, of Fairhaven, the Reverend John Nieman, and Robert Britto; also, Jim Castega of the Association of Vessel Owners and Howard Nickerson of the Offshore Mariners' Association.

Ackerman, Edward A. *New England's Fishing Industry.* Chicago: University of Chicago Press, 1941.
Allen, Everett S. *Children of the Light.* Boston: Little, Brown, 1973.
Ashley, Clifford W. *The Yankee Whaler.* Garden City: Halcyon, 1942.
Boss, Judith A., and Thomas, Joseph D. *New Bedford: A Pictorial History.* Norfolk, Va.: Donning Co., 1983.
Ellis, Leonard B. *History of New Bedford and Vicinity.* Syracuse, N.Y.: 1892.
Garner, Stanton, ed. *The Captain's Best Mate, the Journal of Mary Chipman Lawrence.* Providence: Brown, 1966.
Graham, Shirley. *There Once Was a Stone.* New York: Messner, 1947.
Hohman, Paul E. *The American Whaleman.* New York: Longmans Green, 1928.
Kugler, Richard C., ed. *New Bedford and Old Dartmouth.* New Bedford: Old Dartmouth Historical Society, 1975.
Leavitt, John F. *The Charles W. Morgan.* Mystic, Conn.: Marine Historical Association, 1973.
Pease, Zephania. *History of New Bedford.* New York: 1918.
Quarles, Benjamin, ed. *Frederick Douglas.* Englewood Cliffs, N.J.: Prentice-Hall, 1968.

Ricketson, Daniel. *History of New Bedford.* New Bedford, Mass.: 1858.

Stevenson, Charles H. *The Preservation of Fishery Products for Food.* Washington, D.C.: Government Printing Office, 1899.

White, Donald J. *The New England Fishing Industry.* Cambridge: Harvard University Press, 1954.

Whiting, Emma Mayhew, and Hough, Henry Beetle. *Whaling Wives.* Boston: Houghton-Mifflin, 1953.

CHAPTER SEVEN

The Cape Ann Historical Society, with its knowledgeable curators and librarians (notably Martha Oaks and Marian Harding) is outstanding in its awareness of waterfront institutions' archival *and* community functions. Gloucester tends to value the past, both in the city's commercial sector—I give special thanks here to Julian Hatch of Gorton-Pew and to David and Bryan Wright of the Wright Fisheries—and in its social sectors— here I salute the activists of the Fishermen's Wives' Association, particularly Peggy Sibley and Lena Novello. I would also like to express my thanks to Mr. Irving Goodman and the members of the Fishermen's Institute.

Babson, Helen Carliss. "History of the Fishing Industry of Gloucester."

Babson, John James. *History of the Town of Gloucester.* Gloucester, Mass.: 1860.

Bartlett, Kim. *The Finest Kind.* New York: Norton, 1977.

Brooks, Alfred Mansfield. *Gloucester Recollected.* Gloucester, Mass.: Cape Ann Historical Society, 1974.

Firth, Annabelle. "Rewinding the Skein."

Garland, Joseph E. *Down to the Sea.* Boston: Godine, 1983.

———. *The Gloucester Guide.* Gloucester, Mass.: 1973.

Isaacs, I. I. "Gloucester, Massachusetts, Its Interests and Industries."

Moorhouse, Geoffrey. *The Boat and the Town.* Boston: Little, Brown, 1979.

North, Franklin. "Gloucester Fisheries." *Century Magazine* (1886).

O'Brien, Robert. "You Were Your Own Boss—Life as a New England Fisherman."

Parsons, Peter. *When Gloucester Was Gloucester.* Gloucester, Mass.: 1973.

Pringle, James R. *History of the Town and City of Gloucester.* Gloucester, Mass.: 1892.

———. "Souvenir History of Gloucester, Mass."

Stanford, Alfred. *Men, Fish, and Boats.* New York: Morrow, 1934.

Thomas, Gordon W. *Fast and Able: Life Stories of Great Gloucester Fishing Vessels.* Gloucester, Mass.: 1973.

CHAPTER EIGHT

Along the coast of Maine, individuals and institutions kindly assisted me with unique pieces of the total story. Beyond the Maine State Archives in Augusta and the immensely resourceful Portland Historical Society, I must single out for special thanks the historical societies of Stonington, Blue Hill, Gouldsboro, Castine, and Vinalhaven. And I must name with particular gratitude certain men and women: in Stonington, Clayton Gross and Robin Alden; in Castine, Ellenore Doudiet, Gardiner Gregory, Dr. and Mrs. Robert O'Connor, Liddy Fitz-Gerald and Pat Fowler and Kathy Eaton of the library, and Barbara Glidden of the Unitarian-Universalist church; in Jonesport, the Reverend J. Clifford Davis, John Sawyer, Lawrence Norton, Mr. and Mrs. Larson Alley, and Barbara Hall of the library; in Vinalhaven, Esther and Roy Heisler, Kim Smith (and his father-in-law who dispenses candies at the hardware store), Gerry Dowdy, Roger Young, and Maud Warren in the library. I would also like to express my appreciation for the assistance of the Portland Museum of Art (specifically Curator Martha Severenz) and Jim Acheson of the University of Maine's Department of Anthropology.

Bishop, W. H. "Fishermen in the Maine Islands."

Brown, Mike. *The Great Lobster Chase.* Camden, Me.: International Marine, 1985.

Caldwell, Bill. *The Islands of Maine.* Portland, Me.: 1981.

Carson, Rachel. *The Rocky Coast.* New York: McCall's, 1955.

Conkling, Philip W. *Islands in Time.* Camden, Me.: Down East Books, 1981.

Dibner, Martin. *Seacoast Maine.* New York: Doubleday, 1973.

Doliber, Earl L. *Lobstering Inshore and Offshore.* Camden, Me.: International Marine, 1973.

Doudiet, Ellenore W. *Majabigwaduce.* Castine, Me.: 1978.

Duncan, Roger F. *A Cruising Guide to the New England Coast.* New York: Dodd-Mead, 1968.

———. *Friendship Sloops.* Camden, Me.: International Marine, 1985.

Fardelman, Charlotte. *Islands Down East.* Camden, Me.: Down East Books, 1984.

Griffin, Carl R., and Faulkner, Alaric. *Coming of Age on Damariscove, Maine.* Old Town, Me.: Northeast Folklore Society, 1981.

Jonesport-Beals Island High School. *A Pictorial History of Jonesport, Maine.* Calais, Me.: 1970.

Joy, Charles Austin. *Historical Researches of Gouldsboro, Maine.* Rev. ed. Gouldsboro, Me.: 1984. Originally published 1904.

Keyser, Harriette A. "Fishing Industry on the Coast of Maine." *Hammer and Pen* (March 1911).

Martin, Kenneth R., and Lipfert, Nathan R. *Lobstering the Maine Coast.* Bath: Maine Maritime Museum, 1985.

Pratt, Charles. *Here on the Island.* New York: Harper & Row, 1974.

Rich, Louise Dickinson. *The Peninsula.* Philadelphia: Lippincott, 1955.

Rowe, William H. *The Maritime History of Maine.* New York: Norton, 1948.

Thompson, Deborah, *Maine Forms of Architecture.* Camden, Me.: Down East Books, 1984.

Van Winkle, Ted. *Fred Boynton: Lobsterman.* Camden, Me.: International Marine, 1975.

Vinalhaven Historical Society. *A Brief Historical Sketch of the Town of Vinalhaven.* Vinalhaven, Me.: 1981.

Wasson, George. *Sailing Days on the Penobscot.* New York: Norton, 1932.

Westbrook, Perry D. *Seacoast and Upland.* New York: Barnes, 1972.

Wheeler, George A. *History of Castine.* Cornwall, Me., 1923.

Winslow, Sidney L. *Fish Scales and Stone Chips.* Portland, Me.: 1952.

INDEX

Italicized page numbers refer to illustrations